When the Writ HITS THE FAN!

Phil Dwyer with Phil Tripp

A 30 year journey through Australia's
contemporary music industry with a lawyer who was there.

Published by 40Watt Marketing Pty Ltd
ACN 087 615 727

First Published July 2004

ISBN 0-9752084-0-3

Designed by Mark Berry

Cover Design: With kind permission of artist Edd Aragon.

Edd Aragon is a Filipino-born Australian artist (b.1949; arrived in Australia 1979) ; currently Senior Artist for the Sydney Morning Herald. Multi-awarded (trophies) for best illustrator and best caricature portraitist; also a painter, wood sculptor, amateur musician (bass guitar, piano, harmonica), writer and cartoonist; He has exhibited works internationally, currently at the National Museum of Australia in Canberra). Visit his website at www.edd-aragon.com

Proofed by Danielle Hartmann.

MARKETED & DISTRIBUTED BY

IMMEDIA!
20 Hordern Street
Newtown NSW 2042
Australia

Phone (02) 9557 7766 International callers (612) 9557 7766
Fax: (02) 9557 7788 International faxers (612) 9557 7788
Email: tripp@immedia.com.au
URL: www.immedia.com.au/books

CONTENTS

ACKNOWLEDGEMENTS

I would like to thank the following people:

Shaaron for putting up with the early mornings and bad temper. Phil Tripp for his encouragement and badgering. He also came up with the title to the book. Annie Hall for typing and correcting the many redrafts. Renée Geyer for her comments which put me on the right track. Julian Dwyer and Katie Underwood for reading the very early draft. Paul O'Gorman, Sean Costello, Mike Scott and Ian MacDonald for their helpful advice and guidance in relation to content, structure and style. Noam Shifrin and Nicholas McKenzie-McHarg for their research. Louise Craig for her proofreading and constructive input. All the artists I have acted for over the last thirty years for their courage and conviction (not convictions).

This has truly been a community effort and I also want to thank all the staff at Dwyer & Co. This acknowledgement does not imply that anyone, other than me, is responsible for any indiscretions, perceived insults or matters of content.

PHIL DWYER

ACKNOWLEDGEMENTS OF PHIL TRIPP

This is that place where you get to delve into my life and relationships as I try to thank the various people and institutions that made this project possible.

Lisa Treen is the most important person in my life who for the past 15 years has been the tiller behind the good ship Tripp as I madly veer across the seascape of the music industry food chain. She's been the navigator as I've explored my limits of creativity and without her, I would never have been able to exercise my mind and writing in the past decade as I have. She's also maintained my business in the background by running me. Lisa's steered me through so many dangerous times when my enthusiasm or foolishness has run me into the winds of defamation as I've battled the dark forces of the music industry and taken them on in print or online. I can't thank her enough.

Lisa has loved me and encouraged me and occasionally tried to restrain me but always acted in my best interest as she cleaned up my messes, cocooned me, kept the business engines fired up and covered my rather ample ass. She's also been an incredible mother to our dogs Mick and Jeri as well as our parrots Roger and Jackson. Plus she's been mother hen to our great staff at IMMEDIA! as it has evolved over the past 15 years. I couldn't have done it without her. Kisses…

There have been a number of great staff who have crafted the Music Industry Directory which we've published since 1987, stoked the starmaking machinery of PR that I've overseen and made our conferences seamless, successful events. While I get the credit for the victories, they are the soldiers who make my tactics work, overcome my blunders and tolerate my shortcomings. My present crew of Danielle Hartmann, Megan Johns and Justine Lynch have been heroes in the gargantuan tasks that I've foisted on them. Danielle especially, since she took on this project to proof and format the book to the stage of layout. Thanks Dan!

But the best asset in my business efforts is the young man who's made me look good despite my inability to draw a circle, make text into rivers of ink and generally overproduce at the expense of design. Mark Berry is our webmaster, Mr Fixit, chief scientist and in-house designer who has over the past few years maintained our two websites (www.immedia.com.au and www.themusic.com.au), given our image continuous polishing, created wonderful solutions to design and textual complexities plus tirelessly completed all the daunting work that is the substance and content of what we produce and publish. Though he is a graphic genius, he still can't overcome my tainted taste in Hawaiian shirts and desire to cram as much as is possible into a page.

Thanks to Edd Aragon, the fabulous artist whose illustration adorns the cover—originally from an article I did for Penthouse magazine July 1992 titled "Send Lawyers Guns & Money—The Writ Has Hit The Fan!" Edd is best known as the senior artist for the Sydney Morning Herald but also is a multi-talented creator whose site is www.edd-aragon.com.

Phil Dwyer had tremendous faith in my being able to produce this book with him, though he did all the front end work by writing it. He trusted me to bring it into the real world of book publishing and yet do it in a way that is both unique and dangerous. I love him for so many things and have incredible respect for his legal talents as well as an undying appreciation for his sense of humour. He's also served me as a friend when I've cut it a bit close to the line by overstepping the bounds of legal good taste in times that I've drawn blood from an offended subject of my writings.

But it would be unfair if I didn't thank the team of lawyers who have either prevented the writ hitting the fan or cases hitting the courts when I've taken words and punched too hard, allegedly against the law. Peter Thompson of the Sydney entertainment firm TressCox and I go back to the Midnight Oil days when we met and he's been a great friend, a trusted adviser as well as a staunch defender. He's granted me too many gratis billable hours as I battled mighty opponents in the industry and kept me from being shredded by 'his learned friends'. I also honour his former partner, Randall Harper, now in London who handled the trio of my best potential lawsuits—two defamation actions for which I received writs which never saw the light of day at the courthouse steps and one in which

Lisa and I were the aggrieved parties (in that famous settlement 'terms not to be disclosed' manner).

It's also taken a team of medical practitioners over the years to keep me whole against my bad judgments and I have to thank my incredible GP Brian Churnin for keeping me on the right road and forgiving my lapses when I lean to the wrong side. He in turn matchmade me with my endocrinologist Catherine Samaras who has somehow kept the chemical brew that keeps me ticking in balance. And considering the chemical substances that have coursed through me over the years, they've had a job on their gloved hands!

My publishing guru over the years has also been my great friend Greg Bright who not only encouraged me to write but also guided me in my journey through creating regular publications from the Music Directory to my websites. I have to note here though that he actually discouraged me in that unique parental way that makes you do things in spite of yourself just to prove him wrong. In repayment for this, I got him his first threat of a defamation action with the opening article I did for Australian Film Review's debut issue.

He also introduced me to the other side of his family whose craft is printing and the Bright mob have put on paper over the past two decades what I've produced as a data-drug dealer. In fact, if it wasn't for Bill Bright (dad) and John Bright (son) investing in this crazy book, Phil and Phil would have probably never gotten it off the ground our way and would have had to lease our souls to some multinational publisher at a pittance.

Finally, I owe a tremendous debt of gratitude to Apple Computer Australia and its present cubicle evangelists Eric Persijn and Stuart Harris who have supported my Mac habituation as well as been partners in our conferences and conspiracies (preceded by Cameron McDonald Stuart and Dave Mahony in previous Apple incarnations). There's a certain luxury in writing this on a gleaming hotrodded G4 Powerbook linked to a 23 inch Cinema Screen in the foreground, with iTunes in the background as a jukebox to 10,000 songs drives me home.

I could keep going on here because there are so many people who have driven my life, but I'll cut to the chase and let you go to the main story. Let the credits roll with Christie Eliezer (and wife Anita) who's been my best mate in writing; Chris Gilbey who has inspired me to greater heights in technology and business; Brian Peacock who's been a client, supporter and great friend over the years; David Mulholland who gave me my first Tandy Model 100 computer in 1984 and taught me email; Don Singleton who invented rock 'n' roll electronic communications and made me go global; my former bands Secret Society from Nimbin and Scrap Metal from Broome; and the respected trio of label Chairmen who have been great supporters and inspirations—David Williams of Shock, Denis Handlin of Sony and Michael Smellie of BMG.

So rock on and read on...

PHIL TRIPP

INTRODUCTION BY PHIL TRIPP

I've been hanging around the swimming pool of spit and faux sincerity we fondly call the music business for 30 years now and I've taken the position in the last decade or so of being the fat, white whale in the banana lounger poolside, observing the gory action in vivid and horrifying detail. I used to be appalled when I saw artists jumping into the deep end of the pool, generally unable to swim, hanging onto the life ring of a couple of singles until they deflated and then bobbing up and down until they eventually sank. Most of them, maybe 90% at least, failed to surface past their first release.

With regularity, the A&R and marketing sharks would slither out of their exclusive multinational label cabanas in their branded satin jackets and designer shades, slide noiselessly into the pool and feed on the carcasses of the artists—dead and the still living. Being a poolside observer, I was safe and knew not to venture into the tainted waters. I gave advice some times, warned some artists to take the indie route of the swimming hole or DIY in their own garden mini-pool instead of entering the dead zone of mainstream music signing.

But Phil Dwyer is a special breed. He's been a lifesaver for about as long as I've been sunning myself on the sidelines. Where other lawyers in the music business often attached themselves to the sharks of the labels like legal remora fish—feeding on the side stream of victims—Phil has actively fought to pull people out of the pool before they got savaged, rescued them before they went under and became prey or in some instances, outfitted them for survival in the food chain of the music industry so that they don't fall to the predators.

In the 'Industry of Illusion' where fortunes are usually reserved for the middlemen, fame is generally as fleeting as a six week window of opportunity that most releases get between pressing and landfill, Phil is a saviour of many, a hero to most and an enemy of few—usually those who oppose him in contract or court.

When I'm asked how I measure my success in the music industry, my stock reply is that if the people who hate me are egotistical, power-crazed, alcohol or drug-fueled executives in suits with AMEX cards and writs at the ready, that I'm half a success. And provided that those who respect me are at the lower ends of the music food chain and devoted, honest industry workers, it makes up the other half.

I've always followed the advice of Thomas Watson, founder of IBM who said, "Make no little enemies -- people with whom you differ for some petty, insignificant personal reason. Instead I would urge you to cultivate 'mighty opposites' -- people with whom you disagree on big issues, with whom you will fight to the end over fundamental convictions. And that fight, I can assure you, will be good for you and your opponent." And the principle that backs it up that I'm often quoted using is "The truth burns clean. The truth will set you free but first it's going to piss you off!"

I've known and respected Phil Dwyer as one of Australia's top music industry attorneys for the past two decades I've been fortunate enough to have Australia as my home and the music industry as my career. I've also had the fortune of his friendship as well as the privilege to be enlightened by his incredible range of knowledge about the business of music. Plus, I've been endlessly entertained in those years by Phil's talent as a raconteur of industry oddities and identities, artists or entrepreneurs, heroes or villains. And truth be told, he's advised me when I'm in need of counsel and represented me when I needed it to either fight a battle or collect a debt.

This book is as unusual as its creation and amusing as its author.

What makes this book unusual is that it's like an indie album in the best tradition of Australian self-empowerment. Instead of going for a major multinational book publisher (because a GREAT book deal is like the WORST record deal) Phil opted to retain the rights and revenue to a greater degree than when you sell out. With his wealth of information and immense number of contacts in the music industry coupled with his inside knowledge of secrets and settlements, it would have been easy to make this book a scandalous expose like the historic 'Hit Men' or self-aggrandising autobiography such as the recently released "Howling At The Moon" by former Sony CEO Walter Yetnikoff.

However, Phil betrays no confidences in this book. Sure, he reveals a lot, but it's not at the expense of either the truth or trust. He's worked with some of the most talented artists and songwriters in Australia and represented some of our greatest musical empire builders. But he's taken some of the more interesting—and sometimes hilarious—incidents or issues and brought them into the open where readers who are in the industry can learn from them while those with merely an interest can be entertained.

Phil has also fought his share of crooks and cowards in the music industry from outright master criminals who steal entire bodies of work, reputations and careers or who simply rip off creators by the song or the deal. Hell, I've used his firm in the past to pursue some deadbeats as well as recommending him to artists happy to gnaw their own arm off to get out of the clutches of bogus managers, willing to shoot their foot off to free themselves from the shackles of a major label.

You'll find some of those stories in here as well as some more unusual tales of those who fought the law, struggled with the law and faced down the most powerful masters in the music industry. He shows in the book that when you get into a legal fight, you get law and not necessarily justice when you go to court—but the smart of the lucky get settlements, with 'terms not to be disclosed'.

Those are the stories you might not find in this book, unless you read beween the lines. In the two years that Phil has worked with me on crafting "When The Writ Hits The Fan", he's been meticulous in his integrity for not violating confidentiality as well as not taking cheap shots in parting. Plus, we've had it legalled four times. You have to when you do a book of this scope and depth.

So why is my name on the cover? Well, you'll notice it's in smaller type with the time-worn word 'with' preceding my name. It's totally Phil's book, and in terms of content, he wrote it not once, but twice before he was happy with the result. I edited it and gave advice on what worked and didn't. Though I would have loved to throw in my comments or two bob worth, what is written, past this intro, comes from his mind and Dictaphone.

Which makes this book more unusual in one sense, it was dictated as Phil would admit, he's not a strong typist! But it flows as well as one of those dinners that you sit fascinated as he unreels the long epic movie that is the music business.

The final thing that is unusual about this book takes me back to the beginning when I compared it to an indie album. When Phil came up with this idea maybe five years ago, he approached me to help him with it and over the years, the relationship evolved into what he wanted it to be which is a popular book for those with an interest in the music industry and a learning tool for everyone from artists to lawyers and industry workers about how the business really works. All this without it being a legal tome that is weighty and drab. To that end he succeeded in making his first release a hit!

But the unusual aspect is that we are publishing this book outside the mainstream media. There a book from a multinational publisher has an expensive launch party (like a CD from a name artists) followed by a six week window in retail stores where it either sinks or floats according to the whim and opinions of reviewers, positioning of product in stores, the number of units shipped and the bulk of returns recycled back into wood pulp. Ask any writer what a book deal is and it's usually a meager advance against thin royalties which they seldom if ever recoup. They may make $5 on a $49.95 book but it's eaten up by the advance, the advertising, promotion, publicity, touring and balanced by returns, Yes books do ship gold and return platinum as recordings do.

The reason we could do this 'indie book' is not that we're rich. We did a unique deal with the long term printer of our AustralAsian Music Industry Directory for so many years—Bright Print—in which we made them a partner in the project. We're relying on word of mouth, viral marketing and the quality of the 'release' to spur sales through our own online Music Business Books system online at www.immedia.com.au/books as well as through our normal mail order means and promoting through media over a course of time in 2004.

So if you're reading this first edition of the book which we released in the beginning of the 2004-05 financial year—because Phil and Phil were running their businesses while crafting this tome—you probably fell prey to our guerilla marketing, found it on the Internet, by word of mouth, through one of our evangelists or even through a seminar we held. We hope you haven't taken the option of 'file-sharing' this text by having the book shared to deny us our rightful recompense as the industry is blaming the peer-to-peer networking for its artists' losses.

Seriously though, we're both proud and happy to present this for your reading pleasure in your own lounger or as a guidebook to avoiding disaster in the music business.

PHIL TRIPP

CHAPTER 1 - THE ICEMAN

Pat Daly was an iceman. He delivered ice to homes in Northcote, an inner suburb of Melbourne, in the 1950's. It was used in ice chests. Like his father and grandfather before him, he worked hard and had a good business. The kids particularly liked him when he gave them pieces of ice on hot summer days. Then one day an old customer showed him her new acquisition – a refrigerator.

The context for this story is the Australian entertainment industry with particular emphasis on contemporary music. The principal cast consists of musicians, songwriters and their managers. It is told from my perspective as a lawyer who was there. Why I was there is also part of the story.

In the Australian music industry 1975 to 1985 was not unlike 1852 to 1862 in Bendigo, Victoria. Gold was to be found under every rock and it seemed like it would go on forever. It was with this spirit of optimism that I started writing this book in 1985. Fortunately I was distracted. In about 1990 I thought I would have another go and had my daughter write out the steps to operate the computer. Her first instruction was 'turn on – at side'. That caused such a bout of anxiety that I deferred the project for another twelve years.

When reviewing my involvement with the industry I have not had to refer to a diary, files or correspondence. The people and events have been well documented in newspapers, books and writs. For inspiration, all I had to do was look at company names to bring the memories back. Above the Clouds Pty Ltd was the name I gave to Glenn Wheatley's trustee company. It came to me during a flight home from Europe. John Farnham's Sirius Pty Ltd was from my trip to Norfolk Island. It is now frequented by the 'just wed or nearly dead' set but then it was a well-used tax haven, although not by John. Tutankamun Pty Ltd, The Angels' company, had its origin from my Egyptian period. Pizzicato, Staccato and Thieving Magpie, used by Australian Crawl, were from a phase when I was trying to improve my image. Then there were the bridges of Paris, the streets of Amsterdam, Los Angeles and New York and the ships of the Royal Navy. They all represented Australian groups or productions at one time or another.

I can also look at what I like to call my record collection. It is really just a pile of old vinyl albums. I am pleased to say that on many I have been personally acknowledged by the artists. I am particularly proud of the handwritten one from Chrissie Amphlett on Divinyls' *What a Life* album. It reads, 'Thanks Peter'.

Over the years the same names kept recurring. By that I don't mean the names of the stars, the Hunters, Finns and Reynes. I mean people like Vince Lovegrove, Brett Cottle, Ernie Rose, Ross Fraser, Phil Mortlock, Peter Karpin, Jeremy Fabinyi, John McDonald, David Joseph, Michael Smellie, Denis Handlin, Simon Young, Roger Savage, Kevin Jacobsen, John Bromell and Fred Bestall. They are the people this book is really about.

At the outset it should be understood that I only have a rudimentary knowledge of music. My father played the cornet. I made a dismal attempt at playing the trumpet and my wife played the tambourine. The closest I came to any entertainers was when I worked at the Northcote Post Office in the 1960s. I delivered telegrams to Bert Newton who lived with his mother in Alphington and to Doug Trevor, then a member of The Cherokees and now a successful manager, who lived with his mother in Northcote.

It should also be remembered that this is written through the eyes of a lawyer, not a musician. Unlike my colleague, Paul O'Gorman, I do not listen to 'demo tapes'. He thinks all such tapes are 'fantastic' although many of them lack the 'flagship single' he always seems to be looking for. I gave up doing that when, in frustration, I finally took a call from a client who had telephoned several times. I told him that the tape was fantastic although I couldn't hear a hit single. I said it needed some more work. He thanked me but said he was ringing just to let me know he was going to drop the tape in personally that afternoon.

I did my law degree whilst working in the Taxation Department where I spent some time as the 'entertainment assessor'. In those days touring artists were required to lodge a Tax Return and obtain a tax clearance before departing Australia. I assessed their returns. The Department was a strange place. Priority was given to ex-servicemen, particularly those with a disability, mental or otherwise. We had one who would stand to attention and salute at the beginning of each tea break. Married women were not employed. My wife, who also worked there, retired at the age of 22, when we married.

Twenty-year-olds were being conscripted for service in Vietnam. They were always sent off with a very long counter lunch at the Francis Hotel on their last Friday. On returning from one of these we were confronted by a senior assessor complaining about our absence. Our group leader, an ex-serviceman, resented this unpatriotic attitude and dropped him for the count of ten. We all cheered.

The Department was organised on similar lines to that of the army with sections, platoons and companies. We even had our own military police. We called them D12 because they were half as good as D24. One day we were notified that our section was to be 'raided'. They were looking for spoons stolen from the tea trolley. I immediately collected all the spoons I could find and put them in the drawer of the least corruptible person on the floor, Kevin Fitzpatrick. It could not have done him any harm. He is now an Assistant Deputy Commissioner.

Once, when relieving on the enquiries counter, I was confronted by a Mr Fosteropoulos who wanted to talk to the 'manager'. After talking on the telephone to no one I advised him that we had a problem with his tax return. It couldn't be handled by the computer. It had been taken off the production line and given to 'the long name assessor' for personal attention. He made a quick exit. I left the Department in 1974 by mutual agreement.

Soon after commencing practice in 1975, Glenn Wheatley was referred to me by David Self during David's four-day career as a life-insurance agent. Glenn has not really changed since then. He still says H-E-L-L-O-W and P-L-E-E-E-A-S-E when he wants to make a point and is always picking imaginary lint off his jacket. His favourite sayings are 'give me a break', 'out of left field' and 'it's not always going to be this way'.

Glenn had a successful career as a bass player in The Masters Apprentices. He was in the process of forming, managing and publishing the then 'super group' Little River Band. The group was 'super' in the sense that it was made up of members of already successful acts. There was an awareness in the band of the value of copyright and the need to perform original compositions. This at the time was quite rare. Glenn, with his usual enthusiasm and optimism, was always convinced that the group would be internationally successful. For that reason the songs were directed towards the west coast American market.

Unfortunately, Glenn's success with The Masters did not mean he had money. He needed $4000 to buy a truck for the band. The security offered was a personal guarantee from Glenn, each member of the band, the truck, a block of land Glenn owned in Queensland and 'all the band's copyrights'. We had an upbeat meeting with Ray Nielsen, the manager of the St Kilda Road branch of the then Commercial Bank of Australia. Glenn gave a moving (but in retrospect probably not very accurate) dissertation as to the value of copyright. He certainly moved me. Unfortunately he didn't move Ray and the loan was refused.

Soon after that I had my first experience socialising with 'celebs'. I invited that week's rock superstar home for dinner. We had three children under two and my wife put in an extraordinary effort – three courses, candles, the kids bathed and fed. I bought the drinks. He arrived about 7.00pm (sunglasses still affixed in spite of the fading light) and promptly announced, 'Don't worry about me – I had a hamburger on the way'. That was a good lesson for my wife early in my career.

Unlike Glenn I did not formally study copyright or embrace technology. I am still trying to understand how the domestic sewing machine works. Nevertheless, I realised from the beginning that practising law has more to do with relating to people than solving complex legal problems. The trick at the end of the day is to ensure that your client is better off for the experience of having known you. More often than not I think I achieve that. Along the way I have managed to attract such epithets as 'mad dog Dwyer', 'cowboy' and 'whore for hire' but rarely from my clients.

One has to make choices in life and those choices are often influenced by minor matters such as paying the kids' school fees and the registration on the car. I was once sounded out for the Federal Court. Aside from having to go back to living on a wage, my background makes me nervous about judging other people. I declined. There was a time when I thought about going to the bar (becoming a barrister). After some consideration, I decided to continue practising as a solicitor. That was the right choice. It allowed me to maintain a direct relationship with my clients. That is my strength whereas research and procedural matters are an eternal source of frustration.

Certainly, no one can practise in the fields in which I have practised and survive without enjoying what they do. Fortunately I have always had an affinity with, and an understanding of, people who earn their living by entertaining others. That is not to say that I regard myself as part of the entertainment industry. I have always considered myself a member of the legal profession. However, I do understand the strength of character, determination and innate insecurities of professional entertainers.

It is true that creative people don't like confrontation. It's also true that they rarely say thank you or goodbye. I acted for Neil Finn and Crowded House from the beginning. Near the end, just before Neil moved back to New Zealand, I was called to a meeting at the office of their accountant, John Smith, in North Balwyn. By that stage John, to whom I had referred Neil and his manager Grant Thomas, several years earlier, had retired. I was detained in the waiting room for half an hour and then told I wouldn't be required. That was the last time I saw Neil – through the office curtains. That was also the day those accountants stopped getting referrals from me.

Many times over the years I have been sacked and rehired without that fact ever having been communicated to me. In the early days I would be annoyed by that. Now I see it as just as much a part of the entertainer as a good set of teeth. I also appreciate what a lonely place the industry can be. In a rather sad conclusion to his autobiography, Tommy Tycho, after fifty years in the Australian entertainment industry, acknowledged that he has 'never had a close friend – anyone I could confide in'.[1]

Phil Tripp has been on my back to finish this book for years. Along the way he even dropped me from his 'A' list. I think that was because I tried to say something as a presenter at a seminar chaired by him. I have often told Phil I was making progress. He knew what that meant. Eventually, I just picked up a dictaphone and started to dictate. That process has its shortcomings. I have developed a neurotic need to punctuate which even extends to recorded telephone messages. Then there is the lawyer's compulsion to qualify everything. As Mark Twain once wrote: 'Sorry about the long letter but I didn't have time to write a short one'. Having said that, this book is intended for people to read and enjoy. It is neither a treatise nor a text book. Nor is it a deep and meaningful analysis of every Australian pop song ever released. It is more about reality than imagery. Substance has prevailed over form.

The second chapter sets out the history of the music industry which is the framework of the story. The next three chapters cover the dynamics within a group and their relationship with that strange species called a 'manager'. There are chapters on the importance of a professional image and the hazards of litigation. The chapters on contract and copyright cover the basic tools of trade of the industry. It's difficult to infuse these concepts with light and colour but they are fundamental.

The chapter on the Prices Surveillance Authority is included because it was an important turning point for the industry. The common denominator of the chapters on indigenous music, film and theatre is music. The chapter on legal practice nearly fell victim to the delete button. For me it is a little close to home. Phil Tripp's view was that it gives an insight into why people like me do what we do. Phil has always had a lawyer fetish. I have not defined every term in the text so the glossary might help.

Finally, I have resisted the temptation to redress a few perceived wrongs. There is no malice in this book. Those planning to make a career in the industry might learn something from reading it. People who don't participate might gain a better understanding of those that do. Hopefully any young lawyers who read this will not immediately lose interest in practising law. I had planned to use the Thesaurus and to include a few big words and some stylish alliteration. Finally, I accepted Renée Geyer's advice to just tell it as it is.

CHAPTER 2 – GOOD VIBRATIONS

Many people devote their lives to the music industry but never take the trouble to find out what it's really about. My excuse is that I am a lawyer. It is useful to have some understanding of music, the industry which has developed around it and its historical context. Music is an international language which crosses all barriers. It can bring out the manifestation of Satan. At the same time Jeff Buckley takes his place in the chorus of Angels. So what is music?

In a technical sense it is fairly basic. If a guitar string is plucked it will vibrate. Those vibrations cause the surrounding air to vibrate. When they reach a person's eardrum it, in turn, will vibrate in sympathy with the vibrations being transmitted. A sound is simply the impression these vibrations register on the human brain. A sound might just be a noise like the slamming of a door. That is not music to the ears. To create music the sound must have a regular vibration.

The human ear is capable of picking up vibrations within a certain range. The more vibrations per unit of time the higher the note. This is the difference between the sound of a tuba and that of a French horn. The frequency of vibrations caused by the horn is much greater than that of the tuba. The relative position of a sound within that range is called pitch. This should not be confused with amplification which represents the degree of violence with which the vibrations come into contact with the eardrum. The Angels perfected that.

To move forward it is necessary to establish a rhythm. To enable members of a group to communicate and to relate musically, the rate of progress needs to be designated and regulated. This is done by dissecting the road to be travelled into bars; a concept musicians on the road can readily relate to. If a waltz is being played there are three beats to every bar. In contemporary music there are four, with the emphasis on the second and fourth. This is the responsibility of the rhythm section. It sets the structure around which the other members perform.

In 1986 I acted for 87 Fat Girls who tried to break away from the accepted 4/4 rhythmic pattern. Their launch was couched in much secrecy. They could have saved themselves the trouble. Their career was spectacular but short. They were using a language no one could understand. Most musicians are content with the 4/4 pattern; they overlay some notes configured in a melodious and harmonious way and create music. When they add lyrics they have a song.

Contemporary music is popular at a particular time. When I use the term I use it to describe music which is particularly popular with young people. If that popularity endures and young people become old it becomes 'popular' music. The Seekers, who include stories about 'senior moments' in their concerts, perform popular music. The same applies to The Rolling Stones. Contemporary music is ephemeral by definition. Having said that, the music industry commercially exploits music of all types, including the contemporary, popular, jazz, theatrical and classical genres.

Music is not a modern phenomenon. It had a pre-eminent role in Aboriginal and African cultures long before Bardot did that famous medley of their hit. Jazz is based on ancient African rhythms. Celtic, Greek and Arabic music predates Bach by hundreds of years. The music industry as we understand it probably had its beginnings in Europe around the Renaissance in the seventeenth century. Prior to that organised music in the western tradition was largely the preserve of the Church. The popularity of music by Bach, Handel, Haydn and Mozart created the need for an industry infrastructure. Sheet music began to be commercially distributed and the music publishing industry evolved.

Throughout the latter part of the nineteenth century people were keen to find a way of capturing, preserving and reproducing sound itself. The break through came in 1877 when Thomas Edison invented the phonograph. Sound vibrations were captured by a large funnel and transferred to a membrane. The vibrations of the membrane were 'recorded' by a needle cutting grooves, the depth of which varied with the sound vibrations, into a rotating cylinder covered with tinfoil. By reversing the process the vibrations caused by the rotating needle were transferred back to the membrane which recreated the sound in the funnel.

In 1887 the cylinder was replaced by a flat circular gramophone disc which used grooves with a constant depth but which varied laterally.

It was not until the 1920s that the range of recording equipment was increased and background noise eliminated such that commercial records could be manufactured. It was then possible to bring recorded music to the people. The development of the electric guitar in the fifties enabled a vast repertoire of rhythm and blues music to be reincarnated in the guise of rock 'n' roll. That was the beginning of the contemporary music industry as we know it today.

Prior to 1975, Australia was not a significant source of music. It was, however, an important market for international, recorded product, that is records of music composed and recorded by predominantly English and American composers and performers. Often Australians re-recorded songs which had been successfully recorded and released overseas. These were called 'covers'. Successful Australian artists including The Seekers, Helen Reddy, the Bee Gees, Rolf Harris, Olivia Newton-John and AC/DC based themselves out of Australia and became part of the British or American industry.

There were some Australian artists who recorded their own material including The Masters Apprentices, Axiom, The Twilights, Daddy Cool, Zoot and Ren e Geyer. Unfortunately their attempts to conquer international markets were less than successful and that is not really surprising. The Masters Apprentices took five and a half weeks to travel to the UK by ship only to find on arrival that not only the general populace but the parent of their own recording company, EMI, had no real knowledge of, or interest in them.[1] Their experience was not unique. Even the glam acts Sherbert and Skyhooks and later Split Enz, although they had some success in England, had mainly local appeal.

Nevertheless the climate was becoming favourable for Australians to start thinking about their own music. There was an audience in Adelaide, particularly in the working-class suburbs like Port Adelaide.[2] The Skyhooks by their album *Living in the Seventies* had shown that it was possible to be successful, at least in Australia, with songs which were unashamedly Australian.[3] Both Sydney and Melbourne had a fairly active pub scene where, particularly in Melbourne, original songs were welcome and encouraged. Sydney was finally shrugging off the sterile club scene which had developed around American servicemen on rest and recreation leave from Vietnam. In short, there was a ready-made audience in Adelaide, Melbourne and, to a lesser extent Sydney, for Australian music.

The late seventies saw the development of a generic Australian recording industry. This was facilitated by the fact that recording budgets were low and facilities were readily available, particularly in Melbourne. Richmond Recorders, with the laconic and omnipresent Tim Stobart and Tony Cohen, and AAV / Armstrongs / Metropolis with Ernie Rose and Roger Savage and later Platinum were booked out twenty-four hours a day. Richmond Recorders tended to be somewhat left of centre and catered to all tastes. Metropolis was regarded as more 'professional' and was the studio of choice for Little River Band. However, it should be acknowledged that the most successful album ever recorded in Australia, *Business as Usual*, was recorded by Men at Work at Richmond Recorders. There was also ready access to airplay on radio stations which were not restricted by national and narrow formats.

Over the next five years it became the norm for Australian artists to record songs which were composed by songwriters within the group. This was the case with Little River Band, Cold Chisel, The Angels, Divinyls, Icehouse, Australian Crawl, Mental as Anything, Rose Tattoo and Men at Work. There was also an invasion of New Zealand acts including Mi-Sex, Split Enz, Dragon, Sharon O'Neill and Noiseworks. International success was a realistic expectation and Australia remained an important and valued market.

In those years it was customary for the one solicitor to act for all the members of a group personally, their manager and everybody associated with the group. This was the case with Little River Band which was very much based on a family concept around the head of the family – Glenn. Whilst this can have short-term benefits for a lawyer, it can also create pressure. It is not unlike a solicitor working in a country town where everyone is related to everyone else. Any alleged slight or failure with regard to one client is likely to have widespread repercussions. There were many examples but two come to mind.

The first concerned Ernie Rose. Ernie was, and still is, a well-respected producer and engineer in the industry. He was an indispensable member of the Little River Band 'family'. He decided to buy a house and I handled the conveyancing. I was also given the responsibility of organising the finance. For some unknown reason, I procrastinated in relation to the latter to the point that three days before the Friday on which settlement was due, it was impossible to complete the necessary documentation to allow it to proceed. It was then that Ernie let me know that he had to settle on the Friday because he was getting married in the house on the Saturday. Almost everyone who was anyone in the Melbourne music industry (except me) was invited to attend the wedding. I offered Ernie the use of my lounge room. Fortunately we settled and the wedding proceeded.

Then there was the siege of North Brighton. A guitarist purchased a property which, on my advice, was registered in his name. His girlfriend, for whom I also acted, moved in. Just before his return from an American tour, I received a call from the guitarist's manager. The guitarist had fallen in love with another woman and was bringing her back to Australia. I was to let the ex-girlfriend know about these developments and request that she do the honourable thing and leave. This she refused to do. She was not impressed by my suggestion that the guitarist should be free to carry his sweet love across the threshold without being greeted by his ex-girlfriend. Being a cunning coward I suggested that the locks be changed while she was at work. The locksmith (a perfectionist) took a little longer than was expected and managed to change all the locks except that on the back door. He left at 6.00 pm, just before the ex-girlfriend arrived.

The siege then began in earnest. It resulted in Supreme Court writs and much embarrassment. The argument by the incumbent was that 50% of the house was being held on trust on her behalf. I advised the guitarist to settle. That eventually led to a resolution of the dispute which did me no good in the long-term. I was alienated forever from the old love and grandly condemned as being 'weak kneed' and not up to the standards of American lawyers by the new.

During this period I was representing a manager, a group and a record company regarding an album which was very successful in Australia and which Atlantic Records was keen to release in North America.

Predictably the group decided that this was an opportune time to terminate its relationship with the Australian record company and litigation was threatened. Because I acted for all parties I refused to act for anyone. The manager approached a lawyer who proceeded to give him a two-hour lecture on the music industry. The lawyer said he was writing a book. That's one of the reasons I put off writing this for another twenty years. The lawyer concluded with the advice that he charged $250 an hour and that he and the manager would fly to Los Angeles the next morning and 'sort out the Atlantic deal'. The response from the manager was twofold. Firstly, he said that he couldn't afford the lawyer. Secondly, he pointed out that Atlantic was in New York. I accepted them all back. Fortunately the chemistry was OK.

The 1980s started with great promise. At least in the field of contemporary music, the cultural cringe was no more. Mainstream acts Midnight Oil, Australian Crawl, Men at Work, Broderick Smith's Big Combo, Goanna, Mondo Rock, Hoodoo Gurus, Cold Chisel and The Angels were intrinsically Australian in their music and their demeanour. INXS, Moving Pictures, The Models, the Little Heroes and Sharon O'Neill were poised for success. They were to be followed by Kids in the Kitchen, Boom Crash Opera, Southern Sons, Hunters & Collectors, Real Life, Crowded House and many more.

The Premier/Harbour monopoly over the live scene in Australia had some competition at least temporarily. The Angels, Cold Chisel, Flowers, INXS, Mental as Anything and Mondo Rock could all be booked through 'Dirty Pool Live Representation'. Unfortunately it was all too late; the live scene was in gradual decline. That was masked to some extent by the introduction of compact discs, but it was there nevertheless. At the same time there was a more sinister and furtive development. Although AIDS was going to make Richard Branson a lot of money selling condoms, for the music industry the consequences were catastrophic.

The early eighties also saw Little River Band, Air Supply and Men at Work fall apart. Air Supply had probably run their race. Little River Band might say they only made some changes to their line-up, but without Glenn Shorrock it was a different band. The demise of Men at Work was disastrous. It sent a bad message. Here was Australia's most successful international act falling apart because it seemed like a good thing to do at the time.

Renee Geyer calls this the 'neo-Romantic period'.[4] It was categorised by groups such as The Church and INXS and followed by Kylie Minogue and Peter Andre. According to Renee, 'Australians didn't have the tolerance for real-roots, R'n'B, and people who played that sort of music were considered "old blues folk"'.[5] Certainly it was a time when recording budgets which included budgets for videos were becoming out of step with reality. They were reaching a point where it was almost impossible to recoup recording costs in Australia. This came at a time when the costs of breaking an act in America, which were often cross-collateralised or recouped against artist royalties from Australian sales, also spun out of control.

The increased activity and volatility in the industry meant that conflicts started to catch up with me. Having acted for so many people in a small industry, professional conflict was inevitable. This usually resulted in me acting for no one, which was not good for business. But more serious were the cases where a conflict had personal implications. Perhaps one of the more unfortunate examples occurred about that time. It was during Glenn Wheatley's conquest of the world. At regular intervals Glenn would decide that it was time to corporatise and bureaucratise his various operations. This meant setting up a few more companies, buying a new whiteboard, appointing executives to draw on it, taking (but not listening to) advice from a very large firm of accountants, having many meetings over a period of a week or two and then disappearing overseas.

In one of these moods Glenn had hired a new CEO. His concepts of business and corporate structuring were fine but they were never going to work in an operation run by Glenn or any other successful manager in Australia for that matter. The CEO and his family were holidaying in Surfers Paradise. They were staying in a unit which I had made available to them. Sadly, during that stay a member of the family had a fatal heart attack in the surf. That same day Glenn, who was in Los Angeles, mailed a letter setting out the reasons why things could not continue. The next day I met with the CEO at the Sebel Town House in Sydney. On the one hand I commiserated with him about his loss and on the other let him know that the business relationship was over. He had not received the letter at that time. Even for me the reality was starting to catch up with the imagery.

The eighties also saw the emergence of 'punk' and 'new wave' groups. The music press loved them. This did nothing for the live industry. An audience was not high on their agenda. Michael George Smith put it fairly well. He asserted that the 'hip press', which included Tracee Hutchinson, Stuart Coupe, Toby Creswell and Clinton Walker, had a 'contempt for nearly all things pre-punk that were Australian'.[6] This sycophancy with everything grunge reared its head again in 1994, when under the heading 'Young And Restless', Clinton Walker described Roger Grierson as 'perhaps the most influential of a new generation of power brokers'.[7] I like Roger but even he would have needed an emetic after that one.

Timing has always been critical in the music industry. Getting a break for a band is often about being in the right place at the right time. However, in the early eighties the American market was corrupted. This was the time of the 'pay for play' payola scandals. Airplay was based on how much was paid rather than the quality of the product. Of course, just because a record company paid didn't mean the record was played. Who could complain? INXS and Crowded House broke through because of good management, great songs, hard work and a little luck. Other groups equally as talented like Midnight Oil, Mental as Anything and Divinyls had the songs and did the miles but struggled. There was more pain than pleasure.

In America the graft associated with radio was referred to as 'independent promotion'. It became so bad that 'independent promotion' budgets were formally negotiated and included in record contracts. For obvious reasons they were impossible to audit. The generosity of record companies in the direction of radio programmers extended from cocaine and cash to white goods and other comforts. Every day was Christmas Day.

This period also saw the development of the video as a promotional tool. All this did was greatly increase production costs. A video budget in some instances could exceed the recording budget. It would usually be fully or partially recoupable against artist royalties. Since most Australian artists were very capable and experienced live performers this trend mitigated against them. Why nurture, tour and market an act over the long-term when a record company could make a video of a sweet-looking

American blonde and, with a good marketing budget and a targeted audience, achieve success which was almost guaranteed? Talent became an unnecessary complication.

Songs were composed to a formula by the production house Stock Aitken & Waterman in the UK. Performers were regarded more as actors than singers or musicians. Often the 'singer' had little or nothing to do with the vocal performance actually recorded. Records were promoted via television advertising or successful television shows. Kylie was just another T-shirt. Again, Australia was becoming a marketplace for American and English product.

To many, especially during the 'excessive' eighties, the contemporary music industry was synonymous with sex and drugs. The first of these passed me by and the second has always been there but in a detached sort of way. I have had several clients who have died from drug-related illnesses. I have also had clients who disappeared on unplanned vacations from time to time, particularly those in the old days who based themselves around Richmond Recorders. I have seen tour budgets which made provision for 'coke' and 'speed' and I have been around long enough to know this has little to do with soft drink or erratic driving.

While it is true that early death and debilitating illness have intervened on occasions, there are many examples where people of the sixties and seventies generations, who should surely be dead, are still breathing. If Keith Richards didn't move every so often he would be embalmed. Some even seem to get better with age. Who would think Brian Cadd would still be a sex symbol in the new millennium? Brian invited me as his special guest to what turned out to be a dinner show in Sydney. I gained entry via a backstage door and asked about my seating arrangements. Brian's suggestion was that I stand in a corner and pretend to be a waiter.

There have been rumours around the industry for years that the traditional business activities of certain promoters and nightclub proprietors are secondary to some other very profitable enterprises. I have had the good fortune to represent many professional nightclub operators, such as Sam and George Frantzeskos (The Metro in Melbourne) and have never seen any evidence of this.

There was a case in Sydney which one day will make an interesting film. Truth indeed seemed stranger than fiction. It concerned a tour manager named Ian Saxon. When he was arrested in 1990 the police found 5.5 million dollars cash in a garage in Coogee. The records he kept verified that the gross receipts from the sale of the cannabis shipment he and others imported were $77,523,530. He was a meticulous bookkeeper. He was committed for trial on 5 September 1991 and bail was refused. Obviously some people didn't want him around because he escaped from the Sydney Metropolitan Remand Centre on 3 March 1993. He was recaptured in America on 21 April 1995. On 1 August 1996 he was sentenced by Justice Dunford in the Supreme Court of NSW to 24 years' gaol.[8] His non-parole period expires on 31 March 2008. He has made no attempt to implicate any associates. This led to an investigation of the Frontier Touring Company books by the National Crime Authority and Frontier 'was cleared of any involvement'.[9]

The only experience I had personally with a drug-related offence was a minor matter which I fell into by mistake. I try to avoid criminal and Family Court matters. They are invariably bad experiences for all concerned. In this instance I acted for a touring American group of the 'death metal' genre. The lead singer decided that it would be a good idea to import some marijuana for his own use. Someone had told him marijuana was in short supply in Australia. A sniffer dog took a particular interest in him and he was subsequently filmed emptying his boot in the Customs toilet at Melbourne Airport. When presented with the video he surrendered. The procedure in these cases is for the person to be taken directly from the airport to the Broadmeadows Magistrates' Court and the matter is then heard. One of the likely consequences is that the offender is put on the next plane out of Australia. This obviously would create major problems for a promoter. I accompanied my client and the officers to the police car and was promptly told to take my own transport. I then took two hours trying to find the Court. The waiting police regretted their lack of courtesy. They missed their lunch. As for my client, he was allowed to stay in Australia on certain conditions and the tour continued.

Towards the late eighties cynicism started to become the defining characteristic of the industry. This reached its peak when Betty Boo convinced everyone she could sing, Milli Vannilli didn't even try and Jason and Kylie became megastars of TV merchandising. At that time I represented a producer who was trying to produce a record for a visually attractive but utterly unmusical group of young ladies. He was having difficulty with their first single. Finally he solved his problem. He gave them some money, told them to go shopping, and recorded the track in their absence. It became a Top-10 hit in Australia.

As a general rule, the less talent an artist has, the more the marketing machine is activated, the more hysterical is the reception by the fans and the shorter is the career. As was shown this is particularly the case with artists who target younger, prepubescent fans. The love affair is intense, immediate and overwhelming. The rejection is usually total and brutal. No self-respecting teenager of 14 years of age will want it known that three months before they had a poster on their wall of a group which now appeals to 13-year-olds, or even worse, their 13-year-old sister. Pseudo Echo and Uncanny X-Men fell victim to this phenomenon. The Cockroaches learnt by it and made a fortune as The Wiggles.

Another feature of the late eighties was the development of groups which were essentially vehicles for a singer/songwriter. Crowded House was probably the best example, although Divinyls and Icehouse were run on pretty much the same lines. Some of the highlights were the long-overdue success of John Farnham and the emergence of the Aboriginal bands Yothu Yindi and Blekbala Mujik.

The nineties commenced with the announcement that there was to be an Inquiry into the industry. This jolted the industry out of its stupor. People started to question whether or not it was healthy for the industry to continue to be run over a long lunch at Beppi's in Sydney (or was it the Purple Cow?). I am not suggesting that the industry should have found another restaurant. Things were never going to be the same again.

The industry was going grey. Gerry and the Pacemakers had become Gerry and his Pacemaker. The songwriters and performers of the seventies were now approaching middle age. They still had the technical know-how, maturity and experience to write songs. However, the means of exploiting those songs – the tour – was becoming a thing of the past. Glenn Wheatley and Michael Gudinski the Melbourne icons were still active but in between they were attending parents' meetings and being castigated by 21-year-old teachers. The real problem was that the audience had moved on. The sound of the rhythm section in the old venues in Melbourne was replaced by the sound of money being pumped into poker machines.

Ironically, this led to a resurgence in the popularity of seventies-type cover bands. To rub salt into the wounds they were playing Cold Chisel and AC/DC songs. They were called 'tribute bands' but were known in the industry as 'scam bands'. Signs were placed outside hotels proclaiming 'live band'. Presumably this was to distinguish it from a 'dead band'. Young songwriters simply did not get a go. Things reached the point of absurdity when I represented a Doors tribute band who issued proceedings against another Doors tribute band on the basis that the second tribute band was damaging the artistic integrity, credibility and reputation of the first.

Some of the nineties bands were so exciting that members of the audience started to commit suicide by first invading and then diving off the stage. Even this became institutionalised by the creation of the 'mosh pit'. The Beastie Boys actually published a set of rules of the pit 'because real people really do get really hurt!' Ironically this was all supposed to be anti-establishment. In reality it was proof positive that even the early eighties 'punks' were getting old. They had become the establishment.

The new millennium has seen a resurgence in the industry. In a strange sort of way it has been caused by a breakdown in the traditional methods of funding, recording and distributing recorded product. The traditional players in the music industry include:

- originators or creators; songwriters on the one hand and performing artists and musicians on the other.;
- the publishers and record companies who provide capital;
- the collection societies, Australasian Performing Rights Association (APRA) and Australasian Mechanical Copyright Owners' Society (AMCOS), which represent both publishers and songwriters, and Phonographic Performance Company of Australia (PPCA), which represents record companies;
- those involved in the recording process, producers, engineers, studio staff, artwork designers, printers and manufacturers;

- promoters, booking agents, ticketing agencies and providers of technical services including sound, lighting and security;
- lawyers, accountants and psychiatrists;
- those concerned with distribution, retailing, advertising, journalism and promotion;
- the many support and educational organisations including The Push in Melbourne and Southern Cross University;
- consumers who buy or rent records, attend concerts and clubs, go to movies and listen to music in shops, offices, restaurants, taxis and 'on hold'.

This all sounds very complicated but in practice it is quite structured. Record and publishing companies are in the business of making a profit by taking a commercial risk. They provide risk capital by way of advances for songwriting, recording and sometimes for touring. These advances are recoupable against artist royalties but are not returnable. In other words if the record doesn't sell, the advance is not repayable by the artist. This means that there is a very real commercial risk. Record companies also incur the costs of manufacturing, distributing and promoting the sale of records.

From the perspective of the artist, there is a risk that good songs and career opportunities might be squandered. There is not much point writing and recording a great Christmas song if it gets released on Boxing Day. There is also no value in an artist recording songs which have taken years to accumulate if the record is released a week after the promotional tour ends. This happened with a promising group, The Degenerates.

It is easy to recognise recording-company staff. The person who wears jeans, sniffs a lot, misses appointments, never sits still, drives a battered Alfa and says 'yes' to everything is the Artist & Repertoire Manager (A & R). He or she is responsible for the artists and their repertoire. The person who grunts, is on time for appointments, wears Gucci jeans and drives a second-hand BMW is the Business Affairs (not Business & Affairs) Manager. He or she is responsible for legal matters. The one who is pale and drawn, wears a grey suit, drives a station wagon and says 'no' to everything is the financial director. The CEO is the one who is never there.

The principal role of the modern publisher is to provide money. That is the commercial risk a publisher takes and the industry would not exist without access to capital. Ironically the traditional role of publishing, getting covers or songs in a film, on a Farnham album or in an advertisement, seems to have been forgotten by most publishers. John Anderson of EMI is, and John Bromell of Warner was, an exception.

Technology has added a new dimension to the industry. In 1985 it was not uncommon for a recording-plus-video budget for a first-class international record to be $300,000 or thereabouts. The Models boast about a record which cost $600,000, supported by a video which cost $150,000.[10] The record sold fifteen copies. I acted for a group which broke up before a record, which had cost $500,000 to produce, was released. The members of that group are now killing time in cover bands. Today a new group can record its own songs and make a video for a fraction of that sum.

By using the internet and other methods of distribution, artists can promote and distribute their music. This has fragmented the industry but at the same time has given it new life creatively. My first experience of this was with a young group in the early nineties, Southern Sons. They recorded their album in their lounge room for next to nothing using their skills with technology. Phil Buckle's songs helped. They had to inflate the recording budget to generate interest from the recording company notwithstanding that the company loved the songs. Today, young groups can bypass the traditional infrastructure of the music industry. This gives them total creative control of their product.

Technology has also allowed consumers to access product either by downloading or simply burning a CD without any commercial return to the creators. This is the greatest problem facing the industry today. But technology has facilitated a more subtle malaise. Configurations have changed from vinyl to tape, compact disc and now to DVD. This has sustained and enhanced the value of back catalogues to the detriment of new material. It has partly fulfilled the dreams of record company executives of an artist-free industry but is terminal for the creative environment.

Of course the lawyers have a role to play. There are those who represent the corporate infrastructure of the industry, that is the record and publishing companies and their offshoots. They are usually occupied in hearings before the Copyright Tribunal and are based in Sydney. There have never been more than half a dozen lawyers representing artists and often they were Melbourne based. Because of this, Australian lawyers act for many artists and groups. They limit their activities to legal matters, contract, copyright, taxation and associated litigation. They negotiate and formalise rather than initiate contracts. They try not to offer helpful advice as to which song should be the next single.

The American practice, where lawyers often act as managers, is not appropriate in Australia. This is partly due to our fixed-fee basis of remuneration as distinct from the percentages charged by American lawyers. It is also because there are many more lawyers in America and individually they act for fewer clients than Australian lawyers. The result is that Australian lawyers negotiate contracts with a cross-section of record and publishing companies. An American lawyer is locked into one successful client who often has a long-term relationship with one record company or publisher. For that reason American lawyers have a rather limited network and develop a close and sometimes unhealthy relationship with a record company.

There have been some attempts by Australian lawyers to break into management by providing more extensive and quasi-managerial services. This is a short-term career move because it alienates other managers, highlights a conflict of interest (the lawyer is supposed to be acting for the client not the lawyer) and quickly reveals the inadequacies of the lawyer – more on this later.

Because of the international nature of the industry the contracts and principles of copyright are much the same throughout the world. There is little difference in negotiating a contract with Sony in New York and Sony in Sydney. Any logistical problems caused by distance have long been overcome, initially by the fax machine and ultimately by the internet. It's fair to say that Australian artists today are better represented than they were thirty years ago. They are still exploited but at least today they know it. There is now a bank of experience and expertise with managers, lawyers, accountants and industry personnel. The success of Savage Garden confirms that the talent is there although their premature demise shows that with creative people nothing much has changed. I will now look at this in more detail.

CHAPTER 3 – MEN OUT OF WORK

Men at Work began as a four-piece band with Colin Hay (vocals and guitar), Ron Strykert (bass guitar), Greg Ham (flute & saxophone) and Jerry Speiser (drums) in May 1979. Prior to that it was the Wiggles of the seventies and was touring schools with Riff-Raff, a performing group associated with the West Theatre in Melbourne. At the same time the band was playing one night a week at the Cricketers Arms Hotel in Richmond and was developing a repertoire of a dozen or so songs. John Rees joined the band as the bass guitar player in July 1979 and after that Ron Strykert played guitar. The group gave its first performance as a five-piece at the Cricketers on 6 September 1979. They were unique in that John and Colin only had two eyes between them.

The band attracted no interest from the Australian recording industry. In 1980 it was one of the first Australian groups to establish its own record label, MAW Music. On 24 February 1980, at Richmond Recorders in Melbourne, the group recorded its first 'double A' - side single, featuring 'Down Under' and 'Key Punch Operator'. Richmond Recorders was fundamental to the development of contemporary music in Melbourne. They encouraged many acts including Men at Work and The Models to record there for minimal budgets. Their strange working hours and even stranger diets seemed to appeal to many young musicians. There is much for which to thank Tim Stobart and the early engineers like Tony Cohen. However, I would not recommend that they ever be given control of a health farm.

In March 1980 an old university friend of Colin's, Russell Deppeler, was appointed manager of the group. The band consisted of a loose form of partnership involving eight people including Deppeler, the five members of the band and two roadies who left the band when it was formally established in mid-1981. By that time the group had a regular 'gig' every Thursday at the Cricketers and each member was earning approximately

$50 per week. Throughout 1980 the band continued to develop its style and repertoire and toured Australia.

From about mid-1980, Michael Ware and the then Artist & Repertoire Manager of CBS Records (now Sony) Peter Karpin, became interested in the group and exerted their influence on CBS to offer a recording contract. It did so reluctantly and after several other record companies had 'passed'. On 9 February 1981, the recording contract was signed with CBS Australia. That was followed on 9 March 1981 by a publishing contract with a CBS affiliate, April Music. When these agreements were signed no independent advice was taken. That was not uncommon at that time as a recording contract was seen as a necessary step to success. Contracts would be offered as prizes on TV talent quests. As far as the artists were concerned the recording and publishing contracts were minimalist to say the least. Nominal advances were paid.

In March 1981, the group recorded a live concert at the Barleycorn Hotel in Melbourne for an FM radio station. The first single for CBS was recorded in a session from 1-3 May 1981 at the then AAV Recording Studios in Melbourne. The single 'Who Can It Be Now?' was produced by an American, Peter McIan. The 'B' side was 'Anyone for Tennis'. The single with the supporting video was released on 25 May 1981. At that time videos were regarded as quite novel. Touring was still considered to be the most effective method of promoting a record release.

From 6-8 April 1981, the group recorded demonstration tapes in Sydney of 15 songs. Their first album was recorded at Richmond Recorders from 27 July to 27 August 1981. It was *Business as Usual* and the recording costs were $30,000. As was customary, the release of the album was supported by a tour of Australia from August to December. The music and unique performing style of the group were very well received by Australians and a gold record was presented for the single 'Who Can It Be Now?' on 4 September 1981. The group was away – at least in Australia.

The first six months of 1982 were taken up with touring Australia. On 22 March 1982, demonstration tapes were recorded at Crystal Clear Studio in Melbourne for the second album *Cargo*. Crystal Clear Studio was owned by a client of mine, Phil Dwyer, who had managed Dove and with whom I am still often confused.

Despite the considerable success in Australia of *Business as Usual* and the obvious strength of the songs for *Cargo*, there was little interest in the group in America, perhaps as a result of its quirky and very Australian character. Throughout September, October and November 1982 a tour of Canada and the US took place. The Canadian tour was very successful and the sales which followed forced the Americans to take interest. The group toured Europe in December 1982. They exploited their success in Australia by a further tour along the East coast in January 1983. From late April to May they toured Japan followed by a tour which included England, US, Europe and Canada and finished at the end of October 1983.

By this stage the group had achieved success far beyond any Australian-based group. Sales of *Business as Usual* topped six million units. The singles 'Who Can It Be Now?' and 'Down Under' both went to number one in America. *Cargo* when released in 1983, sold four million units. The recording costs for *Cargo* were $70,000. It has been reported that the two albums sold one hundred million units. That is subject to the rule that any figures reported in the press relating to the music industry should always be divided by ten.

In November 1990, in a submission to the Prices Surveillance Authority, I calculated the income generated from sales and publishing of the two Men at Work albums.[1] The figures were not challenged and if anything they are conservative. On the basis that the two albums sold a total of ten million units the income generated for CBS was in the vicinity of forty million Australian dollars. Their investment in recording costs was a total of $100,000. April Music, the publisher, received in excess of three million dollars for a nominal investment. The songwriters would have shared approximately six million and the non-writers one million dollars. The artists, producer and manager would have shared record royalties of twenty million dollars or thereabouts. All of this was in the early eighties when a million dollars actually meant something. Of course the records have continued to be played and sold generating both recording and publishing income.

Fredric Dannen, in his exposé of the American recording industry asserts that 1981 and 1982 were bad years for CBS.[2] In late 1982 this all changed with the release of the Men at Work *Business as Usual* album and

Michael Jackson's *Thriller* which itself sold thirty-eight million units. Dannen notes that there was some irony in the release of *Business as Usual*. The album was delivered to CBS International in mid-1982. Its Vice President was Dick Asher. Neither Epic nor Columbia were interested in releasing it despite Asher's support. Finally, after Asher insisted, Al Teller, the head of Columbia, agreed to release the album 'to shut Dick up'. According to Dannen, by April 1983 Wall Street analysts were advised that *Thriller* and *Business as Usual* had brought about the long-awaited change in the financial fortunes of CBS Records.

There is some truth in the Dick Asher story, but he was being hounded by Deppeler who deserves some credit for the success. The timing of the ultimate release was opportune since it coincided with the launch of the twenty-four hour video channel MTV. The group had produced distinctive videos which were unashamedly Australian. They had also appointed their own publicist, Evan Hosie. The American record company only then really supported the release.

The strain of excessive touring, the lifestyle that goes with it and pressures created by international success began to take their toll. Rocket fuel could not have sustained their touring schedule. This was compounded by the unrealistic demands of record companies to produce hit songs and commercially successful records to a formula and timetable. The group was having 'musical differences'.

There were the usual tensions within the group, most of which could have been resolved had their success been a little more predictable and the pace of their touring a little less frenetic. There is no doubt the group was a victim of its own success. None of this was helped by the fact that their manager Russell Deppeler started managing the group as a favour to his 'mate' and found within two years he was managing one of the most successful groups in the world.

With due respect to Russell, Men at Work was one of the worst-managed acts in Australia. He would retort that it was also the most successful. Contrast Men at Work with groups like Mental as Anything, Boom Crash Opera and The Angels who were managed to perfection and never achieved international success. Russell must be given some credit for the pressure he applied to CBS International to force a release of *Business as Usual*. It should also be acknowledged that the group he managed had a single and album which were simultaneously number one on the American and UK charts. No other Australian manager has achieved that. His only real failing was that he couldn't control Colin. Who could? Russell might ask 'why would you try?'.

There were the usual differences between songwriters and non-writers. More than anything however they just started to get on each other's nerves. There was no 'other woman'. The disputes which followed and led to the ultimate demise of the group and the long-term disruption of their relationships had, aside from some of the games that lawyers play, little or nothing to do with money. They had everything to do with being on the road continuously and the pressure on the songwriters to deliver international hits. The bar had been set too high.

About the time the group signed the recording and publishing contracts, they confronted the problem of non-writers having a share of publishing income. It is common for non-writers to share in publishing income from songs recorded by a group. This recognises that most groups remain unrecouped in relation to their recording contracts. They receive no recording royalties whereas songwriters receive advances on signing publishing agreements and ongoing cash flow from APRA income. The share received by the non-writers is usually quite small but in the case of Men at Work no one in April 1981 could imagine the income that would be generated. It was agreed that non-writers, including the manager, would have a share in publishing income generated from songs recorded by the group.

On 30 June 1981, the partnership which by then included Deppeler, assigned their rights to a company, Men at Work Pty Ltd. The company was trustee for a unit trust the unit holders of which were companies acting as trustees in their own right for the six 'members'. This was, and still is, a standard structure. It is complemented by each member entering into an agreement with the company agreeing to provide his or her services as a performer.

Because of the level of success achieved in Australia, Europe and Canada, by mid-1982 the group was given the opportunity to renegotiate its recording contract. The original contract the group signed was bad but understandable given their poor bargaining position at the time. The renegotiation, which was carried out in the midst of major international success, was disappointing to put it mildly. It was negotiated by Grubman Indursky & Schindler who had a strong connection with CBS.[3] They were actually paid a success bonus by Men at Work. The renegotiated contract with CBS Australia was dated 1 January 1983.

Throughout this period, Deppeler had submitted several management contracts, all of which had been rejected. On 25 July 1983 a handwritten agreement was prepared to cover the following year. The arrangement involved using the services of a co-manager, Nathan Brenner, a well-known and experienced identity in the Australian music industry and an American, Lars Sorenson, who was experienced in the American industry. Deppeler was not only the manager of the corporate entity but also managed each of the musicians personally. This was to become an important issue when the lawyers became active.

As is always the case with international success in the contemporary music industry, money in great quantities is generated quickly and without any real planning. In 1981 the term 'business plan' had not been invented. Taxation always becomes a paramount and immediate concern. The group's accountant was Martin Jurblum of the firm Lachman & Feldmann Pty which about that time merged with Stanton Partners Pty. Jurblum identified the tax problems the group was about to face in late 1982. He approached the then accounting firm of Coopers & Lybrand for advice.

At that time Michael Brereton was an employee of Coopers & Lybrand. Michael was 27 years of age, had qualifications in law and economics and had joined Coopers & Lybrand twelve months previously to obtain taxation experience. Michael had presented a paper on international tax planning in October 1980.[4] He also presented a paper to the Victorian Law Institute based on the taxation aspects of the music industry in February 1984.[5] Michael left Coopers & Lybrand and established the legal firm of Harding Brereton & Shiff on 1 March 1983. His sister Marie was a friend and client of mine. Michael was supposed to do his articles of clerkship with me but somehow got lost along the way.

It was standard in the music industry in the late seventies and early eighties to make use of what was colloquially known as 'the Dutch sandwich'. Australian income tax was only payable on income generated from an Australian source for non-residents or derived by an Australian resident from any source. It was a relatively easy matter to create a situation when dealing with income from an American or European source whereby the recipient was a company which was a non-resident of Australia, thereby removing any liability to pay Australian tax.

The difficulty with a structure of this type vis-à-vis America was that American withholding tax might be payable and arguably there might also be a liability to pay American federal income tax. This problem could be solved by making use of the American double tax agreement with Holland which allowed royalties to be paid without American withholding tax.

Because Holland was only a conduit for the income, a minimum tax rate of say 6% would be paid in Holland. This would be the subject of a formal agreement with the Dutch tax authorities. A company could be established in the Netherlands, the shareholder of which would be a further company incorporated in the Netherlands Antilles. In turn that company would be owned by a company incorporated in the Channel Islands. The ultimate owner would be a Hong Kong charitable trust.

To enable the Dutch company to derive the US source income it was necessary to transfer the income-earning asset to that company for a commercial value, that is to sell it. The 'asset' would be either the copyrights in recorded masters or publishing copyrights. The proceeds of sale would be received in Australia as a capital gain which was tax-free. There were no capital gains taxes in Australia then. Those monies on being received in Australia would alleviate any ongoing cash flow problems. Because Netherlands Antilles was a 'scheduled tax haven' it was necessary to obtain Reserve Bank approval. Nevertheless, such a structure was quite legal and effective at the time.

The downside was that the structure required by its very nature the principals to lose control over, and ownership of, their assets. In other words there was always an element of 'wink, wink, nudge, nudge' or mutual trust involved. That sort of arrangement works pre-marriage and sometimes survives the honeymoon but it can be a disaster during the divorce. Death can also be a complicating factor, as was experienced on the unfortunate demise of Michael Hutchence. 'Where have all those assets gone?' is usually the question. The answer is that they have been disposed of long ago and no longer form part of the estate of the deceased for purposes of the deceased's Will. This can be an unpleasant surprise for the beneficiaries when the Will is read out.

Michael Brereton took advice from Counsel and the structure which was contemplated was legal. The proposed structure and all the advices obtained were based on the assumption that the company would sell its interest in the copyrights in certain recorded masters for good consideration. This would be a capital, tax-free receipt. Obviously any commercially reasonable price for those assets was millions of dollars. More importantly, it is paramount that the assets being sold are properly analysed and defined. At the very least, it is generally considered a good idea that the assets are owned by the company which purports to sell them. CBS owned the copyrights in the masters.

By mid-1983 tensions within the group started to spin out of control. Jerry Speiser appointed his sister to act as his personal manager. On 15, 16 and 17 August 1983 a meeting took place at Cape Cod in America. It was addressed by Michael Brereton and ostensibly was called to discuss the offshore structure. At that meeting, a document was tendered which was headed 'Men at Work – Present Operating Structure and Effect of a Change in Ownership'. Michael advised that he had taken advice from Counsel in relation to the effect on the structure should a member leave the group. The discussion then turned to the 'compulsory purchase or redemption of any equity holder'. Michael suggested that Counsel's view was that a member's services could be terminated by the company at any time.

It was clear that the group had split into two factions, the rhythm section on the one hand, Speiser and Rees, the drummer and bass player respectively, and Deppeler and the songwriters Hay, Ham and Strykert on the other. The word 'faction' is probably too strong in the case of Jerry and John who were enjoined by circumstance. The discussion at Cape Cod sent a message to the rhythm section that they were on notice.

In retrospect it seems fairly clear now that Hay, Ham and Strykert had decided to remove Speiser. Jerry is an intelligent and professional, if somewhat intense, person who was perhaps not that easy to live with on the road. Appointing his sister as his personal manager during a tour probably did not help. However, throughout the discussions that followed there was never any suggestion that Jerry lacked the necessary energy and skills as a musician or was unreliable. There was never any criticism of Rees either implied or expressed.

For whatever reason Hay, Ham and Strykert had decided that they could no longer work with Jerry and, while they were at it, might as well dispense with John. This was a mistake. John is a loyal and committed person of integrity who had a formal background in music. He was always of the view that there was an understanding from the beginning that if any member left the group it would disband. He could not accept that a member of the group could be removed.

The corporate structure of the group did not facilitate the acquisition of a member's equity in the group. A member's services as a musician were provided via his employment agreement. It was feasible under these agreements for the group to remove a member as a performing member on the basis of real or perceived grievances. That would not of itself change the exiting member's entitlement to shares in the company or units in the Trust.

Ominously the attempt to remove two members of a group of five raised immediate issues as to a valuation of the assets including goodwill. This focused attention on the offshore structure. Sacking one member of a group was a distraction. Sacking two was self-destruction. The proposals put forward by Michael at the Cape Cod meeting were not pursued but the seeds of discontent had been sown. The matter came to a head in bizarre and inappropriate circumstances in April 1984.

On 30 April 1984 Deppeler sent letters by courier to John Rees and Jerry Speiser. The letter to John stated that he was to attend a meeting at the Southern Cross Hotel, the place made famous by the Beatles when they visited Melbourne on 2 May 1964. This was unnecessarily formal and provocative. John was advised to attend with his professional adviser. Of course, at that time, Deppeler was John's business adviser and manager and Michael Brereton was his legal adviser.

Enclosed with the letter to John was a document headed 'General Nature of Business'. It referred to a letter from Hay, Ham, Strykert and Deppeler which included this sentence: 'As you are aware, there has been growing ill feeling between various individuals in the band. In addition, it has been apparent that there are artistic differences which we believe cannot be resolved'. The letter and attachment were signed by Deppeler. John had never been advised prior to that correspondence of any artistic differences within the group. There were none.

John attended the meeting on 2 May 1984 with his manager (Deppeler), his lawyer (Brereton) and his accountant (Jurblum). Jerry Speiser also attended with his lawyer, Brian Ward. At that meeting it was stated that Hay, Ham Strykert and Deppeler wanted John and Jerry out of the band. Because of the obvious conflicts of the people involved, the meeting was adjourned at the request of Ward and on his insistence certain undertakings were given. Those undertakings become crucial.

On 11 May 1984 John Rees instructed me to act for him. We attended the adjourned meeting at the Southern Cross Hotel on 24 May 1984. The undertakings given at the previous meeting were confirmed. Those undertakings were to the effect that there would be no action taken by any lawyer, accountant, manager or member of the group in relation to the professional activities of the group until there was unanimous agreement: not a good concession to make when you have the numbers. This effectively prevented the continuing members from recording another album until the dispute was resolved. CBS would have been really pleased when they heard that.

On 13 August 1984 Strykert, Hay and Ham called for a further meeting of the company to take place on 28 August 1984 – again at the Alpha Room, Southern Cross Hotel. The meeting was attended by Hay, Ham and Strykert, Deppeler, Brereton and Leon Zwier from Harding Brereton & Shiff, Martin Jurblum from Lachman & Feldmann, Jerry and his sister manager Irene and lawyer Brian Ward, John Rees and myself. It was formally a directors' meeting of the company and degenerated into farce. At the end of that meeting it was obvious that litigation was inevitable. That litigation encompassed the following:

- Jerry Speiser and Jerry Speiser Productions Pty Ltd issued a writ in the Supreme Court of Victoria against the partners of Harding Brereton & Shiff and Lachman & Feldmann. It was seeking their removal as solicitors and accountants respectively for the Men at

Work structure and the adjournment of any proposed meeting. This was based on the conflicts of interest.

- There were audits of CBS carried out by both American and Australian accountants.
- A Supreme Court writ was issued by John Rees and his company alleging negligence against Coopers & Lybrand over the tax structure. Subsequently Coopers & Lybrand joined Michael Brereton and Martin Jurblum as third parties to the action.
- An arbitration occurred in relation to monies which had been paid as a 'special advance' to Hay, Ham, Strykert & Deppeler which excluded Rees and Speiser.
- The Taxation Department salivated.

Litigation continued for five years or so after the break-up. The group continued with Hay and Ham and various new members. That was after a negotiated settlement involving the usual royalty entitlements and overrides to the outgoing members. As for the group, after so many meetings at the Southern Cross Hotel there was no creative energy left.

During the course of negotiations, in an attempt to impose a value for goodwill, I had made the statement that Men at Work could release a third album featuring 'Bah Bah Black Sheep' and it would sell a million copies. I was wrong. A third album entitled *Two Hearts* was finally released in 1985. It included a track called 'Snakes & Ladders' which has the lyrics 'there's a snake at the top of every ladder who will tell you he's your best friend'. Paranoia prevailed. The album was not received well critically and was a failure commercially. *Two Hearts*, including videos, cost $450,000 to record. It was self-produced. It shipped approximately 300,000 copies and did not recoup its recording costs. The number of records shipped back by the retailers as 'returns' was never disclosed. It failed to make an impression on charts anywhere. Only Molly Meldrum thought it was 'very good'.[6]

Two months after the release of *Two Hearts* it was all over. There was only one original member left in the band. Colin had proved his point. It really was his band. Ralph Novak, a reviewer in *People Weekly* (USA) on 1 July 1985 noted that the group suffered a 'manpower shortage'.[7] Further, 'the ensemble's drumming has been taken over by a human wave of percussionists including Ham and Hay. They lay down a monotonous, slamming beat that all but overwhelms the album'.[8] There was some talk years later of a revival and discussions took place in relation to ownership of the trademark. This was finally resolved 'amicably'. Rees and Speiser had no further involvement in the group.

It was and remains my view that had commonsense prevailed there would have been no attempt to break up the group prior to recording the third album. Once that album had been released it would have facilitated the usual spin-off of *Greatest Hits*, *Best Of*, *Live*, *Boxed Sets* etc., for the next twenty years. Furthermore, had John and Jerry been approached by the people they regarded as friends on the basis that the group would record a third album and then disband or they leave, they probably would have accepted that. A little courtesy can go a long way. To attempt to solve what was essentially a relationship problem via a letter sent by courier calling for a meeting in the Southern Cross Hotel was foolish in the extreme. That guaranteed the demise of the group and the litigation and angst that followed.

To some degree the errors of judgement were a reflection of the inexperience of the manager and lawyers involved. Had this occurred in 2003 I have no doubt that Michael Brereton, Brian Ward and I could have resolved the 'artistic differences' and preserved the imagery and commercial value in the 'brand'. That is not to say we would have maintained the friendships between the members which by that stage were fractured by frustration and suspicion.

Some might say that the only people to gain from this were the lawyers and accountants. It is easy to forget that a case of this kind, with many almost insurmountable legal problems and embittered personal relationships is demanding on the professional advisers and not necessarily remunerative in the longer term. The facts speak for themselves:

- Coady Dwyer & Associates dissolved in December 1988.
- Harding Brereton & Shiff and its successor Dessau Harding Brereton self-destructed. Leon Zwier went on to represent the Administrators in the collapse of Ansett. I am still arguing with Michael Brereton but these days we do it over lunch.

- Stanton & Partners dissolved.
- Coopers & Lybrand were submerged.
- The Southern Cross Hotel was demolished.
- John Rees is teaching music at a Christian School in Leongatha, Victoria, and enjoying life. He is still a loyal friend.

It really is correct to say that there were no winners from the Men at Work saga. By 1985, in a *Penthouse* interview by Glenn A. Baker,[9] Colin Hay had worked out what it is all about. He said, 'I am a lot clearer about what I want to do. I want to make Gaelic Soul. That's my roots. I want the rhythm section to be more flexible, the style more mellow, but dense'.[10] By the summer of 2002 he was back performing at beach resorts along the east coast of Australia.

CHAPTER 4 – IF YOU LEAVE ME CAN I COME TOO?

This sardonic lyric by Mental as Anything was intended to apply to the end of a love affair. It applies equally to many groups in the music industry. Three years after having been ousted from Men at Work, John Rees was quoted as saying, 'I still love them'.[1]

To understand the dynamics of a group it is helpful to have some appreciation of the pressures that exist. One of the main reasons Men at Work broke up was the tension caused by continuous touring. There are people who are simply not suited to touring. Read Glenn Wheatley's account of Little River Band[2] and ask yourself if Graham Goble should ever have been on the road. James Freud and Marc Hunter were too well suited. Brian Cadd also fits into this category. Some even tour without knowing they are touring. I once asked Christine Amphlett where she was (meaning which hotel) so I could ring her back. She asked Mark McEntee who, after some thought, replied Chicago. That must have put me off balance. I drafted a contract for them which extended automatically from 'mouth' to 'mouth'.

Some say it is too arduous for female artists to tour. If this is correct Renée Geyer must be a male. She seems to have been born to it. As only Renée could, she has described the characters who make up a group.[3] I have known all of them. Renée identifies 'nut man', 'open man', 'book man' and 'mean man'.[4] I like the one who is into God but likes money too. He rings every day and starts each conversation with, 'It's not really important, don't want to bother you, but …'.

So what does cause a group to break up? Many groups including Boom Crash Opera, Australian Crawl, Mondo Rock and The Angels had given it their best shot. Sometimes, and Dragon is probably the best example, lifestyle factors were responsible.[5] In the case of Midnight Oil, time simply took its course.[6] It's unfortunate the same cannot be said about The Rolling Stones. Two groups I acted for self-destructed at the peak of their success and everything that goes with it. Little River Band and Crowded House had worked long and hard for their success. Both groups were at the stage where the fruit was there for the picking.

Two of the most perceptive articles I have read about the music industry were both written by Peter Wilmoth from *The Age*. One concerned Men at Work[7] and the other Crowded House.[8] These articles emphasise the stresses which are an inherent part of touring and recording at that level. It is easy to forget that the industry is about people, and artistic people at that. Obviously relationships are an important factor. It is fair to say Graham Goble and Glenn Shorrock or Colin Hay and Jerry Speiser were not soul mates. Neil Finn had his problems with Paul Hester although that is not necessarily a criticism of Paul.

In 1996, Neil complained of the pressures caused by only having one songwriter in the band. Neil said that the bands which generally survive have 'a creative core of two main writers at least, where the friction, the bounce between these two people is what makes the music evolve and keep changing and being exciting'.[9] This is a little disingenuous of Neil since he controlled the group and created the environment where there was minimal creative input from the other members, but his analysis is very close to the truth.

In both Men at Work and Crowded House there was too much pressure on the principal songwriters to deliver hit songs. It is not surprising that after the break-up Colin was off to find his Celtic roots and Neil was going to make 'very experimental'[10] music and a 'lightness descended'[11] upon him.

Little River Band signed its first recording agreement with EMI on 18 June 1975. The members of the group were Glenn Shorrock, Derek Pellicci, Rick Formosa, Graham Goble, Gerard Bertelkamp (Beeb Birtles) and Roger McLachlan. By 1977 Rick had left to study music at the Sorbonne in Paris and Roger had been asked to leave because Graham and Beeb wanted him out. His downfall was that he liked to have fun. David Briggs replaced Rick and George McArdle replaced Roger. George didn't like to have fun and left the band in 1979 to become a Bible student. The band was unique, not only for its songs but because of the vocal harmonies between Glenn, Graham and Beeb. It was also one of the best live acts I have ever seen.

There was always some friction between Glenn Shorrock on the one hand and Graham and Beeb on the other. To some extent this gave the band its spark but it was only due to Glenn Wheatley's skill and determination that the band lasted as long as it did. Glenn Shorrock is outgoing, open, at peace with himself and enjoys the company of other people. He is not judgemental and has even publicly acknowledged that he is a friend of Brian Cadd. Beeb and Graham were the total opposites of Glenn. With them there was always another agenda. The irony was that along the way Glenn, with the help of an astute and loyal wife, became wealthy although you would never know it. Aside from his hair he hasn't changed.

For Graham and Beeb life was to be endured. Graham was quoted in 1978 as saying: 'I enjoy rehearsals more than the actual performance. As soon as they start standing up and screaming, I know they're not interested in the music and I'm not interested in playing for those sort of people – I don't get any kicks on stage'.[12] Graham was probably not high on the Christmas-card list of the record company promotions department.

From a lawyer's point of view Little River Band was great. Over the years I acted for the group I had no difficulty with any of them. But the mix within the group was terminal and the intensive care from Glenn Wheatley was only putting off the inevitable. By 1982 it had arrived. Graham wanted to replace Glenn Shorrock with John Farnham. Glenn Shorrock, who was the soul if not the heart of the band, was effectively sacked. At that point I lost interest in Little River Band. I was hopelessly conflicted anyway. Glenn Shorrock retained Glenn Wheatley as his manager and myself as his solicitor. I was always pleased about that. Oh, and before I forget, Graham isn't Graham anymore. He is now Graehame Goble. Glenn Shorrock is still Glenn Shorrock.

The group has continued in various configurations. The goodwill and intellectual property, the trademark and name, was retained by the company which continued to conduct the professional activities of the group. As the members left they sold their shares. The practical implications of this became evident in 2002 when Glenn, Graehame and Beeb wanted to re-form under the name. They were prevented from doing so by the original company which still owns it. The case was ultimately settled.[13] It was a sad exercise in futility. The three now performing as BSG "the original voices of Little River Band" are trying to claim their rightful position in the annals of 'heritage rock'. It has very little to do with contemporary music.

Prior to the mid-seventies, groups usually consisted of a loose informal partnership the members of which, with few exceptions, maintained their day jobs. With the success of groups typified by Little River Band, The Angels and Split Enz, things changed rapidly. The songs they recorded were composed by members of the band and they became part of the infrastructure of the industry rather than on the periphery as performers.

This gave rise to two potential causes of disputation which had to be addressed. One was the inequality in financial rewards accruing to the songwriter and non-songwriter members of the band. The other was that a member of a band who was a 'mate' and capable of performing around the pubs in Melbourne might not have the necessary expertise or motivation to perform on records for international release or to tour internationally. This was sometimes referred to as the 'bass player/drummer syndrome'. It implied that at a certain stage in a band's career the rhythm section would have to go. For some reason, bass players and drummers (with notable exceptions such as Paul McCartney, Roger Waters, Sting and Phil Collins) tend not to be songwriters and are thought to be dispensable.

The disparity between the income of songwriters and non-songwriters in a group is understandable. A group needs a hit song like a jockey needs a good horse. Peter Cupples has often said that Stylus was one hit short of stardom. He is also quick to point out that they were however a 'good hair band'. Conversely a songwriter needs a group as a vehicle to commercially exploit his or her songs. Songwriting requires exceptional skills and application. It is not unreasonable to expect a songwriter to be remunerated for those endeavours. Because of the personal and somewhat solitary nature of songwriting, it is also fair that a songwriter should retain control over the commercial exploitation of his or her song.

The great majority of Australian groups never receive any artist royalties from record sales. Because of recoupable contracts, that is recording contracts where recording costs are recouped from artist royalties before the artist receives any income, most artists remain un-recouped throughout their recording careers. They rely almost entirely on income from performing and welfare.

Publishing income accrues directly to the publisher/songwriter and not the performers. Publishing income includes performance income, that is income collected by APRA and its affiliates on behalf of the songwriters in relation to public performances of their songs. It also includes mechanical royalties which are paid by the record company to the songwriter for the right to reproduce the songs on record. Any publishing advance is also paid to the songwriter. This can result in the songwriter driving a Porsche and the non-writer, irrespective of the fact that he or she may be the lead singer of the band and publicly regarded as an Australian idol, still paying off the family Ford. Fame and fortune do not necessarily go hand in hand. This can cause resentment, particularly when partners become involved.

The challenge is to maximise the skills of the songwriter and the performing artists to achieve commercial success and to give everyone a fair share of the accolades and financial rewards that accrue. Finding a solution is a matter of balance. One extreme is the Hunters & Collectors or Goanna type of group which might regard a band as a co-operative. All income from both recording and publishing accrues to the group and is shared equally. The songs are registered equally with APRA in the names of the members of the group. That structure sometimes also treats the manager as a member of the group. This usually results in disputation because it fails to properly acknowledge and reward the skills and endeavours of the songwriter. Should not the songwriter, who has written a song which exposes his or her soul to the world, have the final say as to whether or not a record by the group featuring that song is used in a car advertisement?

The middle ground acknowledges the right of the songwriter to control the use of the song, such as in advertisements and films. The songs are registered in the name of the songwriter. However, the members agree contractually that some portion of the income from publishing songs recorded by the group should be divided equally between the group members including the songwriter. This requires that a manager or company on behalf of the group receives monies from the record and publishing companies, collection societies or the writer and apportions that income between the group. This might be appropriate for a group like Mental as Anything.

At the other extreme is the group which really consists of the songwriter or songwriters who own and control the copyrights and receive all publishing income. They effectively treat the non-writers as session musicians. This might be appropriate for a Crowded House or Icehouse type of group. It fails to acknowledge the particular skills and contribution of the performing artists and can lead to premature break-ups which leave everyone in tears and is characterised by missed opportunities. It is always good to remember that the industry is contemporary and time is of the essence. A smaller percentage of something is better than 100% of nothing.

In my opinion the songwriter who has created the song should own it. This implies that there is general agreement between the group as to the contribution (if any) made by each member in composing the song and the percentages in which it is owned. Often a member of the group will come to a group session with a lyric, a riff or simply a rhythm or backing track and the group will work up the song. Immediately on completion of the session agreement should be reached as to the proportions in which the song is to be registered with APRA. This is usually not difficult provided it is done at that time.

It should be assumed that the lyrics and music each comprise 50% of the song. To a large extent the music consists of the melody. This would usually account for 30 to 40 of the 50% which makes up the music. If there is a contribution by the members of the group towards the music or lyrics that should be acknowledged and formalised.

Once the ownership of a song has been agreed it should be registered with APRA in the percentages which reflect the actual contribution of the parties, for example if there is one songwriter it should be registered in the name of that songwriter alone. If one person has written the lyrics and another the music they should be registered separately. If the writers have collaborated, that is worked together on the song, their respective interests should be registered. McCartney and Lennon each have a 50% interest in the lyrics and music irrespective of who wrote the music, lyrics or even the song. Thereafter the entitlements of non-writers to any publishing income becomes contractual. It is covered in the internal agreement between the group and does not impact on the ownership or exploitation of the song but rather is reflected in the division of income from it.

There should never be any binding agreement within a group to automatically accord members songwriting credits or ownership. If a non-writer owns part of a work and the writer wants to licence it for use in an advertisement or a film, the non-writer can veto that commercial opportunity. A songwriter should always retain ownership and creative control of his or her work.

In one particular case in which I was involved a very successful Australian producer composed a hit song to be recorded by a singer who was making a 'comeback'. To keep the ageing artist happy he was allowed to change four words in the lyrics and was credited with 5% of the song, that is, 10% of the lyrics. It was an inspiring and uplifting song. Some years later a soft-drink company wanted to pay the songwriter, who by then needed the money, a large sum for the rights to use the song in a national advertising campaign. The minority owner refused permission for the song to be licensed even though his recorded version was not to be used. The permission of both writers was required. The reason for refusing permission was expressed in terms of artistic integrity.

One of the problems with giving non-writers a share of publishing income is that it is derived not only from the version of the song recorded by the group but also from all other versions, that is covers by other artists. Although cover versions are fairly rare in the Australian industry, when they do happen they can generate large amounts of income, as in the case of Graham Goble's 'Reminiscing' which has been covered many times. There are potential problems in relation to performance monies in that APRA will account to the writer and may not differentiate between versions by the group or cover versions. The writer may then be required to account back to the other members. This can cause problems. It is always easier to deduct money prior to, rather than to try and recover it after, payment. Generally this is not be a problem because of the rarity of covers.

One possible solution is to agree that all members of the group including the writers share an agreed percentage, say, 15% of mechanical royalties generated by the group in relation to records recorded by the group. This is a fixed sum which is easily determined. Because the entitlement only relates to mechanical royalties the percentage is higher than it would be if non-writers were sharing all publishing income. The entitlement to performance and sundry income is retained by the writer.

When a group is engaged in these discussions the importance of a song cannot be overstated. The biggest recording budget in the world will not turn a bad song into a hit. All the successful groups in the late seventies and early eighties had great songs. The inflated recording budgets of the late eighties and early nineties were not able to resurrect songs which did not have the essential ingredients necessary to connect with people.

Songwriting is a lonely pastime. As has been said one of the main reasons Men at Work broke up was the pressure on Colin Hay to live up to his previous successes. Neil Finn has complained about the difficulty of writing songs without the input of a second songwriter in a group.[14] Surprisingly, for someone as talented as Neil, he was always nervous and uncomfortable when taking songs to the band.[15]

Tommy Tycho is dismissive of the whole process. He regards 'rock music' as 'banal noise' and considers that the lyrics are 'ludicrous' and show 'no integrity'.[16] All of that is understandable. Art is indeed in the eye of the beholder. But he goes on to dispute the integrity of The Beatles:

> I cannot believe that those four boys wrote all the compositions that they claim to have written. When you look at the musical style, there are two or three songs that they could never have written. Songs like "Yesterday", "Michelle" and "Norwegian Wood" are sophisticated, good pieces of music and I doubt that they were written by someone who did not have a sound, professionally trained musical background. Not in 100 years.[17]

The question might be asked, 'If they didn't write those songs who did?' Was it perhaps George Martin? Obviously he made a major contribution but whether that amounts to creating a new work or just producing or arranging an existing one is an age-old question. Paul O'Gorman has often pointed out that great songwriting has more to do with the heart and soul than music theory. My view is that those songs were composed by young people for young people.

Some understanding of the creative process is helpful. Neil Finn will carry a tape recorder with him and record snippets of melody, riffs etc. The late Marc Hunter had a somewhat less organised approach. In 1983 I had a meeting with Dragon and their manager Steve White in the Sebel Hotel in Sydney. They were due to record tracks for their album *Body and the Beat* the next day. Studios were booked and an expensive American producer was in the air. On leaving the Hotel room at about 3.00 am Steve asked Marc how the songs were coming along. Marc replied that he would start thinking about that tomorrow. The lesson I learnt that night was never to have a meeting in my hotel room. You can't leave and all the drinks are booked to your room.

James Freud utilised the William Burroughs technique in an upstairs room in the recording studio while the recording session was in process. Burroughs was a product of the beat generation. He shot his wife for target practice. To him words didn't really mean much. It was the impression words conveyed in the mind of the person which really mattered. Why bother stringing words together in a meaningful way? Just cut out words from a magazine, put them in a hat and see how they fall. Bowie thought this was a good idea. It was the methodology used in composing the songs for *Ziggy Stardust*.[18]

Little River Band reached a point where they would submit their songs in demo form and those to be recorded would be chosen by consensus with a little help from Glenn Wheatley and the producer. They would then attend the studio individually and record their contribution track by track. That way they didn't have to acknowledge each other's presence and their relationship could be kept professional. It didn't do much for the spontaneity of the performance. By that stage they really were Little River Bland. So much for the ongoing arguments about 'technique and feel' which Renée Geyer writes about.[19]

Australian cases disputing the actual ownership of a song are very rare. One example was the Noiseworks case (see chapter 9). There have been many examples of bitterness caused by a failure to agree on the ownership of, or credits for, a song which subsequently became a hit. Often this remains dormant for years. The crediting of The Beatles' songs to Lennon/McCartney did not always please Paul McCartney, particularly in relation to a song such as 'Yesterday' which was very close to his heart. Nor did the fact that they were subsequently owned by everyone (Robert Holmes à Court, Michael Jackson) except McCartney. In 2002 McCartney released an album and reversed the credits to McCartney/Lennon.

To reiterate, my advice is always that songs should be registered and credited in the names of the actual writers. The non-writers and the writers can be given a share of mechanical royalties from songs composed by members of the group paid in relation to records recorded by the group. 15% or thereabouts is probably reasonable. If they are given a share of all publishing income including mechanical, performance and sundry income, 10% might be reasonable.

The second issue concerned leaving members. This was the crisis faced by Men at Work and it has caused problems with several other groups. What happens when for one reason or another a member wants to leave, or is to be removed from, the band? Most internal agreements allow a band to remove a particular member for any reason. Of course, bands are not exempt from discrimination laws. My firm was involved in a case where a lead singer of a group was removed because she was pregnant. That is actionable.

A leaving member should retain all existing entitlements to artist royalties and a share of publishing income (if any) in relation to recordings recorded prior to his or her departure from the band. The problem of trying to value the goodwill of the band can be overcome by agreeing that it is nil and by allowing the exiting member to retain a share of artist royalties on the next album recorded by the band.

For a smooth transition there needs to be an appropriate clause in the internal band agreement. That clause must make it clear that the name of the band, any trademark, logo and domain name is retained by the continuing members. Any ongoing royalty entitlements can be paid direct to the leaving member subject of course to contractual obligations to the record company. Those royalties should be insulated from any label advances or future advances being cross-collateralised, that is, cross-recouped. This avoids the situation where an advance is paid to a continuing member of the band but is recouped against royalties due to the former member. Whether or not a record company will agree to this is another question.

Because recording contracts impose joint and several obligations (that is, obligations are imposed individually and collectively) on artists, it may be necessary to obtain a release from a record company in relation to any leaving member. None of this affects ongoing obligations under publishing contracts although there may be problems if a publishing agreement calls for a certain number of albums from a group in a particular line-up. Usually this is not a problem unless the exiting member is a key member.

Much confusion often surrounds the significance of a band's name. A company should register the business name under which it trades. A company name applies throughout Australia. Business names are effective in the State of registration. Incorporating a company or registering a business name in no way confers any proprietary interest in, or ownership of, the name. However, as a matter of practice, registration does make it difficult for someone else to register or trademark the name.

In a technical sense business-name registration simply represents compliance with business-name legislation in the particular State or Territory. The Registrar of Business Names can direct that the name be deregistered at any time should the Registrar consider the name is likely to cause confusion with another name which has been registered. The same applies to company names. Business Name Registrars or the Corporate Affairs Commissioner register names without giving any real consideration to the potential for confusion or conflict. That is not their responsibility. They tend to be reactionary not proactive.

The first step in the establishment of any group should be to register a business name. An international register of band names can be found at http://www.bandreg.com/right.htm. Whilst this may be of some assistance it has no particular legal significance. If the group survives the garage phase then it should be incorporated as a company. That company can then conduct its activities as trustee of a unit trust if the group's accountant thinks that is appropriate. The alternative is for the company to operate in its own right that is as a trading company.

Incorporating a company costs about $1000 but it is the cheapest form of insurance available. It provides shareholders with complete protection from being sued and directors with partial protection. A director can be liable for fraud or where a company trades when insolvent (that is, unable to pay its debts as and when they fall due). There are other risks of personal liability for directors such as when tax instalment deductions are not paid and in some other circumstances including copyright infringements and defamation actions. Problems can also arise when annual returns are not lodged. The reality is that directors of companies are often required to provide personal guarantees for bank overdrafts, leases etc. Clearly, it is a good idea not to be a director or secretary of the company. Give that responsibility to someone you don't like. Only one director is required.

The name of the group should be considered from several aspects. The first is its marketability. If a group is to be marketed to a particular audience, it should be considered with that in mind. Savage Garden and Killing Heidi are good examples of names which were directed towards a particular market. I am not sure to what market Le Club Foote was directed. Consideration also needs to be given to whether or not there are groups in other countries using that name. Many groups over the years have had to change their name because of groups in America or elsewhere with similar names. Examples are Flowers (Icehouse), Mississippi (Little River Band) and Angel City (The Angels). Often a bad name will look good in retrospect, especially when a million records have been sold! Air Supply comes to mind. The telephone book and internet are useful avenues of enquiry.

It is also important to register a domain name. This is obviously of prime consideration given that the internet is now one of the most effective methods of communicating with a fan base and distributing product. While registration of a domain name does not of itself confer ownership it does stop other people acquiring that name. Use of a name over time can create a form of 'ownership' at common law, in that a group becomes identified by the public under that name. It is not always as simple as that, particularly if the group has had many members over the years. Who or what constitutes the group?

The name of the group is best protected by registration of a trademark. A trademark is a name, device or logo which is used to distinguish goods and services. Certain letters, words, signatures, logos, shapes, colours, distinctive packaging, sound, sense, or a combination of these can be registered. A trademark confers exclusive legal rights to use a name in certain circumstances although it falls short of actual ownership in a technical sense. Trademarks are registered in particular categories. They can exist without being registered but registration is preferable for enforcement purposes.

Trademarks underpin the creation of value in a brand and ideally a group name will become just that. Death doesn't diminish the fact that a brand name can have value. The American attorneys for Dan Aykroyd and Judy Jacklin Belushi have been quick to enforce the rights they own to the name The Blues Brothers. There are trademarks registered in relation to all the characters created by Beatrix Potter and in her name itself. Posh Spice has tried to prevent Peterborough United Soccer Club (Posh has been its nickname for seventy years) from registering the Posh trademark. David Gilmore and Roger Waters have been involved in litigation over the name Pink Floyd. There has also been disputation over the name The Byrds. Trademarks can confer protection well beyond the period of copyright provided they are renewed and exploited.

Those claiming ownership to the exclusive rights to the name Elvis Presley have and will continue to be active. I represented an Australian client who travelled to America with his barrister (first mistake) and paid a large sum of money for what he thought were the exclusive rights to sell Elvis Presley memorabilia in Australia. He soon realised that everybody in Australia was marketing and distributing Elvis product, from Elvis Presley garden gnomes to guitars endorsed by Elvis 'from the other side'.

On my advice the client refused to pay the next annual instalment to the American company. I received a ten-page letter from an oversized American law firm purporting to act for the Elvis Presley estate. The lawyers claimed that under the *Tennessee Court Act* (TCA 110, 221, 115) my client was liable to pay a massive sum of money in damages. Worse still my firm, as his adviser, was liable to pay a multiple of that sum because I had induced him to breach the contract.

At that time my relationship with my professional partners was not good. The correspondence was unlikely to be received with any real understanding – one of those times when the stomach becomes a bottomless pit. Without consulting my partners I sent a response along the following lines:

> You have us at a disadvantage with TCA 110, 221, 115. However, in Australia, under VCA 111, 222, 449 solicitors are compelled to act in the best interests of their client. Cognisant of that obligation we have confirmed the advice to our client not to pay any further monies to your client.

I didn't hear another word from the American lawyers. I always knew that the Victorian Cricket Association would come in handy sometime. That didn't put them off totally. In 1997 Elvis Presley Enterprises tried to restrain an English shopowner Sid Shaw from selling Elvis Presley merchandise. They failed. Their appeal was also rejected.[20] How could anyone lose a case against someone named Sid Shaw?

To summarise, a group should be established using a company either in its own right or as trustee of a unit trust, the beneficiaries of which are the members of the group or their trusts or companies. A unit trust is a glorified partnership. It has the advantage of insulating the individual members from potential liabilities. If a fan breaks their neck diving into a mosh pit or becomes an active participant in a pyrotechnic display, that person would sue the company, which is the trustee of the trust and which conducted the professional activities of the group, not the individual members. The members of the group enter into individual contracts with the company agreeing to provide their services in relation to recording and performing.

The company should register a business name, domain name and trademark of the name of the group and any logos it may use. The members of the group would also enter into an agreement with each other in relation to their recording and songwriting services. That would cover the two primary issues as to sharing publishing income between writers and non-writers and as to what happens should a member be required, or want, to leave the group.

If the group signs a recording agreement those services would be provided via the company and the individuals would be required to sign a letter of inducement in favour of the record company. If the group is successful, separate companies or trusts might be used for touring, recording and songwriting.

I have included in the addendum a short-form partnership agreement which could be used by members of a group in the early stages prior to incorporation and draft minutes of the first meeting of the group. Obviously these need to be changed to fit particular circumstances but they highlight the issues that should be considered.

CHAPTER 5 – TALK TO MY MANAGER

In 1985 Renée Geyer, one of Australia's most enduring and talented artists, released an album entitled *Sing to Me*. When Renée negotiated the recording contract she didn't have a manager. Nevertheless a manager, Ms I. Jacabovski, was credited on the artwork of her album. Later, in an article which appeared in *RAM* it was reported that 'Now for the first time she has a manager who she doesn't feel treats her like a child'.[1] I was surprised at that because of the work that had been done in relation to the contract and the fact that the new manager was noticeable by her complete absence during that process. To this day no one has been able to locate Ms Jacabovski.

Managers have an important and unique role in the contemporary music industry. The manager is the bridge between the creative individual and the business side of the industry including record and publishing companies, lawyers and accountants. The manager is also very much involved in the day-to-day decisions which impact on an artist's career. These can include whether to marry or not to marry, to have or not to have a child or to change the artist's hairstyle. I acted for a manager who negotiated an advance from a record company which was used to have his artist's teeth straightened. The record could wait.

More often than not in Australia the personal manager and the business manager are one and the same person. Managers tend to devote 90% of their time to, and derive 90% of their income from, one artist or group. The standard commission is 20% of gross income. This funds any other activities the manager undertakes, including managing other artists. A manager must add value; in other words 80% of income with a manager should exceed 100% of income without one.

A manager should not be confused with an agent who books groups into venues, has a limited relationship with many artists and usually charges a 10% fee. The relationship should also be distinguished from that of a sports manager. In Australia there are many sports managers. The AFL accredits sports managers like Greeks baptise kids at Easter. In my view this is an attempt to diminish the power of three or four all powerful personal managers. Ricky Nixon and Ron Joseph are two who stand out. Australian Football managers usually charge a commission of 3% of recurring income and their role is concerned as much with marketing as with management.

Theatrical agents have a quasi-management role. Their fee varies up to 10%. Then there are the large management companies including International Management Group (IMG) and Sports and Entertainment Limited (SEL) who derive most of their income, at least in Australia, from their activities as producers rather than managers. Their commission varies from 20% to 25% of the gross.

The Australian contemporary music industry owes its success to the small group of dedicated people who devote their best years to nurturing, guiding, financing and commercially exploiting talented individuals. Vince Lovegrove (Divinyls), Jeremy Fabinyi (Mental as Anything), Grant Thomas (Sharon O'Neill and Neil Finn), John Woodruff (The Angels, Baby Animals and Savage Garden), Chris Murphy (INXS), Gary Morris (Midnight Oil), Ray Hearn (Icehouse), Steve White (Dragon), Peter Hoyland (Southern Sons and David Hirschfelder), Ralph Carr (Rick Price and Tina Arena), Rod Willis (Cold Chisel), Nathan Brenner (Split Enz and Men at Work), Russell Deppeler (Men at Work), Keith Welsh (Boom Crash Opera and The Sharp) and Roger Davies (Sherbert, Tina Turner and Olivia Newton-John) who based himself out of Australia, come to mind.

I haven't listed Paul O'Gorman. He managed Debra Byrne, Tommy Emmanuel and The Bad Loves. He was too honest to be a manager and is now one of my colleagues. He once travelled to Sydney using a ticket in my name. When he rang the Golden Wing lounge to change his return flight they asked for his date of birth. He said he couldn't remember!!

Glenn Wheatley who still manages Glenn Shorrock and John Farnham deserves a special mention. I have acted for Glenn Wheatley more or less consistently since he formed Little River Band in 1975. In those days Glenn didn't know much but I knew less. Most people romanticise about their first love affair. I think about the first Writ I issued. It was on Glenn's behalf in 1975. It concerned the Moir Sisters who we claimed had been spirited away from Glenn by Elton John's then manager. Glenn's difficulty was to prove he had suffered a loss.

Glenn has always had the ability to maintain his flair and enthusiasm when everyone around him despairs. Glenn would have kept the *Titanic* afloat. He can spot talent and motivate people who, despite the public image, are often insecure. He has also been lucky in love. He had the good sense to seek my advice in relation to his existing wife. Gaynor gave the tumbleweed some purpose. That is not to say I didn't like his first one. Alison and Glenn split up at the peak of Little River Band's success. Her main concern was a life-sized ceramic leopard.

When Little River Band was starting to break internationally Glenn wanted my advice as to what structure should be used to receive their first publishing advance from America. In those days Glenn was convinced that I would have all the answers. I did what all good lawyers out of their depth do and prevaricated. Within days Glenn was desperate and suggested that I make contact with a well-known expert on these matters, Perry Lerner in Los Angeles. He had apparently set up structures for The Rolling Stones and Queen Victoria. I had only been out of Victoria once and that was to Albury. I had never made an international call. Nevertheless I made the call to Mr Lerner in Los Angeles and organised to 'do lunch' in Amsterdam the following week. I then checked with my secretary to find out where Amsterdam was and booked seat A Row 340 to Italy.

On finally arriving at the hotel in Amsterdam there was a note from Mr Lerner. He had been unable to make the trip. He was more frightened of me than I was of him. Naturally I was nervous about how I could put a positive spin on my non-meeting to Glenn. On my return Glenn advised that the circumstances in America had changed and they were looking at a much bigger offer. I said I knew that would happen and had deliberately avoided the lunch with Lerner. My expenses were reimbursed and my reputation as a strategist established.

Glenn was approached by a senior executive from a large advertising company. The agency wanted to meet with him about promoting youth awareness and developing the youth market. Glenn was perfectly suited for this. He asked my tactical advice about the meeting. I thought a certain monthly fee would be 'gettable' and advised Glenn to get a letter from the agency confirming the arrangement.

Glenn rang me after the meeting. In the lift on the way to the executive suite he had thought about the fee and decided to double it. He then had a long and mutually satisfactory meeting with the 'suit' who wasn't such a bad type after all and an agreement was reached. The agreement was to be formalised in a letter to me. A week later I rang Glenn and said that I had received the letter. I let him know there was some good and some bad news. Glenn always wants the good news. They had confirmed the fee. The bad news was that he was paying them.

Glenn learnt quickly. He was the first to exploit the 'catalogue deal', where a label signs a successful act to a major record company and includes one or two unsignable acts in the deal. Part of the advance payable by the major can then be allocated to the acts with no future. This enables the label to recoup otherwise unrecoupable advances. The same principal can apply when licensing or selling a catalogue of copyrights.

Glenn also pioneered the 'Clancy of the Overflow' clause. This applies when a successful act charges a percentage of 'the door' not only in the room in which the act is appearing but also in all the other rooms on the premises. The rationale is that a surplus audience has been created. Glenn can also claim some credit for the 'moshing' phenomenon. It all started when he dived off the stage during a sound check for the AFL Centenary Ball. That is why he is known to his friends as 'Mosher' Wheatley. Most stage divers wait until there is an audience before they dive.

I read Glenn's book *Paper Paradise* with interest. Not surprisingly it doesn't refer to the time Glenn was extending his property in Canberra Road, Toorak. The new property was landlocked. This did not deter the builder from driving a bulldozer across a neighbour's prize garden to gain access. Any avenue of retreat was blocked by the threat of an injunction. At one point I was contemplating co-opting the Army to use an Iroquois helicopter to get the machine off the property – the Killing Fields of Toorak. Finally a humble apology sufficed.

Then there was the time I took four wealthy Japanese businessmen to The Ivy nightclub. They were interested in buying it. Glenn was keen to sell. I took them to some sleazy clubs and finally arrived at The Ivy. To impress, I parked illegally outside the door. Glenn and Gaynor were there and everything was in readiness to woo the potential buyers. The girl on the door saw through all this and refused us entry – something about a private function.

Over the years Glenn has had deserved success with Little River Band, Glenn Shorrock, Australian Crawl, Moving Pictures, Real Life, John Farnham and Delta Goodrem. He has had the international success that has eluded Michael Gudinski. At the same time he has had some difficult periods, mainly caused by his involvement in The Ivy. In July 1989 Glenn was a 'multi-millionaire businessman' who didn't want to end up a 'blithering old fellow with lots of money in the bank and nothing else'.[2] By November 1991 he was a 'former band member'. [3] Glenn was quoted as saying 'my core business is music publishing, record labelling and artist management'.[4] Obviously the time he spent labelling all those records has paid off. He now pays someone else to stick them on.

Glenn's latest drama has centred around Delta Goodrem. The fact that the contract was not extended is probably understandable given Delta's success and health problems. It is quite common for the term of a management contract to extend automatically unless notice of termination is given three to six months prior to the current term. Why that had to be written up in the press as Glenn being sacked is for the press to explain. Glenn was more concerned about not being properly credited by Delta at the 2003 ARIA Awards. The fact that Glenn still cares about ARIA Awards shows he has retained his youthful charm and naivety.

Despite the highs and lows through even the worst of times Glenn maintained his resilience and sense of humour and has, and will continue to be, a great source of strength to many people in the industry. Having said that, those who deal with him should never forget that he was, and always will be, a bass player.

Then, there is my favourite Michael Gudinski, who managed Jimmy Barnes. Some would say Jimmy managed him. Michael has been accused many times of having a conflict of interest because of his roles as a manager, promoter, agent, nightclub owner, merchandiser and owner of very successful recording and publishing companies. Michael is the embodiment of the saying, 'if you don't have a conflict you are not in the music business'.

Michael has sometimes been referred to as 'Godinski'.[5] His former close friend, Nathan Brenner, has suggested that Michael has had an ethical bypass. [6] There has been this long rivalry between Nathan and Michael which has more to do with their common background than any genuine bad blood (I think). In the context of the inquiry into the parallel importation of records I once said on national television that 'no one takes Michael seriously anymore'. That didn't go down very well. The fact is that I have always liked and admired Michael. Because he doesn't like himself very much, he has difficulty comprehending this.

Over a period of twenty years Michael was the principal source of funding for Melbourne artists to record their product. I personally must have been involved in more than thirty signings with Mushroom. The deal was always honoured and a pragmatic approach adopted. None of those signings ended in court.

Michael is clever in that he has always employed honest and professional people like Simon Young and Gary Ashley. They know how to do a deal and understand that there has to be something in it for everyone. Some good people are very loyal to Michael so he must have something going for him. Whether or not Gary and Simon would agree that it has been reciprocated is another question.

If Michael has a weakness it is his tendency to want to control people. This manifests itself in his need to make people a part of his life. If he signs an act which is independently managed he will not be happy until the group is managed by someone in the loop. The Badloves spring to mind. Where are they now?

Sometimes it is a little difficult to distinguish Michael's friends and enemies. In 1990 an anonymous seven-page fax was circulated which caused Michael much aggravation. In union politics it would be called a 'shit sheet'. One of the authors was allegedly a former friend and partner Adrian Barker. That resulted in some PR which only Michael would regard as helpful.

In an article in *HQ* magazine Michael was described as an 'ageing wunderkind'.[7] The late Shirley Strachan, one of Michael's more intimate friends, was quoted as saying 'he's not a manager's f…ing arsehole'.[8] Phil Tripp was more restrained. His view was that if Michael was in the US he would do some 'hard time'.[9] On the other side of the ledger is Molly Meldrum, who was in partnership initially with Nathan Brenner and then with Gudinski in the label Melodian (which signed Indecent Obsession). According to Molly Michael 'is one of the greatest mentors of Australian rock 'n' roll'.[10]

What is certain is that being a close friend and confidante of Michael is not a great career move. Only Frank Stivala is left. Frank is famous for sending a birthday card to his mother signed 'Love Frank Stivala'.[11] Ray Evans, Adrian Barker, Gary Ashley and Simon Young have all moved on. So has Molly. It's just that no one has told him yet.

Michael sold his record company which was probably worth two or three million dollars to a News Corp company for a very large amount of money (reputedly thirty million dollars). He retained ownership of his publishing company which was the jewel in the crown. That only reinforced my view that Michael has a shrewd and commercial business brain. Underneath Michael's chaotic exterior is an arcane and very determined character.

Managers have to make a choice. Are they prepared to devote the most productive years of their lives developing the career of an artist in the knowledge that if they are successful they will probably be sacked? Perhaps the best example of this was Vince Lovegrove. He managed Divinyls from 1980. Vince and I once found ourselves on a New York subway with me carrying a papier-mâché axe to be used by the group – not a wise thing to do in New York. Sadly his wife and child contracted AIDS, which is truly the rock 'n' roll disease. While he was taking a rest to look after his dying wife, his management of the group came to an end. Thankfully he was supported by many in the industry, particularly Jeremy Fabinyi, who managed Mental as Anything.

Management is intensely personal. It is not unlike a marriage. Indeed sometimes it is a marriage. Courts have always been reluctant to get involved in relationships of this kind. Once it breaks down it is simply not in the best interests of either party to continue in a relationship which to be successful requires mutual trust, respect, commitment and personal contact.

The courts are also reluctant to allow a manager to continue receiving management commissions when a service is not being provided. If an artist is put in the position where he or she is paying 20% to one manager it is an unfair burden to expect that artist to have to pay an additional 20% to another manager to carry out the services for which the first is being paid.

There is however general recognition that a person should be paid a fair remuneration for services rendered. Developing the career of an artist in the entertainment industry requires personal and financial commitment. A manager who has supported an artist in the early stages, used his or her skill and contacts to obtain recording and publishing contracts and developed the artist's career internationally over a considerable period of time, should not be terminated without fair recompense. This is particularly the case when that termination is at the whim of the artist and/or a new adviser who wants to benefit from the former manager's endeavours. Often when a break-up occurs commonsense goes out the window and bitterness sets in. That's when courts do become involved.

There have been some spectacular examples of management break-ups internationally, including that of Robbie Williams who lost a case against the former manager of Take That, Nigel Martin-Smith.[12] In Australia there were the theatrics between the football commentator and 'fish lover' Rex Hunt and his manager, Greg Numa. Then there was the break-up of Nick Bideau and Cathy Freeman. Both cases were settled. These were more in the nature of partnership disputes, commercial in the former and both personal and commercial in the latter. The management relationship was a complicating factor rather than central to the dispute.

There have been four Australian music industry cases which are of interest. For Justice Byrne of the Supreme Court of Victoria, 1992 was a busy year. On 30 October 1992, after thirty-three hearing days, he handed down his judgement in the management dispute between Nathan Brenner and Simon Fenner on the one hand and First Artists' Management Pty Ltd and Daryl Braithwaite on the other.[13]

The facts of the case were straightforward. Daryl Braithwaite had been the lead singer of one of Australia's most successful 'glam' bands in the seventies, Sherbert. After several attempts at resuscitation by the group's manager, Roger Davies, including perhaps unfortunate name changes to Sherbs and Highway, the band was finally put to rest in 1980 or thereabouts.

In 1987, Daryl's then wife Sarah Taylor devised a scheme to revitalise Daryl's career as a recording artist. The idea was to arrange for private investors to fund the recording of an album and to licence the master to a major record company for distribution. The investment was to be tax-effective for the investors. Since the record company was not required to pay for the recording and video production costs, there was less financial risk and a higher royalty rate could be negotiated for the artist and investors. Those royalties would be payable from 'record one' rather than after recoupment.

A firm of solicitors, Holding Redlich, introduced Sarah to Gavin Anderson and his company Gavcor Limited which had access to private investment monies and was keen to get involved in a project of this nature. Gavin was a merchant banker with Labor Party connections. He made up for his short stature by wearing shiny suits and driving a Rolls Royce. He set about building his Daryl Braithwaite media empire by hiring a large staff, all of whom drove Saabs. He had the generosity of someone spending other people's money.

A team including Simon Fenner (joined later by Nathan Brenner) was put into place to handle the management aspects. I have had a long association with both Simon and Nathan. Simon had managed Australian Crawl for a while and also managed the Little Heroes. The creative team was headed by Simon Hussey who was closely involved with James Reyne (he married James' sister) and is one of the most talented producers Australia has produced. The songs selected and demonstration tapes produced by Simon and Daryl and the 'hype' in the industry generally about the project, resulted in CBS (now Sony) making an offer to distribute the record. That's when things started to unravel.

The lawyer from Holding Redlich who was acting for the investors may have had some expertise in implementing tax schemes but he was out of his depth when it came to negotiating recording agreements. CBS has always had the longest agreement and the strictest protocols in relation to negotiations. In frustration the then Business Affairs Manager for CBS, Mike Edwards, actually requested that someone with experience in the industry be appointed to act. This request was rejected by Anderson who knew less about the entertainment industry than his lawyer.

Gavin had a unique way of conducting business. He once submitted a management agreement to an artist for whom I acted. I responded with the usual comments. The precedent used was based on one I drafted. I received a response from his lawyer (the same one) pointing out that Gavin regarded my comments as a personal insult and was not prepared to countenance any amendments. Gavin applied the same degree of professionalism to the management agreement with Simon and Nathan to the point that it was never formalised in writing. Nevertheless, Simon and Nathan had been appointed Daryl's managers by an agreement originally made in July 1988 and modified in January 1989 whereby they were to receive a management commission of 20%.

The complication was that Daryl, under his agreement with the investors, had already appointed First Artists' Management Pty Ltd as his manager and had agreed to pay it 20%. In effect he had appointed two managers, both of whom were to be paid 20% of his gross income. Obviously that was not sustainable. As His Honour put it in his 100-page judgement, 'the real difficulty arises because, under the agreements with the investors, a 20-25 per cent fee is payable to First Artists' Management Pty Ltd . . . whereas Braithwaite had agreed to pay to Fenner and Brenner a further 20 per cent management fee on his gross earnings'.[14]

Throughout this time Daryl and Simon Hussey were busy making the album *Edge* which would be immediately successful on its release. Ominously, on 11 August 1988 Fenner telephoned Peter Karpin, the A & R person at CBS, and requested that the single due for release on 15 August be postponed for a week. Ostensibly this was because the video was not up to an acceptable standard. The real reason was that a management dispute had arisen. When Anderson found out about that call he had letters couriered to Simon and Nathan terminating their management.

In the subsequent trial the Judge made some interesting observations about the principal witnesses, some of whom spent upwards of a week in the witness box. His comments in relation to Daryl were diplomatic. He found Daryl to be a complex man of passive disposition, at least in relation to business matters.[15] On 15 August 1988 Daryl went to Brenner's office at Nelson Road, South Melbourne. He celebrated Nathan's birthday in the full knowledge that letters terminating the relationship with Nathan and Simon, which had been authorised by him, were due to be served an hour or so later. Daryl even presented Nathan with a cupcake and candle and sang Happy Birthday. At that time Daryl was actually living with Simon and had been since 17 June, when he separated from his wife. His Honour described this conduct as representing either an extraordinary callousness and insensitivity or an extreme passivity without a full understanding of the consequences of his acts. He gave Daryl the benefit of the doubt and preferred the latter.[16]

Not surprisingly, it was held that there was no binding or enforceable contract for management services between Fenner, Brenner and Braithwaite. However even in the absence of an enforceable contract a person can still be obliged to pay a fair and reasonable sum for goods and services under the law of restitution or unjust enrichment. It was found that management services were provided which were of benefit to Braithwaite and a reasonable amount should be paid. The fee had to be quantified. This was a complicated and tedious process. The services were to be valued on an hourly basis. Commissions were to be used only as a guide. This was, and still is, totally at odds with industry practice.

By this time Simon Fenner was bankrupt. The Judge found in favour of Fenner's trustee and Brenner and awarded damages of approximately $60,000 against Braithwaite. Damages of this amount were within the jurisdiction of the County Court and the case had been litigated in the Supreme Court. This meant that costs were only awarded on the much lower County Court scale. There were no winners.

This case demonstrates the inability of the court system to cope with disputes of this kind. Simon won but was bankrupt. He went on to star in a television show about clearing out household junk. Daryl also was effectively, if not technically, bankrupt. His marriage was over. His career was on hold more or less permanently . The investors failed to recover their money. Gavin Anderson went to jail.

The costs incurred by Simon and Nathan would have been in excess of $300,000 and they recovered only a small portion of that. The costs incurred by Daryl, who used senior and junior Counsel throughout the thirty-three hearing days of the trial, would have been well in excess of $500,000. He was forced to have a charity concert to pay costs – 'Lawyers Aid'.

One irony was that despite the fact that Mushroom Records had passed on the album, Daryl's publishing was signed to Mushroom Music on 1 October 1988. Legend has it that Daryl signed because he wanted to play in the Mushroom cricket team. The truth probably had more to do with an advance.

Edge sold 250,000 copies and was a major success for CBS. The follow up album *Rise* was also successful but by then the race had been run. Simon Hussey, James Reyne, Jef Scott and Daryl, assisted on vocals on one song by Peter Mitchell of Channel 7 news, collaborated in a project under the name Company Of Strangers which was also successful. By 1996, Daryl was back in court responding to an application for bankruptcy filed by the Taxation Office. At that time he was talking about making another comeback hosting a show about people's dreams.[17]

If the Braithwaite case was a tragedy, The Models litigation was more in the nature of a comedy. Adrian Barker was manager of the group from May 1980 through to 23 July 1983 when his management was terminated. Barker was one of those people who always seemed to be there. He goes as far back as tour-managing The Masters Apprentices. In January 1970 he set up a booking and management agency with Glenn Wheatley. He was in at the very beginning with Michael Gudinski. During his two years of management there were nine members of the band. The writ was not issued until three years after his termination and didn't come on for hearing until 10 November 1992. Judgement was given on 26 November 1992,[18] almost ten years after he was terminated.

There was a written management agreement which had been terminated prematurely by the members. Barker was claiming 20% commission for the full four-year term of the management agreement and in relation to earnings received after the term from contracts entered into during the term. By the time the case came on for hearing there were only three named defendants, Sean Kelly, James Freud and Andrew

Duffield. Both Kelly and Duffield were parties to the agreement. Freud having joined the group some time later was not. None of the defendants was represented. I had represented one member of the group who was not a defendant for the purpose of the trial.

Freud argued that he was not bound by the agreement because he was not a party to it. Justice Byrne in his usual diplomatic way noted that he was not helped by Barker's demeanour which 'did not inspire confidence in the accuracy of his recollection of events so long past'.[19] Nevertheless His Honour found that Freud had accepted the management arrangements which were in place when he joined the band and thereby became bound by the management agreement.

It was then necessary to decide whether or not the artists were justified in prematurely terminating the management agreement. There were several allegations in relation to Barker's conduct which were said to have justified the termination. Perhaps the most serious of these was a failure to account. In this regard His Honour found that Barker was in breach of his obligations with respect to keeping accounts and providing financial information and advice.

There was also an allegation that Barker had engaged in excessive drinking and aggressive behaviour. The Court accepted that Barker's behaviour was beyond acceptable limits and something of an embarrassment. In view of the lifestyle of the group as detailed by Freud in his very readable book *I am the Voice left from Drinking*,[20] that finding must have been particularly galling to Barker.

It was asserted that Barker had excessively toured the group. As the group had voluntarily accepted the schedule this was rejected by the Court. There was a suggestion that Barker had thrown the takings from a performance into a bin at a hotel. They were later recovered. This, standing on its own, was not held to be a serious breach of the contract.

A further allegation was that the recording contract entered into with Mushroom Records in 1980 was not sufficiently advantageous and the band should have been allowed to seek independent legal advice. It was asserted that the members of the band were put under pressure to execute the document. His Honour did not consider that the contract was disadvantageous given the bargaining position of the group at the time. Similar allegations in relation to their A & M Records contract were also rejected.

There was a complaint that the band had been required to perform at the Surfair Hotel in Queensland when on a previous occasion the band had been short paid. This was held not to be a breach. More serious was an allegation that Barker had allowed a merchandising company, Music Vision Pty Ltd owned equally by Barker and Gudinski, to make and distribute group merchandise without a formal agreement or adequate accounting.

An allegation that Barker had engaged in shoplifting a bag of groceries was not supported by the evidence. Alleged dangerous driving was regarded as 'foolish conduct' rather than a breach.

After digesting all this the Court held that Barker was entitled to commission up to the date of termination. The termination was valid because Barker was in breach of the agreement in that he failed to provide proper accounts and financial advice, failed to conduct himself in public as befits a manager and to account for sales of merchandising made through Music Vision Pty Ltd. The artists were entitled to damages. As is customary the matter was then referred to another hearing for an accounting.

On the evidence the decision is reasonable, There is an obligation on a manager to act professionally and to comply with the management agreement. The case highlights the difficulties the judicial system has when one or more of the principal parties are not represented. I was at the hearing on the first day. It did no credit to any of the parties. Nonetheless Freud regarded it as a 'major victory'.[21] The Models had broken up four years previously. Barker is now a carpenter.

In 2002 the case involving Churchers Pty Ltd (a company controlled by Ralph Carr), and Positive Dream Pty Ltd (a company controlled by Tina Arena)[22] came on for hearing. This case was also in the Supreme Court of Victoria. It was settled on the day the hearing was due to commence. Had the case proceeded the issues were of considerable importance for the music industry. There was no doubt that Ralph had managed Tina's career over a long period of time and that the relationship had been mutually beneficial for Ralph and Tina. The matter was complicated because there was no written agreement in place and Ralph and Tina were husband and wife.

The first question was, 'What is a reasonable period of notice for an artist to give a manager on terminating a management relationship?' This varies from case to case and very much depends on the facts. Obviously the period of notice required in a long-term and internationally successful relationship such as Ralph and Tina's is different to that required in, say, a dysfunctional relationship like that of Barker and The Models. Nevertheless, it seems to be generally accepted that a reasonable period of notice where there has been some degree of mutual commitment, support and success over a long period is somewhere between six and twelve months.

The second was, 'Is a manager entitled to ongoing commission in relation to royalties received after the termination of the agreement which are derived from recording and publishing contracts entered into prior to the termination?' If the answer to that question is 'no' then is the manager at least entitled to commission royalties on records sold prior to the termination but not accounted for by the record company until after the termination? This is particularly appropriate in relation to sales in foreign territories which can often take one to two years to find their way via some circuitous route back to Australia, or might never arrive. To ascertain the real sales figures it was necessary to rely on internal Sony documents called "crime reports". Unfortunately, for the lawyers anyway, the Carr case was settled. I acted for Ralph.

Finally we have the rather predictable Holly Valance case[23]. Scott Michaelson of Neighbours fame "discovered" Holly Vukadinovic when she was fifteen in 1988. Scott, through his company Biscayne Partners Pty Limited became Holly's manager. Her services were provided via her company Valance Corp Pty Limited. A formal management agreement was signed by the parties. It was undated but took effect in or about April/May 2000.

It was a standard exclusive management agreement for three years providing for the usual commission of 20% of gross. Holly's London lawyer purported to terminate the agreement in January 2002. That was followed by a further letter of termination from her Australian lawyers in September 2002. Both attempts were clumsy and ill conceived. The first purported to treat the agreement as void because at the time of signing Holly was 16 years old and the agreement was claimed not to be for her benefit. The second attempted to comply with the cure provisions in the agreement. It gave notice that the agreement would be terminated if a certain material breach was not rectified.

As is often the case the facts were all important. There was much evidence about a meeting at the Bambini Trust Café in Sydney. Then there was a conversation between Holly and a Ms Valentine in the Green Room at the Neighbours Studio. At the end of the day His Honour Justice Einstein concluded that there was no material breach. Rather there had been a deliberate attempt by various parties associated with Holly to exclude Michaelson and to shut him out of her recording career. This was referred to as "the close out". Michaelson was never told that he was considered not up to the task. This is consistent with the persona of many creative people who prefer to avoid direct confrontation. They leave that to their lawyers.

Judgement was in favour of Michaelson's company. Because this case turned on its facts it is of no real interest from a legal perspective. Again there were no winners. Michaelson was awarded $350,000 or thereabouts plus costs. He will be lucky if there is any change. For Holly it is probably all over although it will take a few months before the eerie silence sets in. This sad state of affairs has nothing really to do with the adverse judgement. Rather it is because she is no longer selling records. Of course mum will always be there. Talk about an appeal is unlikely to help either record sales or the legal situation.

Litigation of this kind is difficult because, as stated, the courts are reluctant to enforce personal service contracts. They are also reluctant to try and create or manufacture the terms of a contract where none are evident, and with due respect, judges are not usually experienced in the commercial aspects of the contemporary music industry. Where there is no written agreement, courts will try to take 'industry practice' into account. This is almost impossible to establish in the entertainment industry. Everyone wants to help until they are called upon to attend court. Add to that the expense of resolving disputes in the courts and the unwanted publicity and everyone is in a 'no win' situation.

Falling back on the unjust enrichment arguments in the Braithwaite case may lead to a judgement but minimal damages, as happened in that case. This places the burden of costs squarely on the manager. Indeed, the manager may still be obligated to pay the costs of the artist. This will apply if a prior settlement offer has been made which exceeds the amount actually awarded or if the amount awarded is insufficient to justify litigating in the particular jurisdiction, for example the Supreme Court.

The Models case doesn't assist a manager trying to argue an ongoing entitlement to commission, although given the way that case was presented, it probably doesn't have much weight anyway. In my opinion a manager should be entitled to commission in relation to records sold but not accounted for during the management term. I would go further and say the manager should also be entitled to ongoing commission in relation to income derived from recording and publishing contracts entered into during the term of the management for at least a reasonable period after termination of the management agreement. A reasonable period would be somewhere between one and two years although a reduced rate might apply. This is consistent with industry practice and equity.

Over recent years there have been attempts to establish organisations to represent managers and to give them a voice. In 1992, fifty-five managers came together and established the Australian Music Managers Forum. Despite everyone's good intentions it has been a struggle. Managers are in competition with each other and have a small-business 'free enterprise' mentality. At the same time they are up against well-funded, experienced and bureaucratised organisations which represent the main members of the Sydney- based 'copyright club', namely record and publishing companies and their offshoots. Nevertheless its formation was a step in the right direction.

There have been attempts by solicitors to act as managers. Isaac Apel some years ago set up 'I Am Management'. It is now called 'I Was Management'. I have no objection to solicitors becoming managers but when they do they should cease being solicitors. A solicitor in the entertainment industry gets much of his or her work from managers. It doesn't seem a good idea to put yourself in direct competition with your sources of work. There is also the ethical problem that in the course of their professional activities solicitors become aware of much confidential and personal information relating to their clients, some of whom are managers. For that reason solicitors should not compete with those very same clients. In the Australian context anyway, solicitors managing artists is good for no one.

Because of the personal nature of the relationship, it would be good if parents stayed away from the management of their children. It is perhaps understandable in sporting activities where young children are required to travel the world. A sensible parent would soon realise that this places too much pressure on the child and should be avoided. What is the child supposed to do – sack their mother?

Any manager who manages an artist without obtaining a formal written agreement is involved in a charitable exercise. There are more worthwhile causes. Having said that as a general rule, contracts for personal services with minors under 18 are very difficult to enforce even when they are signed via an adult guardian and after all the necessary words in the contract such as 'in his best interests' are inserted.

The management relationship is fundamental to the music industry. This was obviously lost on the producers of Australian Idol. In that competition a manager came as part of the package for the winner. The prize you have to have. The manager also had an option to manage the other finalists who are competing with each other for the same audience. This also ignored the fact that the manager concerned already managed several artists. By the time the management agreement took effect the artists were already bound by the recording agreement with BMG. To rub salt into the wounds the manager then received 20% of the advances and royalties payable to the artist under the recording agreement. This process demeaned the management relationship and had more to do with control than what was best for the artists.

Included in the addendum is a management agreement which would ensure that many of the problems discussed above do not arise. The terms of the agreement would require some negotiation and advice from the lawyers for the parties.

CHAPTER 6 – KYLIE IS A T-SHIRT

Just as an a.k.a. (also known as) is often a prerequisite for a life of crime, a p.k.a. (professionally known as) is an entrée into the entertainment industry. It allows a person to step outside the restrictions and inhibitions associated with reality and to become a star. It is part of the hyperbole (hype) of the industry. It sublimates individuality to an image or brand which is commercially marketable.

When dealing with an entertainer it is important to recognise three 'people'. There is the actual person, the alter ego or self-image of that person and the person as seen by other people that is the public or the professional image. The public image often has nothing to do with either the real person or the alter ego. Think of a motorcyclist in a full-face helmet weaving through the traffic. The reality is a bank clerk who is late for work. He sees himself as 'Mad Max'. Other motorists see a helmet weaving through the traffic. His public image is as ephemeral as his life is likely to be short.

For an entertainer to survive in the industry it is important that the three 'people' live in harmony. I was once walking down Lygon Street – Melbourne's Italian restaurant strip - with a young Chinese boy, Michael, who had been raised in Melbourne. He looked around and remarked, 'Spot the Aussie'. Michael's self-image was not quite in synch with his public image. I visited a friend in hospital who had throat cancer. He wrote a question on a note pad. I wrote out the answer. His response was, 'I'm not deaf'. A professional image often has more to do with the perceptions of the audience than with reality.

Sometimes entertainers are most comfortable with their professional image. I acted for one of Australia's best comic actors. He could do or say anything on stage. When called upon to say a few words at his school reunion he almost had a nervous breakdown. Many comedians do not have a very high opinion of themselves as people. Having acted for several I can understand their view. This is why I try to avoid them wherever possible. Rod Quantock is an exception.

A professional image can assume a separate and distinct persona of its own. Steve McQueen can endorse a watch long after his death just by associating his name with that product. This is not restricted to the entertainment industry. People around the world related to the image of John F. Kennedy and Lady Di. Australians love 'Warnie' and Wayne Carey. This is not because people are ignorant of their shortcomings. It's just that they relate to the image, not the person. The person doesn't really matter. That is why so many entertainers are neurotic. It is also why suggestions about entertainers having responsibilities as role models is nonsense.

The most cynical example of this phenomenon was the group This is Serious Mum, also known as TISM. They attempted to market an image whilst denying that any real people were involved at all. Their dress ranged from Ku Klux Klan robes to balaclavas. This was the ultimate form of nihilism. Even today the names of the participants with one or two exceptions are well-kept secrets. They were lawyers and teachers. Perhaps there was an element of hypocrisy in that. When I acted for them they were negotiating their recording and publishing contracts. It was obvious that despite their lyrics which professed total distain for the industry, they were there for the money and the fame, just like everyone else. The parody became the parodied.

Probably the best Australian example of the development and manipulation of a professional image is Kylie Minogue. The key to a long and successful career in an industry which is, by definition, part of the fashion industry, is to continually update the image to appeal to a changing audience. Kylie has done this better than anyone. She is still contemporary. She has taken control of her career in a creative sense and has achieved success well beyond the 'Kylie is a T-shirt' view expressed by me in the mid-eighties. That is not to ignore the contribution of her manager, Terry Blamey, who has controlled the reality side on a consistently professional basis throughout her now long career. Kylie was fortunate she met Terry.

He comes from a family with a great military pedigree. Terry has genuine administrative skills and if he has an ego he has always subjugated it to Kylie's professional aspirations.

In 1989, Kylie tried to stop Grundy Television distributing a video based on 'the Scott and Charlene love story'.[1] Under the contract, Kylie's consent was required although it could not be unreasonably withheld. Kylie had refused to consent. She believed it would harm her image. The Judge disagreed and the application for an injunction was refused. Nevertheless, the case sent a message that Kylie was moving on.

Perhaps the worst recent example was the Dixie Chicks. At the height of the euphoria of the Iraq War a member of the group at a concert in London suggested that President Bush was a cowboy who was bringing the great State of Texas into disrepute. As commendable as this view might be it did not show a great understanding of their professional image and its importance as a 'brand'. They went from being the most popular, to the most unpopular, group in America overnight. Ironically because they are now so unpopular they have discovered a new, if somewhat smaller, audience.

In the late seventies The Angels, who were managed by John Woodruff, projected and maintained an image which appealed specifically to young males in the western suburbs of Melbourne and Sydney and all of Adelaide. They did this despite their public-schoolboy background which was cleverly disguised. They rarely gave interviews. Australian Crawl exploited the same private-school background by appealing to an audience from that demographic. In both cases the audience was identified and the image targeted at that audience.

There are times when the image can come too close to reality for comfort. Who would cast Debra Byrne to star in Sunset Boulevard? Debra is one of Australia's greatest talents but she was expected to die eight times a week. Of course, it is true that sometimes the really great performances contain an element of self-destruction. Piaf, John Lennon and Elvis Presley were probably in that club.

Roy Orbison was an example of when it was better not to let reality intrude on the imagery. When I represented Roy he was contracted to do approximately 100 concerts down the east coast of Australia over 110 days and his fee was close enough to $1000 a performance. This consisted of standing in the one spot singing his classic songs in a totally uninspiring manner. My wife and I met him after his Melbourne show in his hotel room for coffee. He was the saddest person I have ever met in the music industry. He was upset about noise in the hotel. Fortunately, or unfortunately, soon after that tour his career had a resurgence with the Travelling Wilburys. That success and what goes with it probably killed him.

Then there are those who fit into the 'what you see is what you get' mould such as Renée Geyer and John Farnham. The image matches the reality. Perhaps it is not a coincidence that both Renée and John have always taken a very professional interest in the lyrics of the songs they record. John is one of Australia's most popular performers but he had long periods during his career when the phone wasn't ringing. The fact that John has always been secure within himself professionally and confident of his ability to relate to an audience has helped him through those times.

I represented John when he and Colleen Hewett had a rather unfortunate investment in the Backstage Restaurant in Melbourne. It is now The European Bar. That was followed by a depressing period in his career which led to his involvement in Little River Band. He went missing at a critical time during the launch of his solo 'comeback' album. He was found under the sink in the kitchen fixing a leaking pipe.

In theatre, there is an understanding that an artist should never break the 'fourth curtain'. This is a theatrical way of saying 'don't let reality destroy the imagery'. That discipline has enabled performers like Anthony Warlow to use their talents to entertain and captivate an audience. Anthony can transport an audience to another place. The really great performances are those which move people. The challenge is to do that without destroying the performer. Anthony has perfected that. He is also one of the few artists in Australia where the public image matches the reality. That can place a heavy burden on the person. Anthony has found an escape route via his family. He also knows he can entertain people and enjoys doing it. The size, location and social standing of the audience is incidental.

A professional image can encompass the name, likeness, signature and even the likes and dislikes of the person. The commercial manifestation of this is character merchandising, that is, where the image of a personality is used to promote products. This image underpins the growing but distinct markets in merchandise, memorabilia and personal endorsement.

The profits from merchandising have always been an important source of income in the contemporary music industry. The image can become a valuable brand in itself. This is particularly the case in genres such as heavy metal, death metal and any other loud music which appeals to young, white males. Perversely, black is a particularly popular colour in this market. Merchandising is so popular that promoters have to be continually aware of the potential for pirated product. The same applies to any unauthorised surplus during the manufacturing process.

Merchandising is also an important source of income in certain sports. Car racing and wrestling are good examples. It is not so important in operatic and choral recitals. This is because young men relate to, and like to be associated with, the people who engage in these activities. The same principle applies in relation to certain football codes. Player-based merchandise (featuring the name or image of the player) as opposed to club-based merchandise (featuring the logo or colours of the club) is very popular in AFL football. In Rugby League and Union, club-based rather than player-based merchandise is pre-eminent. This might have something to do with the fact that young men (and women for that matter) like to be associated with tall, athletic sportspeople who have two ears and a neck.

Over recent years, memorabilia has become much sought after. Ten years ago the main outlets for memorabilia were charity auctions. You know those auctions where, in the grip of mass hysteria, your hand goes up involuntarily. You wait until 2.00 am to write out a cheque for $500 and then carry home an item which has no commercial or sentimental value. Next morning it provokes abuse from your wife who feels a compulsion to dust it.

Today memorabilia, provided it is properly authenticated, does have a commercial value. This has focused attention on the value of a signature. It is very bad form for a popular personality to refuse to sign a program, a T-shirt or a football when requested to do so by a young fan. Most performers oblige but every time that occurs the value of the signature is diminished.

Don Bradman was not only the world's most proficient run getter but he was also the world's most prolific memorabilia signer – all for nothing. Since his death this has been partly redressed in that firstly he is no longer able to sign anything (I think) and secondly his name is protected. For example, any name which suggests a connection with Bradman cannot be registered as a company name.[2]

Most successful entertainers and sportspeople have three signatures. One for the kids, one for memorabilia and one for the bank manager. I have an item of memorabilia which has value not because it includes the signature of a particular sportsperson but, rather, because it doesn't. Peter Daicos was a great Australian sportsman. Collingwood Football Club commissioned a poster featuring the images and signatures of several of their 'legends'. The Club took the view that, because the poster promoted and raised funds for the Club, it should be signed by the ex-players as an exercise in charity. Peter refused to sign. This highlights the erosion of sources of income which have traditionally been regarded as exclusive to a club and which are now not unreasonably considered by players and their managers as personal to them.

Finally, and perhaps of the greatest importance in the future, are personal endorsements. The contemporary music industry has been acutely aware of their commercial value and personal implications. There has been a reluctance by performers to allow their names or images to be associated with cigarette and alcohol advertising, South Africa during apartheid and politics generally. It has always been understood that an entertainer reserves all rights in relation to personal endorsements. To a limited degree, record companies have a contractual right to use a performer's image or name in relation to promoting records by that artist. But there has always been a grey area legally in relation to what does, and does not, amount to a personal endorsement. Does the use of an image in the context of a particular product of itself amount to an endorsement?

Given Australians' love of sport, it is not surprising that this issue surfaced in sports marketing. The pioneer in the field was the long jumper Gary Honey. Gary was a successful Australian long jumper. Without his consent in 1987 his photograph was used on a poster published by Australian Airlines. The poster was to promote participation in sport although obviously that association would also be good for the airline. To add insult to injury the airline, again without reference to Gary, consented to a publisher of Christian lifestyle books using the image on the front page of one of its publications.

The Judge at first instance emphasised Gary's status as an 'amateur' athlete.[3] He also found that the use did not amount to a representation that Gary was endorsing or sponsoring the airline or the Christian publication.[4] Gary's appeal against the decision was dismissed.[5] Gary was ordered to pay the costs of the airline and the Christians. After that effort, if 'amateur' is intended to connote 'poor and impoverished', Gary was indeed an amateur.

Whilst Gary was being financially challenged Paul Hogan successfully prevented his 'Crocodile Dundee' image being used in advertisements.[6] This was held to be a misappropriation of a reputation, misleading and deceptive conduct and passing off which damaged Hogan's business and goodwill. The Court of Appeal agreed that a significant section of the public would think that Hogan was paid for the commercial and endorsed the products.

Undeterred by Gary Honey's personal and financial disaster, Kieran Perkins stepped up on the blocks. In 1994 Telstra acquired the naming rights to the Australian swimming team, the 'Telecom Dolphins'. Kieran's photograph was taken in a pool with a cap bearing the Telecom logo and a drawing of a dolphin. It was subsequently used without reference to Kieran in a supplement published in the Brisbane *Courier-Mail* as an 'advertising feature'.

Kieran and his management company sued in the Supreme Court of Queensland. They claimed that the use misrepresented that there was a commercial association when there was none. Kieran lost at first instance. The trial Judge took the view that readers would not take the advertisement as an endorsement by Kieran of Telecom.[7] That decision was reversed on appeal.[8] The Court held that the advertisement misrepresented that Perkins was sponsored by Telstra, had consented to Telstra using his name, image and reputation and supported Telstra's drive for subscribers. That decision is probably more a reflection of the change in the attitude of the public to the commercial exploitation of celebrities and sportspeople than an example of judicial inconsistency. Nevertheless, even for a lawyer, the Honey case is difficult to rationalise.

In 1995 the issue boiled over in the hubris of AFL football. In my previous firm, we had the misfortune to represent the St Kilda Football Club. Many of these Clubs are managed with the level of sophistication necessary to run a chook raffle at the local RSL. Loyal supporters are told to queue up in the rain overnight to buy finals tickets. The firm donated hundreds of hours of professional fees. For that we were obligated to purchase series tickets which, other than the tickets to the Grand Final, were hard to give away.

After four years of acting for the Club an important paying case did arise in 1982. It concerned Silvio Foschini.[9] This was the first of a line of cases which successfully challenged the VFL/AFL Rules. It is difficult to lose against the AFL. Brian Ward & Partners were instructed to act. We were overlooked. Perhaps the reason was that anyone who is silly enough to act for a Club for years on a pro bono (free) basis shouldn't be trusted with serious litigation. Loyalty is a one-way street in football. The AFL itself just raffles bigger chooks.

Ricky Nixon, one of Australia's most successful managers and sports marketers, wanted to capitalise on the fact that he represented many of the elite Australian Rules footballers. He developed the relatively new concept in Australia of group marketing. This had been exploited very successfully in American football particularly by the leading quarterbacks. It was possible by approaching their group marketing agent to obtain the endorsement of all the top quarterbacks in America – for a very large fee of course. The same scale clearly did not apply in Australia but the principle remained the same.

Ricky set about acquiring the group marketing rights of the top Australian Rules footballers. This still allowed the individual footballer to endorse or market a product personally and to retain his own manager. The group marketing rights only applied when there was an endorsement by more than two players in the group. Ricky being Ricky (an ex-schoolteacher) did market research. He came up with the name Club Ten. There were in fact more than ten players involved but ten was used. It is a number which is looked upon by consumers as connoting success, that is ten out of ten. The contractual rights, which consisted of a licence to exploit the endorsement and merchandising rights of each player collectively as a member of the group, were acquired by a company which was partly owned by the players who were personally committed. This was to give the players an income stream after their relatively short careers.

The launch took place in a blaze of publicity and was hosted by Eddie McGuire. This was not likely to endear Eddie to the AFL and his public support says something about him. Belatedly and at great expense, the AFL established their own group of players under the mantle of Craig Kelly. They were very much the B team and everyone knew it.

The market was already being exploited by the AFL and the Clubs. They assumed that they either had the rights to exploit the players' images and names individually and collectively or, if they didn't, that there were no laws preventing them from doing so. They had gone so far as to issue licences to various licensees to use those images and names. These included manufacturers of cards, posters and large cut-outs of the players.

The AFL's argument was that they had an implied right to use the images for marketing purposes to promote the game. Ricky's contention was that the use by the AFL went further than that and amounted to a commercial exploitation of the image. This was misleading and deceptive in that consumers would assume that the player had endorsed the product or was receiving a share of the profits.

There were some practical impediments to commercially exploiting the concept. Each player had entered into a contract with the Club which allowed it to exploit the player's image to promote the Club and the game. There were certain exclusive rights conferred on the Clubs including the right to enter into boot contracts. These contracts are important for a Club. They are a source of revenue and also reduce running expenses. At the same time they benefit young players who otherwise would not be able to access those products. Slightly used Nike boots can be handed on to younger brothers. If the 'air pocket' happens to get punctured the younger brother can replace the boots with a new pair simply by returning the faulty pair to Nike. It is incredible how often these 'punctures' occur.

I became involved in a dispute which concerned one of the game's greatest players. He insisted on wearing Nike boots in the practice matches leading up to the opening game. The Club was contracted to Adidas for boots and a formal presentation was to be made to the Club prior to the opening game by a legend of Australian Rules football, the late Ted Whitten. The problem was resolved in the practice games by painting three white lines across the 'swoosh'. This 'solution' was not likely to endear the Club to either Adidas or Nike. Clearly the player was contracted to wear Adidas boots and my advice was that the only way he could refuse to do so was to establish that the boots were unsafe.

A week before the opening match I sent a letter to the Club advising that the player could not wear Adidas boots because they 'created an unsafe system of work and didn't have enough spring'. After a long lunch on the Wednesday before the game the Club's general manager telephoned. He made his point in relation to the unsafe working environment in a very profane, forthright and frank manner. He then addressed the lack-of-spring argument. He said that he was looking at a print opposite his desk of the player concerned standing on the shoulders of an opposition player taking a spectacular mark. The player was wearing Adidas boots. I responded that he should wait and see what the player could do when he was wearing Nike boots. The matter was settled in a mutually satisfactory way. Adidas boots were worn.

Perhaps the most serious impediment was the form the players were required to sign as a prerequisite to being registered as footballers with the AFL. It included undertakings that they would not enter into endorsement arrangements with suppliers or companies which were in competition with major sponsors of the AFL. These included airlines, soft drink and apparel suppliers and financial institutions. This was to stop what is known as 'ambush' marketing. Obviously this was a very limiting factor. Players could not endorse Qantas because Ansett was a major sponsor of the AFL. After the fate of Ansett, perhaps sponsoring the AFL is not a great long-term business strategy.

For its part the AFL also had some problems in that most of the Clubs' logos, colours, songs and uniforms were incapable of copyright or trademark protection. These include 'magpies', 'hawks', 'tigers', combinations of colours and old songs which are in the public domain. The only item that was beyond doubt and which was trademarked was the

AFL logo. Not surprisingly sponsors were more interested in the image of the players and the Club colours and logos than they were with the AFL logo. Because of this the AFL set about introducing new jumpers, Club logos and songs.

The litigation which followed did not concern copyright. There are copyrights in photographs but no copyright in an image as such. This is in accordance with general copyright principles that copyright protects the expression of a creative endeavour and not the endeavour itself. Nor was there any issue in relation to trademarks as none of these images was trademarked. At that time Ricky's arguments were novel. We were a little nervous in that the Honey and Perkins cases had been decided against the sportsperson. The Perkins appeal was still to be heard.

Ricky and the players issued proceedings in the Federal Court naming the AFL and several of the AFL's licensees as defendants. Proceedings of this nature are not often a good, long-term career strategy for a manager. Ricky is an unusual manager. He doesn't care. He was born in Bendigo. The AFL on the other hand is a peculiar type of defendant. It has so much money it can afford to lose. It almost invariably does.

Taking instructions from fifteen high-profile footballers and their personal managers is not easy. There is always the risk that they will be approached individually by the press and when asked about the action respond, 'What action?' At Ricky's request we avoided contacting the players on any day before a game. A high-profile Court appearance by Wayne Carey on Friday followed by a North Melbourne loss on the Saturday would not have been appreciated by the Club or the supporters.

During this period we relied on several 'silks' or senior barristers who caused added pressure because of their fees and advice. At a meeting attended by the players one of these barristers was trying to impress some of the best footballers in Australia with stories about when he played professional football. One of my less diplomatic solicitors, asked 'What did they pay you – a guinea a game?' Despite great pressure, particularly on Garry Lyon and Gavin Brown, who both worked for the AFL, the players held fast. Ultimately, the dispute was resolved and the litigation was settled. Never again will Clubs or a League presume to own or control the professional image of a player as of right. Unfortunately Club Ten and similar group marketing companies including the Melbourne Track Club for athletes didn't last the distance. The latter was too reliant on Cathy Freeman.

It is now clear that a sportsperson or performer does have rights in relation to the commercial exploitation of that person's image, name and signature. Obviously it is important that players support their teams and promote the sport in which they participate. It's also important that players recognise and support the major sponsors of the game and try not to endorse competitive products. However, the fact remains that professional careers in the sports and entertainment industry are often short. During that time a sportsperson should be free to maximise the income that can be derived from his or her participation in a sport or activity.

A league should not be entitled to benefit from the commercial exploitation of a name, signature or image from a licensing regime without proper approvals and recompense. This is particularly the case in sports like AFL football, where salary caps are strictly imposed and often marketing opportunities are the only remaining sources of income available to players.

There is no doubt that performers, entertainers, sportspeople and their managers are now aware of the commercial potential of marketing an image. They are also aware of the income potential of merchandising, memorabilia and personal endorsements. These are economic rights which will be protected by the courts. They are an inherent part of the development and commercial exploitation of a professional image. They are also an important factor in trying to extend the commercial and economic life of a performer beyond the proverbial fifteen minutes.

CHAPTER 7 – THEY CAN'T DO THAT

Several years ago I had lunch with Frank Hardy of *Power Without Glory* fame. It was a good lunch in that the food was good and I didn't have to say anything. Frank had spent a lifetime dealing with lawyers and his view was that when lawyers are first instructed their response is always 'They can't do that.' The lawyer and the client then spend the next few years and a large amount of money rationalising just why 'they' can.

I have stopped saying that. Litigation in the entertainment industry is often a career destroyer. It's not just the expense but people with a high profile will always attract publicity. In the image business publicity of this kind is rarely helpful. Litigation also takes time and nowhere is time more important than in the entertainment industry.

Many people think the judicial system has something to do with justice. It has, but not much. The reality is that 95% of cases are decided on the facts which are presented in the form of evidence. Evidence not only requires resources to collect and collate but also witnesses to present. Entertainers generally make bad witnesses.

Before an artist embarks on litigation as a plaintiff suing someone, the action contemplated must satisfy four tests: Firstly, 'Is it winnable?' This depends on the facts. The facts are not what a person knows or thinks happened. They are what the lawyers can prove happened. This depends on the evidence available. If a situation arises where a person in the right is confronted by two people in the wrong, both of whom lie, the chances are that the liars will win. That is the system. The judges have some discretion and must have considerable skill in distinguishing fact from fiction but ultimately the weight of evidence will prevail.

Judges are also people. Roy Schilling, a solicitor who went to the bar (became a barrister) when he was about 80 years of age, once said to me 'If you ever feel intimidated by a judge just stop for thirty seconds and remember that a judge is just like you. Every morning he gets up and has a shit and a shave'. Of course, that only applies to a minority of female judges.

Secondly, 'Are the facts actionable at law?' They must fit within certain causes of action. Examples are a breach of contract, a negligent act by someone who owed a duty of care and which has caused damage, conduct which is misleading or deceptive and conduct which is contrary to some statutory obligation such as an infringement of copyright. It is up to the lawyer to advise in this regard. Of course if the facts as presented to the lawyer are wrong the advice will also probably be wrong.

Thirdly, 'Is it cost effective?' The costs depend on the complexity of the matter and the time it will take to litigate. They will also depend on the court in which the litigation takes place. The Federal Courts, including the Federal Magistrates Courts, have jurisdiction in copyright and Trade Practices. Breaches of contract and negligence are usually litigated in the State courts. Whether proceedings are issued in the Supreme, County (District in New South Wales), or Magistrates (Local in NSW) Courts depends on the amount involved and the cause of action.

If the purpose of the action is to obtain damages, the costs have to be balanced against the chances of recovery and the amount likely to be recovered. When considering costs it is wise to remember that costs are almost always awarded against a losing party. Damages awarded are based on provable losses suffered, not figures plucked out of the sky. Because of the cost implications one of the most important and difficult decisions in litigation is when to make or accept an offer of settlement. A mistake can mean turning victory into a very real loss.

Finally, 'Is it a strategic play?' An action might be motivated by a desire to walk away from a contract because an artist has a belief that a new manager or new record company would be a good idea. This necessitates an assessment of what impact the action is going to have on the artist's audience, creative capacity, general health, financial wellbeing and career opportunities. On this basis Holly Vallance probably would have been well advised to let the Management Agreement with Michaelson run its course.

There is no fifth, 'How could they do this to me?' test. Emotion and revenge should always be excluded from the decision-making process. It is always sensible to take the opposition into consideration. It is generally unwise to sue government departments, churches and collection societies. They are spending someone else's money and there is no commercial incentive for them to settle. They can and often do go all the way. That might include appealing to a higher court which, because of the costs involved, is an option not available to the ordinary litigant. In this sense there are two quite distinct systems of 'justice'. Forget about the scales of justice being evenly balanced. They are not and never have been. The Minister of Justice should be called the Minister of Evidence. Finally, don't complain about lawyers being part of the system. They are and always have been.

The same considerations apply to a defendant, that is, someone who is being sued. Rarely do people choose to be defendants. If that unfortunate situation arises a decision has to be made whether to defend or not to defend. Sometimes people will choose to defend a claim purely for strategic purposes, for example they might not have the money to satisfy the claim and want to buy time. In these circumstances it is important that any defence filed does not amount to an abuse of process. It is always wise to explore options for a commercial settlement.

In the criminal context the system is based on those who have never been tempted judging those who have. I almost had a career as a criminal lawyer. My first case was a win. I represented a Mrs Wong who was charged with shoplifting. The evidence was overwhelming. After my submission, which was a clever mix of legal loopholes and charm, the Magistrate dismissed the case. To my surprise there was no objection from the Police Prosecutor. Six months later I found out that for several years Mrs Wong had been the main supplier of free dim sims to the police and court staff.

In the late seventies, it was quite common for successful groups to walk away from their contracts because record companies had failed to comply with the technical requirements of exercising options. Ironically most artists desperately hope the record company will exercise the next option. Unfortunately, sometimes sales volumes are not enough to justify that happening. This is usually the end of a career.

When a group is very successful, and there were many very successful groups in the late seventies and early eighties, artists and their managers would sometimes look for ways to avoid the contract. Failure to exercise an option in the right manner and at the right time was an obvious way. None of these cases was litigated. Record companies are realists and make the best of a situation where an artist no longer wants to record for that company.

Companies also know that under their record contracts artists are restricted from re-recording songs recorded during the term of the contract for a period of one or two years. This means that where a group has recorded two albums and moves on to another record company, they are prevented from re-recording the songs on those albums. Hence, if they want to put out a '*Greatest Hits*' or '*Best Of*' compilation they will, of necessity, have to include the hits recorded by the previous record company which gets a free ride. One benefit for the group is that they can negotiate another advance with the new record company which will not be used to recoup any unrecouped balance under the old contract. They also get an opportunity to renegotiate with the new company from a position of strength.

Failure to exercise an option is very rare these days because of the inclusion in contracts of 'cure clauses' obligating the artists to notify the company in writing where an option has not been exercised. The company then has a certain time to decide whether or not to exercise it.

The first artist I acted for who was sued by a major record company in Australia was Sharon O'Neill. Sharon is a very talented singer and songwriter from New Zealand. In 1985 she was the reigning 'Queen of Pop' and one of the best songwriters in Australia. At that time she was married to Brent Thomas who was also a successful songwriter and was managed by Grant Thomas (Brent's brother). Grant went on to manage Neil Finn and Crowded House.

Sharon had that particular obstinacy which characterises New Zealanders. I have acted for many New Zealanders over the years including Sharon, Neil Finn and Dragon. They have a rare talent because they think differently. Often they are very black-and-white and think in terms of personal relationships rather than the big picture. Sometimes they have a tendency to self-destruct. I should have been a New Zealander.

Sharon had released three very successful albums and was in the process of writing songs for her next album for CBS. In those days Australian record companies had little understanding of, or patience for, artists who composed their own songs. It was particularly difficult for a solo, female singer/songwriter. Groups would tour on a sniff and a snort. The musicians were all part of the band – a type of co-operative. A solo performer had to hire and pay musicians when on tour. Sharon had support from Brent, who was part of the band, but she was still a solo performer. More importantly, groups usually have access to other songwriters within a group. Again, Sharon had Brent and Grant's support but essentially she was on her own.

She had submitted a demonstration tape of the songs for her next record. Somehow the tape had been misplaced at the record company and this caused quite a delay. During this time Sharon was waiting for a response from the record company and the A & R people were waiting for a tape from Sharon. A meeting was scheduled at CBS on a Friday to sort things out. By then the relationship was already fairly fragile so I attended. At that meeting Sharon was told that they loved the songs but 'couldn't hear a hit single'. It was suggested that Sharon go home that weekend and write a hit. That advice was either an extraordinary vote of confidence in Sharon's ability as a songwriter or a manifest misunderstanding of the skills and effort which are required to be a successful writer. After that any hope of a successful creative relationship was over.

CBS was not prepared to allow Sharon to record her next album. She was ready and willing to do so. Under the record contract if she 'failed' to record an album in a certain time the contract could be put into suspension and time would cease to run. CBS did just that. Sharon was offered a record contract by another major. CBS threatened to issue proceedings in the Supreme Court of NSW to enforce their rights. Sharon's response was typical of a New Zealander. CBS issued proceedings to injunct her.[1]

The case was heard by Justice Young. The Affidavits we prepared were dictated by me and typed by Sharon. She had been a legal secretary in another life. We were all quite elated when Sharon won the case at first instance. We were not quite so ecstatic when she lost on appeal. Two of the judges decided that even though the failure to record was not attributable to Sharon, who at all times was ready and willing to record, CBS could still suspend the contract. 'Fail' was not to be interpreted in a pejorative sense. Pejorative means implying some element of fault or blame.

All failure meant was non-fulfilment for whatever reason. The dissenting judgement was from Justice Kirby who is now a Justice of the High Court. At that point we negotiated a compromise with CBS. Each party recognised the relationship was over and subject to the usual overrides Sharon was free to go.

Unfortunately, litigation is not only draining on creative people but it is also time consuming and we are talking about the contemporary music industry. Things had moved on. Suffice it to say that had I been acting for Sharon today my advice probably would not have been 'they can't do that'. In retrospect, perhaps the relationship might have been a little more productive if CBS had simply done what record companies are supposed to do, make and sell records. Sharon is a person with a rare talent. She is also one of the very few people I have met in the industry with the courage and determination to confront a situation like that.

Some years later I was instructed in another case involving Brent Thomas. By this time he and Sharon had gone their separate ways. Brent is one of those people who is almost impossible to dislike. He is charming, open and someone my kids thought 'very cool'. He had a songwriting partnership with Jon Stevens. Stevens had been a successful performer in New Zealand and has a certain charisma. His personality is more that of a performer whereas Brent tends to be somewhat retiring, as is the case with many songwriters.

When Stevens fronted Noiseworks in Australia the group was immediately successful. Their methodology for writing songs was that Brent would compose and record a music bed and Jon would add some melody and lyrics. This would be the basis for the ultimate studio recording. It worked very well for such hits as 'No Lies' and 'Take Me Back' from the first album *Noiseworks* in 1987. The same methodology was used to compose the songs for the next album. However, the group reconstructed the music bed contributed by Brent. This meant that Brent was effectively excluded as a songwriter on these tracks. He was not happy.

A writ was issued in the Supreme Court of NSW. The litigation centred around the title track of the album *Touch*. Our argument was that the work composed by Jon and Brent was a collaboration and was jointly owned in its totality. The concept of joint ownership of songs doesn't fit well with industry practice or legal concepts. Alternatively we argued that there was an implied contract between Jon and Brent which had been breached. Jon and the group argued that the music and lyrics were separate and distinct copyrights and there was no agreement to only use those lyrics with Brent's music. The case necessitated obtaining evidence from 'musicologists' as to what is distinctive about contemporary music. Their evidence was unhelpful and depressing. They couldn't find anything unique about the chord structure of contemporary music. After much expense and time the case was settled on a mutually acceptable and confidential basis. From then it was only a matter of time before it became Noiseworks who?

In 1985 I became involved in litigation concerning Australian Crawl. Their songs had a sophistication and quality one would not have expected from songwriters of that age. They were very middle class, Mornington Peninsula. Their first three albums *Boys Light Up*, *Sirocco* and *Sons of Beaches* were, and remain, Australian classics even if the Americans could never cope with James Reyne's accent. Unfortunately Guy McDonough, who was an integral part of the band, passed away. Simon Fenner, who was later a party in the Braithwaite litigation, began managing the group. Previously they had been managed by Glenn Wheatley and Richard East who went on to manage Jason Donovan and to successfully co-produce *Mamma Mia*.

The surviving members began to record a new album under the name Australian Crawl. I acted for Guy's estate. My advice was that the estate should share in royalties from the new album. The continuing members disagreed. This led to a writ being issued in the Supreme Court of Victoria. The writ was based on Trade Practices, a relatively new concept then. We argued that people who bought an Australian Crawl album would be misled and deceived into thinking that Guy McDonough, through his estate, would be sharing in the proceeds from that record. This was a bad argument.

One of the problems with a Trade Practices action is the requirement to prove someone has actually been misled. I am not sure anyone was. The case was settled. This is called a strategic withdrawal. A clever lawyer like me might even call it a victory. The new Australian Crawl released an over-produced and not very successful album *Between a Rock and a Hard Place*. They never quite managed to extricate themselves. Sadly, one of the other members of the band, Brad Robinson, died from cancer some years later.

A good example (at least from the defendant's viewpoint) of a case being litigated for strategic purposes involved the Hoodoo Gurus and their record company Big Time. The group originated in 1981 and made steady progress with *Stone Age Romeos*, *Mars Needs Guitars* and *Blow Your Cool*. They had a good following in Australia and were popular on the American college circuit. They were there but still a thousand miles from being there. They were signed to Big Time who had a distribution deal with Electra in America. Fred Bestall, a New Zealander and long-time friend of mine, was Big Time. Fred is smooth and stylish, generous and the ultimate gambler.

The money was running out. The label had not generated the sales to justify the continuing financial support of Electra. All this occurred when the group was touring America and they found themselves with no video to support their single. Perhaps understandably they wanted out of the contract. Fred prevaricated. His trump card was his control over the existing masters. Fred exercised the next option and paid the advance which was then due. The cheque 'bounced'. The group issued proceedings.

There was some residual angst in that the group was then being managed by Michael McMartin of Trafalgar Records, who was previously employed by Big Time. That soon dissipated as is the way in the music business. We argued that the option had been exercised. All that was necessary was to hand over the cheque. Then it became the bank's responsibility to go through the usual processes which are necessary to honour a cheque. Really the band should have sued the bank. This was a creative but not very sustainable argument.

On the first day of the hearing we had a young barrister who was in a state of nervous collapse. His instructions were to say who he was and sit down. The band was represented by Michael Brereton so we were able to agree on a settlement before our barrister had to be taken away. The case was always going to be settled because Big Time owned the masters which the group wanted. Thereafter it was all hard work for the band. Fred went off to manage a nightclub in London.

For several years I acted for *The Truth* newspaper. When acting for a publication of that kind the main concern is not defamation, which is more often than not a matter of commonsense. The real challenge is to ensure that the published material doesn't fall foul of the many technicalities which can be construed as contempt of court. They can include revealing the identity of a victim and sometimes the accused in a sexual assault, the identity of parties involved in Family Court litigation, of children in criminal prosecutions or publishing something which causes a trial to be aborted. This can be a very expensive exercise.

Despite the cunning attempts of *The Truth* journalists to circumvent or neutralise their lawyers, I was very pleased with our success in keeping the publisher out of court and successfully defending those cases which did arise. There is always a risk of litigation. Genuine mistakes do occur. Typing errors are made in telephone numbers in advertisements for services providing the latest innovation in bondage. The local vicar tends to be a little upset when he starts receiving phone calls at 2.00am enquiring about 'the usual'.

The Truth only had one serious problem with litigation during the years we acted for it. Unfortunately, this was on one of the few occasions I personally intervened. A double page exposé was published criticising the costs which had been incurred in prosecuting and defending a relatively minor offence by a serving police officer. The costs were millions of dollars. The article arrived for my sign-off on a Monday which was a public holiday. I was the only one in the office and, as is usually the case, had about half an hour to read the article and give it my approval or otherwise. I approved it for publication. It resulted in the company, the directors personally and publisher being successfully sued for contempt of court. Fortunately for me, by then the publication was near the end of its natural life. That was the final nail in the coffin. Mark Day, one of the principals, moved back to Sydney and is now a successful columnist and commentator. He didn't complain and paid our account.

Over the years I have represented many journalists. The current music writer of *The Age*, Patrick Donovan, is the direct responsibility of my clients Sue Donovan and her former husband, Barry. Barry was the industrial reporter for *The Sun* where he was ably supported by Ben Ainsworth. They are both exceptional characters.

Ben once organised a function to raise money for a children's charity. He hired a band and catered for several hundred people. Because of the status of the people expected to attend, the sandwiches were served on silver platters. Unfortunately, because of communication problems, which are not unusual with journalists, there were more waiters than attendees. At the end of the evening the left-over sandwiches were delivered by Ben to the poor of Melbourne via a lane at the rear of Ozanam House in North Melbourne. The next morning the manager of the hotel was not pleased when he discovered that his silver service platters had been used to transport the sandwiches. He was even more unhappy when he and Ben went to the lane to find the sandwiches in a pile and the silver service gone.

I have been instructed in many defamation cases. One concerned Glenn Wheatley and Lawrence Money of *The Age*. Glenn has had a bad relationship with Money for many years. Money was given the opportunity to embarrass Glenn over the book *Paper Paradise* which was written by Glenn and edited by Ed Nimmervol. Ed is a well-respected music writer. He also had a career as a songwriter having co-written the Little River Band song 'Red Headed Wild Flower'. Some disputation arose between Glenn and Ed which would have been sorted out in the normal course of events. Things turned bitter when Money wrote an article in his '*Spy*' column suggesting that the book was written by Ed and Glenn had failed to properly acknowledge or credit Ed. Glenn being Glenn had actually written enough material for ten books. The case was settled and Money has gone quiet for now.

Then there was the defamation action by Robin Bowles against *The Age* and Andrew Rule. Robin is a very successful crime writer. One of her books was about a young mother who, according to a coroner, managed to commit suicide by shooting herself twice through the forehead whilst holding a rifle, with which she was not familiar, between her legs and operating the trigger mechanism with her toe. She was in the process of feeding her young baby and half-way through her coffee and a biscuit at the time. Ultimately, there was another inquest and adverse findings against a serving police officer.

The second inquest was largely the result of an article researched and written by Andrew Rule, an 'investigative journalist' for *The Age*. Robin's book had much greater detail and insight into the particular events that took place. Both authors are deserving of credit and their works were complementary to, rather than in competition with, each other. Rule in his professional activities generally is a direct commercial competitor of Robin. This didn't stop *The Age* commissioning Rule to review Robin's new book. The review did no credit to *The Age* or Rule. It was more a personal attack on Robin than a review of her book. That case was never going to reach court.

I was instructed in the celebrated case involving a first author, Pam Skutenko. Pam had written a manuscript entitled 'The Goose' which had great potential. One of Australia's most successful, or at least lauded, editors Jane Arms and her husband Brian Matthews, a minor celebrity in academia, were enthusiastic about the book and offered to assist in an editing capacity. Arms also happens to be an agent and agreed with Pam to act as both her agent and her editor. That was the first mistake. Jane was to be paid a fee which was to be recouped from any future publishing advance. That was a sign of confidence in the work in that if it was not published and there was no advance, no editing fee would be payable.

Artistic differences arose between Pam and Jane. Jane was of the view that the work could be greatly improved if her editorial suggestions were implemented. Many were but attempts to obtain a publisher were unsuccessful. There were further demands for editorial changes. Pam was satisfied with the book and wanted it published. Jane decided that if her suggestions were not going to be embraced with the enthusiasm they deserved she would cease her activities as agent and editor. A letter of demand was sent demanding payment of fees which were allegedly outstanding.

The correspondence from Brian Matthews required a good editor. He likes to use phrases like '1999 V8 High Dudgeon' and to refer to the many exhausted, young PhD students with whom he has shared his wisdom at university. This goes down well with first-year students in the arts faculty. It had little impact on a first-time author who has spent a lifetime being patronised by people like Arms and Matthews. Pam was trying to write her book and at the same time survive on the pension. Finally a summons was served on Pam. Over time the claim had grown to $16,000.

Things were not helped when I returned at midnight one evening from France and decided that I would represent Pam the next morning at her mediation hearing at the Geelong Magistrates Court. That Court has considerable expertise in domestic violence orders. Nevertheless things were progressing quite well until one of the Court co-ordinators decided to make an appearance. He set about browbeating and berating Pam for having the cheek to waste his valuable time. He pointed out that neither he nor the Magistrate had any time for people who didn't pay their debts. That led to an altercation of sorts. As politely as possible in the circumstances I explained that the courts are there to serve the people. Pam and I made the not terribly scenic return trip to Melbourne in the knowledge that whatever the theatrical value of my performance it was probably not a particularly productive day.

An author must retain artistic control of his or her work. Editors, like music producers, do have considerable technical skills and undoubtedly can add immeasurably to the presentation, style and marketability of a publication, but at the end of the day it is the author who is the heart and soul of the work. Pam, to her credit, was not prepared to surrender and continued the fight despite the fact that the academic establishment seemed to be lined up against her, although I think that had more to do with my paranoia than reality.

Things were complicated by the fact that Pam's agent was the same person as the editor with whom she was in disputation. That is a clear conflict which can only work against the best interests of all concerned. Jane Arms didn't appear once throughout the litigation, which was finally settled. Pam attended every hearing. The book was self-published in November 2002 and justified all the pain experienced in its long period of gestation.

One of the most dangerous weapons in the armoury of the lawyer is the injunction. If a young lawyer wants to be famous, he or she can apply for what's called an ex parte injunction. Ex parte means that the applicant is seeking the injunction without the other party being notified or being present. By their very nature injunctions whether ex parte or otherwise are interlocutory, that is provisional. The courts will only grant applications on the balance of convenience, that is, if there is some pressing reason why the matter cannot wait until the trial.

Whether the injunction is granted or not the case will then be listed for a full hearing. If the injunction is granted and there is ultimately found to have been no merit in the substance of the application, the applicant will be required to pay any costs and losses incurred by the person injuncted. The applicant is required to give undertakings to pay any such costs and damages before an injunction will be granted. Most young lawyers are undeterred by this because an injunction involving someone with a high profile is almost always reported in the press as a great victory for the person seeking the injunction. This is one of those times when the lawyers make sure they are walking close to their client as they enter or leave the court.

Because of the costs implications an injunction can be a very sharp two-edged implement. This lesson was learnt by Mary-Anne Fahey and Media Arts Corporation Pty Ltd. They successfully injuncted a publisher who sought to publish a book, 'Kylie Mole's Official School Planner' which contained representations of a character named Kylie Mole.[2] The publication was injuncted after the usual undertakings were given. Ultimately, the case was lost and the plaintiffs were ordered to pay the damages this is the profits lost as a result of the injunction. That was the end of the Comedy Company, which was one of Australia's more prolific sources of creative output.

Fortunately I was not involved in the Kylie Mole case. However, I was contacted by Wendy Day (the wife of Mark Day) and requested to act on behalf of Tom Cruise and Nicole Kidman in relation to an application for an injunction to stop *New Idea* publishing certain photos of Tom and Nicole's adopted child.[3] The photos, which were of a private family nature, could have been sourced from various places including the shop where they had been developed. This was speculation and difficult to prove. Damages were also almost impossible to quantify and to prove.

The injunction would have stopped the publication of more than a million copies of *New Idea*. That would have involved millions of dollars in easily provable damages and, because of the evidentiary problems, there was no guarantee of success in the subsequent hearing. Tom and Nicole to their credit were prepared to give the undertakings. Fortunately, the court was not disposed towards giving the injunction. Finally, commonsense prevailed and a workable and reasonable compromise was reached. I breathed again.

Where would we be without the enthusiastic amateurs? I was once instructed by a group of people who had been successful in a business which had nothing to do with the entertainment industry. They decided that the entertainment business was there for the taking. What better way than to promote an Australian tour by Whitney Houston, who was then one of the world's most popular artists? They made contact with Whitney's manager. Whitney has a big extended family and all of them seemed to be involved in her management.

Whitney had always wanted to tour Australia. She loved kangaroos and koalas and if the would-be promoters could just telegraphically transfer some money all would be well. Getting a contract was, according to the manager, dependent upon this sign of good faith. My advice was that no money should be transferred until a contract was exchanged. This was not what my client wanted to hear. Finally we reached a compromise and the money was telegraphically transferred to the trust account of Whitney's lawyer pending an exchange of contracts. Whitney also has a large circle of friends many of whom claim to be her lawyer. That was the end of the money and the tour.

I travelled to New York and after obtaining special leave to appear made an application to the Federal Court sitting in Manhattan for an order that the lawyer to whom the money was transferred repay it personally. The lawyer's appearance was enough to convince me that we had little or no chance of recovering the money. Gold chains were his thing. He had released the money without notification to, or authorisation from, me. That didn't really impress the Judge who, by the way, didn't like me very much either, and appropriate orders were made. New York courts are nowhere near as glamorous as seen on television. Of course no money was recovered. Rather than get a letter of thanks I received a letter alleging that I had been negligent in adhering to my instructions in the first place and transferring the money. That went nowhere. I never did get to see Whitney.

Over the years I have been preoccupied to some extent with keeping various collection societies such as APRA, PPCA and AMCOS honest. This is because of a personal view, perhaps unwarranted, that these societies are foundation members of the Sydney based copyright club. For whatever reason my involvement in litigation against them has not been terribly rewarding.

In 1991 there was a reference by APRA to the Copyright Tribunal to change the way licence fees for hotels, nightclubs and other venues were calculated. I represented the Melbourne Nightclub Owners Association. The Melbourne nightclubs have a rich and colourful heritage. Names such as Frew, Kornhauser, Spry, Sam, Athos, Con and Goldsmith come to mind. The clubs, for obvious reasons, vehemently opposed any change. That opposition was not only based on their reluctance to pay the increased fees but also a natural reticence to allow anyone access to their accounts. They even resent the Taxation Department having these powers.

Collection societies are well resourced. No self-respecting barrister who has ever represented a collection society will appear without an entourage of at least five solicitors, each one of whom must be adept at manoeuvring trolleys full of files. Give me six months acting for a collection society and I would retire to Rio. Part of the problem is that they are always trying to answer the question, 'What is music worth?' – a futile but perhaps fertile exercise for lawyers.

The Melbourne nightclub owners, despite receiving great spiritual guidance from George Frantzeskos, then of the Metro Nightclub, were not well resourced. There was enough to cover my economy airfare to Sydney, but that was about it. By the day of the hearing in Sydney I had failed to comply with every time limit which had been imposed and my primary exhibit was a pair of spare underpants in my carry bag.

I was instructed by one of my sons who, surprisingly after that experience, went on and practised law. The Chairman of the Tribunal was Justice Shepherd. My submission, repeated over and over like a mantra, was that any inquiry into Melbourne nightclubs should be conducted in Melbourne. Everyone present knew I was right. Justice Shepherd forcibly pointed out that had this been a sitting of the Federal Court I would be locked up for contempt. I was ordered to remain in the Tribunal room during lunchtime. It brought back memories of my school years.

During my incarceration all the participants, other than the Melbourne nightclub owners, reached what they considered to be a reasonable and mutually comforting package. The matter dragged on until we were finally included in the compromise. By that stage I had missed my flight to Brisbane where I was representing a client involved in the Skase inquiries. I was lucky to get out of Sydney at all.

In 2001 there was an Inquiry by the Copyright Tribunal into the mechanical royalty rate. For many years the rate of mechanical royalties had been fixed by agreement between the interests representing publishers and recording companies subject to the overall supervision and control of the Tribunal. For some reason this time there was bad blood between the parties and the matter came before the Tribunal for resolution. I regarded this in itself as a minor victory because it showed that the wall was starting to crack.

I represented the Managers Forum which applied for leave to be heard in the dispute. Our application was not helped when Richard Cobden, who was representing the recording company interests, seized on a technicality. Richard is now a successful Sydney barrister. He represented Holly. Years ago he worked for Allens, who represented CBS. He would be there sitting in the corner as an observer when Robert Scard, the then Business Affairs Manager and I did battle. I called him 'the flowerpot'. Richard had discovered that my client company had been deregistered the week before for failure to lodge annual returns. My client had ceased to exist. I submitted that this was a mere formality. The judge thought the input of the managers would be of some assistance to the Tribunal and our application was more or less successful-more less than more.

Along the way I fell between the cracks caused by internal politics. Trying to bring together a small group of people who are competing with each other not only in the marketplace but also for the talent to be marketed is never going to be easy.

There have been very few copyright cases litigated in the contemporary music industry. Copyright is fairly well understood both in its substance and application. There are some grey areas which arise in relation to who owns a particular song. These are usually matters of fact, not law, and are resolved in commonsense ways. Little River Band once solved the question of who owned a prelude to a song by deleting the prelude. I liked the prelude more than the song.

A good manager will ensure that his or her artists stay away from the courts. Copyright cases in particular are characterised by high costs and low damages. Courts are full of frustrated actors. They are called 'barristers'. Their problem is one which is experienced by many entertainers. It is the lack of an audience. Most barristers' best performances are before four or five people, only two of whom are payers and all of whom wish they were somewhere else.

I should close with an inspiring example of democracy in action. I was approached by a public servant who had tried unsuccessfully but diligently to help a member of the public with a grievance. That contact resulted in the aggrieved citizen making a complaint to his local member of parliament. The MP then wrote to the head of the Department concerned and made statements of fact which my public-servant client considered were false and very damaging. I wrote a simple and straightforward letter of demand to the MP.

That resulted in the MP making a complaint against me alleging breach of privilege of Federal Parliament. The matter was duly debated in Parliament and referred to the Committee on Privileges. It was reported in Hansard on 26 February 1992. The complaint was that my letter amounted to an attempt to intimidate the good member and impair his independence in the performance of his obligation to represent his constituents. In short, I was in contempt of Parliament. The professional obligation I had to represent my client and her rights was of no consequence.

My first reaction was that it had to be some sort of bad joke. I have never had any respect for politicians or interest in politics. This just fuelled my cynicism. In my experience Parliament is full of failed lawyers and schoolteachers. Who do they think they are? Someone special! Well, they are. I consulted my friend, John Zigouras, who is the only Communist solicitor still alive. His nickname is 'The Jesuit'. Politically he describes me as an 'anarchist'. His advice was to pack my toothbrush – I was going to jail. I wondered who would pay my mortgage while I was away. I was forced into an apology. To this day I am not sure what I was apologising for! My client was left with no representation or rights. Her union abandoned her. My view of politicians hasn't changed.

The Daryl Braithwaite, Models, Holly Valance, Sharon O'Neill and Men at Work cases illustrate that the courts are not appropriate venues for resolving disputes in an industry which, by definition, is contemporary. They are too slow, too expensive and constrained by rules of evidence and procedure. They are presided over by people who often have little or no experience of, or interest in, contemporary music or musicians. Wherever possible courts should be avoided.

CHAPTER 8 – YOU CAN HAVE MY GIRLFRIEND TOO (JUST LEAVE THE CAT)

Commercial agreements or contracts underpin the music industry. They determine not only who bakes the cake but also who gets to eat it. Music industry contracts are primarily about the creation and commercial exploitation of publishing and recording copyrights.

Publishing copyrights are the copyrights in a song or musical work and encompass the music and lyrics which are owned by the person who created the work, the songwriter. In Australia they endure for the life of the songwriter plus fifty years and generate publishing income. The recording copyright is the copyright in the master recording. This survives for fifty years from release and is owned by whoever paid for the recording process (usually a record company). It generates recording income. Publishing and recording contracts set out the responsibilities of the parties in the creative process. They also determine how the proceeds of those endeavours are to be distributed and who is to own the capital assets, the copyrights.

Publishing income is derived from four sources. Firstly there are mechanical royalties. These are paid by record companies to songwriters and/or their publishers for the right to reproduce musical works on records. The mechanical royalty rate in Australia is fixed by agreement between the associations representing publishers and record companies subject to supervision by the Copyright Tribunal. They are often collected by the Australasian Mechanical Copyright Owners Society (AMCOS). In America they are fixed by statute (the statutory rate).

Secondly there is public performance income which is collected by the Australasian Performing Right Association (APRA) and its international affiliates and is paid to songwriters and/or their publishers. It has nothing to do with performers. It has everything to do with the public performance of songs. APRA licenses the public performance of musical works on radio, television, in venues and public places. 'Public place' has a wide interpretation and in England has been held to include playing music in a taxi. It also includes 'on hold' music over a telephone. The broadcasters, venues and other users pay licence fees to APRA which are then distributed in accordance with the frequency of use.

Thirdly, there is 'sundry income' which is income from licensing the musical works for use in films, advertisements and any other sundry uses such as print music.

Finally, there is investment income. Publishers usually account to songwriters on a six monthly basis. In the interim they invest the writer's share of income. Investment income is not 'publishing income' in the true sense, in that it is not derived from the commercial exploitation of the publishing copyrights. Nevertheless, it is a valuable source of income for publishers.

Publishers also have access to capital gains as distinct from income. They are in the business of building catalogues of copyrights. This can be achieved by signing writers or by purchasing or acquiring an interest in existing catalogues. These catalogues have considerable value. They can be sold, used as security, licensed or leased. This is the real business of publishers. Rarely do writers share in the rewards from this activity unless they control their own copyrights.

Publishers take a financial risk. They pay advances in order to gain access to income from the commercial exploitation of musical works assigned or licensed to them under publishing agreements. A publishing agreement has two aspects. On the one hand, the songwriter agrees to provide his or her exclusive services as a songwriter to the publisher over a period of time (the term) which is usually three years. On the other, the songwriter assigns his or her copyrights in all musical works composed prior to (which are not subject to a current publishing agreement) and during the term for an agreed period. This is subject to negotiation but is usually somewhere between ten and fifteen years. This is called the reversion period because the copyrights revert to the songwriter after that time. Before 1980 or thereabouts, songwriters often entered into agreements whereby they assigned their copyrights for the full period of copyright. Today this is very rare.

In America they use the terms 'writer's share' and 'publisher's share'. Each equates to 50%. These terms are only used in the context of performance income. This came about to ensure that songwriters received at least 50% of their public performance income which must be paid direct to them. It was to stop songwriters being exploited. Some of the old timers, like John McDonald at Image Music, will use this to justify a 50/50 split. However, in America everyone assumes 50/50 and then negotiates as to how the 'publisher's share' is to be split. The end result is usually somewhere between 75/25 and 80/20 in the songwriter's favour. John's standard response is, 'How can you do this to me?' John is doing it pretty tough. He is almost down to his first dollar.

If an advance has been paid to the songwriter, it will be recouped from the writer's share only, that is 75% not 100% of income generated, before the songwriter receives any income (assuming a 75/25 split). The commerciality of the contract will represent a balance between the financial risk the publisher is prepared to take against the potential return from the songs. To some extent a publisher offsets any potential loss by basing any advance on what is called 'pipeline income'. This is the total of all mechanical royalties, APRA monies and sundry income due but not yet paid. Mechanical royalties are relatively easy to calculate because they are based on units sold and the APRA money can be estimated.

There are other types of publishing agreements. Single-song assignments are an assignment of one or more musical works for an agreed period of time and do not involve contracting the writer as a songwriter. Nor do they usually involve the payment of an advance. Then there are administration agreements whereby the writer retains control of his or her copyrights but enters into an agreement with a publisher to administer them over an agreed period of time, usually three years. 'Administer' means attending to the necessary legal and accounting formalities and collecting and distributing any income. The income split would be somewhere between 85/15 and 90/10 in favour of the writer.

Recording income is primarily generated from sales of records derived from the master. Income is also received from licensing the master for use in films and/or advertisements and for public performances. Income from the public performance or broadcast of records (recording income) is small when compared to public performance income from songs (publishing income) collected by APRA. However it is still an important source of income.

With advances in technology the means of exploiting masters is likely to change. The emphasis on sales will be replaced by other methods of distribution, direct into-house transmission via satellite, cable or the internet. In the not-too-distant future the main source of income to a record company will be from licensing its catalogue of masters for direct distribution into a store or the home. (Like a prophet of doom I have been saying this for fifteen years).

Under a recording agreement, a performer or musician provides his or her exclusive services to a record company for an agreed period of time and number of masters to be recorded. This is a 'direct signing'. The company pays the costs of recording the masters and producing videos and agrees to manufacture, promote and distribute records derived from those masters. The company owns the copyright in the masters which makes up its catalogue. That is its real business. This represents a financial risk in that while recording costs are recoupable from artist royalties they are not returnable or recoverable if there are no sales. The company pays the artist a royalty which is a percentage of the income from record sales. The royalty base price can vary. It can be calculated on the retail, wholesale price or the published price to dealer. Because of this it makes no sense to compare royalties unless they are reduced to a dollar figure per unit sold.

Over the years record companies have developed many ways of reducing the royalty payable to artists. These often take the form of a deduction from the royalty base of which the actual royalty is a percentage or simply a reduction in the royalty rate itself or the units upon which royalties are paid. The most blatant is the packaging deduction. Often the royalty base price is simply reduced by 25%. This is supposed to cover the cost of packaging. Why the artist should pay this anyway has never been explained. Packaging and distribution is an obligation of the record company. Either way the 'allowance' has become a fiction. It bears no relationship to the actual costs incurred.

Reductions can also apply for 'new technology'. This can reduce a royalty base by 30%. In some recording contracts CDs are still regarded as new technology despite the fact that sales of CDs are rapidly being overtaken by sales of DVDs. A 50% reduced royalty rate can apply to sales which are supported by TV advertising campaigns, club and budget sales and sales in foreign territories. This is supposed to compensate for the extra promotional costs. A national advertising campaign might consist of one fifteen second advertisement per day shown in Alice Springs. Reductions often apply to foreign sales. The Seekers suffered a 50% reduction in their royalty rate for sales in Australia which was defined in their English contract as a foreign territory.

Record companies have also devised a way of not paying royalties on all records sold. There is often an arbitrary reduction of 10% or more to allow for 'free goods', that is records given away for promotional purposes. This is yet another fiction. It is also contrary to the basic principle that the record company is responsible for promotion, not the artist. Arbitrary reductions are also made to cover reserves against returns. This bears no relationship to the actual returns.

All recording costs are recouped against artist royalties. Artist royalties of between $2.50 and $3.50 on a normal-priced CD are common. On this basis if a record costs $50,000 to record, and an artist royalty of $2.50 per unit applies, the artist would receive nothing until 20,000 units had been sold. Often part or all the production costs of videos and sometimes even tour-support advances are recouped against artist royalties. Again, these are essentially promotion costs, which are the record company's responsibility. If these advances are recouped ownership of the copyrights in the masters and videos is still retained by the record company despite the fact that the artist has now paid for them. There is no logic or fairness in this. It is just the way it is.

It is standard practice when recording an album to utilise the services of a producer and engineer. The engineer is paid an hourly rate. A formal contract is entered into with the producer. Producers' fees range from $500 to $5000 per track and many producers also receive royalties (points). These points might be calculated on a different royalty base to artist royalties. Again, they should be reduced to dollars and cents per unit for comparative purposes. The producer's fees are usually treated as an advance recoupable against those points. Furthermore, the fees and points are treated as recording costs and recouped or deducted from artist royalties.

Sometimes a record label is interposed between the artists and the record company. This is particularly the case with established artists. The record company is almost always a major. The label is a company controlled by the artists, their manager or simply someone with whom the artists have a particular rapport. The role of the record company is to provide funds for the recording process and to manufacture, promote and distribute the records. Major record companies use labels for a variety of reasons but often because a label is able to source, nurture and control product not otherwise available to the company. The short-term aim of the label is to recover its costs from royalties and to make a profit. The long-term goal is to create a catalogue of copyrights. Artists often just want more say in the creative process.

At one end of the spectrum a label can use a major record company to distribute its product and the record company will advance monies to fund part or all of the recording costs. It will provide an advance (called a 'label advance') to fund office and related expenses. The record company would also pay the costs of manufacturing, promoting and distributing the record. This includes the payment of mechanical royalties to the songwriters or their publishers. Because in this instance the risk taken by the record company is relatively high the points paid to the label would be low. The label would pay the artists their royalties and retain the balance as the label's share. The rights licensed to the record company are the equivalent of copyright ownership.

This is appropriate when a label can source talent, that is provide an artist and repertoire function, but doesn't have the bargaining position to negotiate a better deal with the major. This can be dangerous for an artist because he or she has no control over, or right to receive, the advance paid by the record company to the label even though it is recoupable from royalties generated from sales of records by the artist. All the artist has is a contractual right against the label which might disappear from the scene. This can happen in real life.

Some labels pay their own recording costs. This would apply to a label controlled by a group like INXS which has recording facilities readily available and access to capital. The label might enter into an arrangement with the record company for it to spend a certain amount on promotion and to pay all manufacturing and distribution costs. Because there is less financial risk for the record company the points paid to the label are higher. At the end of the licence term the copyrights revert to the label. Access is provided to the record company's distribution network which includes the main retailers. The record company would be required to give a commitment to distribute a certain number of albums per year. All matters of creative control such as choice of material recorded, singles, studios, videos and artwork would be retained by the label.

At the other end of the scale there is a Pressing & Distribution (P & D) agreement. A label may record and promote its own product and simply enter into an arrangement with a record company for that company to press and distribute a certain number of records. This involves the label agreeing to pay a fixed amount for each unit manufactured and distributed. It increases the risk to the label in that it is responsible for all costs associated with the recording, manufacturing and distribution process. It follows that the returns to the label are very high provided the units manufactured are in fact sold. If they are not, an invoice will follow from the record company. All copyrights are retained by the label. In a P & D deal it is not unusual for the label to receive $10-$12 for each unit sold. This arrangement would be appropriate for an artist like John Farnham who has a well-established fan base, that is, he knows he will always sell a certain number of units.

If new musical works are being created and recorded it is sensible to think about establishing a publishing label. The songwriters would be offered publishing agreements with the label. The label would agree to administer the copyrights and collect royalties over the period of administration. If need be the label can then enter into an agreement with a major publisher whereby that publisher carries out all the administrative and accounting functions on behalf of the label. Assuming an income split of 75/25 in favour of the writer it would not be unusual for the label to pay 15 of its 25 percentage points to a publisher and retain 10 as the label's share. The entitlement to income would continue for as long as the copyrights in the musical works are controlled by the label.

Before a record or publishing company, artist, songwriter or manager can negotiate a contract, it is important to have an understanding as to what is, and what is not, possible. Since CD sales are still the primary source of income for record companies and recording artists and a major source of income for songwriters and publishers via mechanical royalties, the price of a CD is the cake. There needs to be a slice of that cake for everyone at the table. The break-up of the retail selling price of a CD is as follows on the next page for the purpose of ease of reading the percentages and prices:

BREAK UP OF THE RETAIL SELLING PRICE OF A CD

	Retail selling price	$29.95	100.00%
Less	Retailer margin	$9.03	30.15%
	Wholesale price	$20.92	69.85%
Less	GST	$1.90	6.34%
		$19.02	63.51%
Less	Delivery fee	$.40	1.34%
	Published Price to Dealer (PPD)	$18.62	62.17%
Less	Mechanical royalty (8.9% x PPD)	$(1.66)	(5.54)%
Less	Packaging deduction (25% x PPD)	$(4.66)	(15.56)%
Less	Artist royalty (19% x PPD less packaging)	$(2.65)	(8.85)%
	Gross profit to record company	$9.65	32.22%

The cake for a DVD is slightly bigger but otherwise the percentages are more or less the same. The mechanical royalty is the royalty payable to the songwriter/publisher for the rights to reproduce songs on the CD. No royalties are paid to the artists until all recording costs are recouped, that is against the artists' royalties only. Manufacturing, promotion and distribution costs are paid by the record company from its gross profit, i.e. the $9.65.

Based on the above the artists could expect to receive a royalty of $2.65 per CD sold after recording costs have been recouped. If recording costs were $100,000 it would be necessary to sell 37,000 units before any royalties are paid to the artists. Once a royalty is paid the manager might take 20% and each artist would receive an equal share of the balance. A producer might also be paid a royalty. The records 'sold' excludes free goods and returns and the royalty rate would be reduced in certain circumstances as per the contract.

The record company would receive $12.30, being $9.65 gross profit plus $2.65 artist royalties recouped from the first record sold until 37,000 have been sold. Thereafter it would receive $9.65 because at that point recording costs have been recouped. All other income from exploiting the copyright in the masters is retained by the record company unless there is a contractual provision to the contrary. This includes income from their use in advertisements and films, broadcasting income paid by radio stations and capital receipts from the sale and/or exploitation of the catalogue. These days it is common for artists to receive a share of sundry income but not of capital receipts.

In the example, writers and their publishers receive mechanical royalties of $1.66 per unit. Often Canadian and North American mechanical royalties for controlled compositions, that is those composed by the artist, are reduced in the recording contract by 25% of the prevailing statutory rate. The rationale for this is corporate greed. The sale of the record would result in further airplay and other public performances which would generate public performance/broadcast income in relation to the song. This accrues to the songwriter/publisher unless there is an agreement to give non-writers a share. So too does any sundry income from licensing the song for use in advertisements or films.

An artist might have the misfortune to win a contract as part of a prize. That removes the necessity for independent advice, messy negotiations and complications caused by managers and lawyers. The record company would probably have options for five or six albums. Royalty rates of 16-18% of PPD would be paid for albums. Foreign income would be split 60/40 in the artist's favour. A signing on advance of $20,000.00 might be paid with similar advances on completion and release of an album. Recording costs, 50% of video costs and the advances would be recoupable. The record company might even try to recoup the costs of a website even though this is clearly a promotional expense and is also something which the artist should own and control. Any contract of this kind where there is no independent advice or bargaining position could probably be set aside. Prizes are supposed to benefit not exploit recipients.

When negotiating a recording or publishing contract there are certain principles which should be kept in mind. They are:

- The goal is to obtain the best deal possible given the artist's bargaining position at that time. Do the deal. It is always possible to renegotiate later if enough records are sold.
- Timing is everything. We are talking about the contemporary music industry. Product which may be contemporary today, may not be three months later. The negotiations to release an album for Mondo Rock in America were so protracted that the hit song 'The Summer of '81' was due to be released in the summer of '82.
- It is always preferable to have offers from at least two companies. However, once an agreement has been reached that should be the end of negotiations.
- Anyone who needs someone else's money is not in a great bargaining position. Money will beat artistic integrity every time.
- First agree on what can be agreed upon and go back to the points where agreement has not been reached at the end of the negotiation. This applies particularly to 'deal breakers'. This maintains a sense of achievement and wellbeing.
- Remember that 'No' is not in the vocabulary of most A & R people. 'Yes' is not in the vocabulary of most business affairs managers.
- Don't overestimate your bargaining position or believe your own PR. You are not the first and you will not be the last.
- A negotiation cannot be so protracted or painful that there is no longer any working relationship between the parties. Signing a 'deal' is supposed to be the beginning not the end.
- In the music industry songs are everything.
- Never work on the assumption that the person in the record or publishing company who loves the material will be in the company next Monday.
- Solicitors should ensure they have clear instructions and can speak for their client. If a lawyer confirms a 'deal' on behalf of a client then that lawyer will have to be able to deliver the client or lose credibility. It is preferable to lose the client.

I once negotiated a very favourable contract for Uncanny X-Men with the then CBS (now Sony). CBS in a spirit of enthusiasm and generosity organised to send all their senior people to Melbourne for the signing followed by a boat trip on Port Phillip Bay. Brian Mannix, who is still a client, was well managed by Larry Tyler but on the day of signing decided to take some advice from the makeup lady at a TV station – her advice was not to sign. Larry and I had to threaten to skin Brian in public before he signed. It was an incredibly good offer.

Roger Hart of the Little Heroes refused to sign a contract because that particular date was a multiple of 7, his unlucky number. Their first album was entitled *Play By Numbers*.

The reformed Seekers (not the original or the latest which is the original) refused to sign contracts at a signing ceremony at the Windsor Hotel in Melbourne. When the cheques for the advances started to go back into the pocket of Michael Smellie, the head of the record company, we all became reconciled.

- There is no such thing as a 'free' lunch. There is always a price to pay for a large advance and this should never be the main objective of negotiations. That is unless the artists are contemplating a very short career.
- Publishing and recording agreements should not be negotiated at the same time and ideally not with the same company or its affiliate.
- When signing publishing agreements each writer should sign separate agreements. This is to avoid cross-recoupment of advances and to accommodate individual careers.
- Always get an example of royalties expressed in dollars and cents per unit.
- Every so often negotiations will involve someone who is overly aggressive and defensive or uses inspired responses like, 'I hear what you say' or 'I'll take that on board'. Don't react. This usually means they are insecure and out of their depth.

- If negotiating a contract interstate, go the day before. Even then things can go wrong. I once sent a solicitor to Sydney to negotiate the sale of a radio station. I rang the hotel at 7.00am to check he was up. He was. I didn't know he had just walked into the room. He missed the meeting.
- When interstate always book a single room. I recently travelled to Sydney with a client. We stayed in a twin room at the Sheraton Hotel. Within twenty minutes of going to bed I was awoken by snoring which was grating, discordant and thunderous. I wet some tissues and stuffed them in my ears. These were held in place by two sets of eye-shades wrapped around my head – no respite. In desperation, I took the mattress off the bed and tried to drag it into the bathroom. It stuck in the doorway. My client woke to find me trying to escape from the room with my mattress under my arm. I finally settled into the bathroom only to crash my forehead into the bottom of the hand basin at 3.00am. The cleaner next morning would have concluded that a firstclass orgy had occurred – not a great preparation for a court case.
- In the mid-seventies two English cases, the Schroeder Case,[1] and the Clifford Davis Management Case,[2] emphasised the bargaining position of the parties in a contract and the need to be represented by an experienced lawyer. NSW Unfair Work Contracts legislation[3] and Trade Practices legislation[4] embrace these concepts in principle if not expressly.
- It is often preferable to exchange letters (called a deal memo or heads of agreement) which set out the basic terms of the agreement and which is binding. This can be subject to an exchange of formal agreements in due course, but that becomes a matter for the lawyers. The creative process can then begin immediately.
- Contracts should be fair for all parties. There has to be something in it for everyone. The contract is supposed to underpin, not undermine, the relationship. A good contract is one that accurately documents an agreement with which the parties are comfortable. For that reason, good contracts stay in the filing cabinet. It is only when the relationship is failing that the contract has to be 'dusted off'. By then it is usually too late.

- When negotiating a contract consideration should be given to the impact of possible export market development grants. These can be paid in relation to intellectual property, that is, musical works and sound recordings which are exported overseas. Claims can relate to cost of recording, promotional videos and tour support. It should be remembered that a claim cannot be made for an export grant rebate in relation to expenditure which is to be recovered or recouped from a third party. Warren Cross of Export Incentives in Sydney is the expert in this area.

Set out in the addendum are basic heads of agreement for recording and publishing and a producer agreement with some comments as to what is, and is not, reasonable. Again, these agreements should be the subject of advice and negotiation. They are included only to highlight the issues that might arise.

CHAPTER 9 – BRICKS AND MORTAR

When Glenn Wheatley met copyright on the road to Damascus in the mid-seventies he found the key to the door. The business of music is about the creation, accumulation and commercial exploitation of copyrights individually or as part of a catalogue. Copyright is the bricks and mortar of the music industry.

Copyright is an exclusive right under law to commercially exploit certain works and material over a fixed period of time. The underlying ideas are not protected and remain freely available. Historically these rights were justified on cultural and social criteria. It was accepted that creative people should be given a commercial incentive to nurture and develop their talents. On the other hand people generally should be given reasonable access to the product of those endeavours. Today copyright is essentially an economic right by which an exclusive marketplace is established and protected. Like all good things it is subject to abuse.

Australian copyright legislation had its genesis in 1701 when laws were passed to establish a royal monopoly over printing in the UK. For the next two hundred years copyright legislation developed around the concept of authorship. Protection was limited to the traditional areas of creative endeavour, literary, musical, artistic and dramatic works. Law makers walked a fine line between providing an economic incentive to authors to create, and recognising the public interest in having access to the works created. For people to have access to a creative inspiration it has to be perceptible to them.

There developed a clear distinction between the expression of an idea, which is protected, and the idea itself which is not. If an author creates an original recipe and that recipe is reduced to a material form, it is protected by copyright. Thereafter people are prevented from reproducing the recipe. There is however no restriction on baking the cake. Furthermore, the copyright in the recipe is owned by the person who wrote it down or reduced it to a material form, not grandma who created the recipe. Similarly, a student can listen to a lecture and develop the ideas advanced. At the same time a recording of the lecture or a typed copy is protected by copyright.

Copyright as an asset is intangible. It is not like owning a house or a car. It is a contrived concept of property. Because of this it is necessary to distinguish the copyright from the underlying asset. The purchaser of a painting acquires ownership of that painting. That purchaser does not obtain any interest in the intellectual property or the copyright in the artistic work other than an implied licence to hang the painting. The exclusive rights of the copyright owner (for example to reproduce the work as a poster) are retained by the 'author' (the painter) unless specifically assigned in writing.

The exclusive rights that are conferred include the right to reproduce the work in a material form, perform the work in public, communicate the work to the public (for example broadcast) and to adapt the work (for example to translate it). These rights can be licensed or assigned in writing individually or collectively, in part or as a whole, now or in the future.

Because the concept of authorship is central to copyright, the duration of the right being conferred is based on the life of the creator/ author. Again, the author is the person who gave expression to, rather than the one who conceived, the idea. The duration is usually the life of the creator plus fifty or seventy years, depending on the country. This makes sense in the context of traditional works where there is an author.

Technology has always been several steps ahead of copyright legislation. The courts first grappled with technology in about 1900 when a publisher called Boosey sued a manufacturer of piano rolls for breach of copyright.[1] The manufacturer argued that the piano rolls were not copies of the musical works because the works were not perceptible from the rolls as would be the case with sheet music. The music could only be performed or perceived by playing the rolls on a suitably modified piano. The court held that there was no infringement of the copyright in the music by the creation of the piano rolls. The same argument applies to literary and musical works which are reproduced on records, tapes and film. None of these works can be perceived until they are used in conjunction with the appropriate technology.

Because of these conceptual difficulties it was accepted that the public interest would be served if producers of records and films were given protection. This was to provide an economic incentive for them to invest the capital required to develop and market the requisite technology. The incentive was provided by extending copyright protection beyond the author to the 'carrier of the work'. To accommodate this, a new concept of 'the maker' emerged.

In each of these instances, and in later developments, the maker is the owner of the copyright and copyright protection in Australia generally extends for a period of fifty years. In some international territories it has been extended to ninety years. As a matter of practice, the maker is usually considered to be the 'person' who paid for the manufacture of the medium, whether it be a master recording or a film.

This process obviously has more to do with capital raising and exclusive markets than it does with creative endeavour. Certainly it has nothing to do with originality as such. Ironically, creative input by performers is not protected by copyright – more on that later.

The Australian *Copyright Act 1968* (Cth) ('Copyright Act') now recognises four categories of subject matter other than the traditional works. They are sound recordings, cinematograph films, broadcast transmissions and published editions of works. In sound recordings and films, the maker is the owner of the copyright which extends for fifty years. In the case of broadcast transmissions, the licence holder owns the copyright for fifty years. The copyright in published editions is owned by the publisher for twenty-five years. The period commences from the date of first release, broadcast or publication. At the end of the period of protection the work falls into the 'public domain'.

The development of computer technology, which commenced in earnest during the Second World War in the UK and North America, was achieved without copyright protection. The original computers were large and expensive machines. The software by which the machines were 'instructed' was an integral part of the machine and did not require separate protection. The cost of reproduction was a sufficient disincentive. The manufacturers were protected by contracts with the end users. In the mid-sixties with the development of the semi-conductor chip and microprocessor, computers began to be mass marketed. Software was easy to reproduce and software manufacturers were faced with the same problem the music industry had experienced for many years: piracy. A contract with the end user was clearly inadequate.

Because of the relative informality and international enforceability of copyright, political and economic pressure was exerted, particularly from the Americans, for copyright protection in computer software. In the next few years there was considerable confusion in the marketplace and in the courts as to whether or not computer software could be categorised as a literary work for copyright purposes.

The series of cases known as 'the Apple cases' delivered some confused judgements by many confused people. The difficulty centred around object code, a series of electrical impulses which are not perceptible and which instruct the computer to carry out certain functions. Object code does not communicate with human beings and is simply a component of a machine. In May 1984 the *Copyright Amendment Act 1984* (Cth) was passed. The definition of 'literary work' was amended to include 'computer programs and adaptations thereof'.

Although the author is the owner of a work protected by copyright, an employer can be the owner of that copyright if the work is produced in the course of employment under a contract of service. There are also specific provisions which relate to newspaper and magazine proprietors and photography. Similarly, in relation to subject matter other than works such as recordings or films made by a person under a commercial agreement, the person giving the commission (and not the actual maker) becomes the first owner of the maker's copyright in the material.

It is necessary to distinguish a contract of service from a contract for services. The former constitutes an employer/employee relationship; the latter that of a contractor/sub-contractor. There are many statutory tests which are applied to differentiate the two. As far as copyright is concerned, general common-law tests apply. Of these, the control test is the most important. If a person is under the direction and control of another as to how a function is to be carried out, a contract of service rather than a contract for services is likely to exist. Each case depends on its facts. Because of this all contracts should include a clear statement in relation to copyright ownership.

As stated the copyright owner is given certain exclusive rights. In relation to literary, dramatic and musical works they include the exclusive right to reproduce the work in a material form, publish the work, perform the work in public, cause the work to be transmitted to subscribers through a diffusion service or make an adaptation of the work. With artistic works, which include photographs, they are the right to reproduce the work in a material form, publish the work, reproduce the work in a television broadcast or cause a television program that includes the work to be transmitted to subscribers to a diffusion service. The rights in relation to subject matter other than works, i.e. sound recordings, films etc., include the exclusive right to make copies and to cause the works to be heard in public or to be broadcast.

It is important to understand what is not protected by copyright. As has been noted there is no copyright in a performance. Copyright law has apparently not extended protection to performers for two reasons. Firstly, copyright law provides protection to works, or other subject matter, which are reduced to a material or tangible form, whereas performances are, by definition, live, temporary and transitory. Secondly, there has been some doubt as to whether a performer, however skilled or individual his or her performance, can be regarded as an 'author'.[2]

It is surprising, given all the legalistic contortions to accommodate computer software as a literary work, that there is no interest in overcoming the relatively minor drafting difficulties to legislate for a performer's copyright. I have expressed the view several times that this has more to do with the music industry establishment wanting to divide the cake two ways rather than three. The industry does not want performers as 'part of the club'.

The *Copyright Amendment Act 1989* (Cth) did confer some limited rights, which fall far short of a copyright, in respect of performances. Performers have been given a right of action in respect of an unauthorised use of their performances. It would be an unauthorised use to make a bootleg recording of a live concert or to broadcast an unauthorised recording of a live performance. It is incumbent upon the performer to prove that the other party knew or ought reasonably to have known that the recording of the performance was not authorised. Performers are left to rely on any contractual rights they may have as to how a recording of their performance, to which they have consented, is exploited. This very much depends on their bargaining position at the time the contract is negotiated.

As has been pointed out the music industry is about the commercial exploitation of 'two' copyrights. Firstly, there are the copyrights in the musical work or song, i.e. the music or, in the case of a song, the music and lyrics which are owned by those who created the work, the composer or lyricist. The copyright lasts for the life of the creator plus fifty years. It generates publishing income. There is no definition of 'musical work' in the Copyright Act. A song is really a combination of two copyrights each of which is separate and distinct, that is a literary (lyrics) and a musical (music) work. The term 'musical work' is often used loosely to describe both lyrics and music. Secondly there is the copyright in the master recording. It is owned by its 'maker' and in Australia lasts for fifty years from first release. It generates recording income.

These copyrights satisfy the need for protection of, and an incentive for, the songwriter and the 'maker'. Public access is achieved by a statutory licence system. Once songs are released on record, anyone other than perhaps the artist who made the initial recording (if there is a re-recording restriction period in their recording contract) can record those songs provided they pay mechanical royalties to the songwriter/publisher.

The artwork on the standard CD can provide a few clues as to how this all works. There will be a 'c' in a circle with the name of the record company or owner of the copyright and a date. This refers to the copyright in the master recording. The 'c' in a circle is an internationally recognised symbol for copyright. The 'year' is the year the master was first released.

There is also a 'p' in brackets. This stands for 'phonogram' and is derived from the Rome Convention 1961. The Convention has the effect of conferring reciprocal recognition of copyright in sound recordings (phonograms) as between the signatory countries. Australia has been a signatory of the Convention since 30 September 1992. Under Article 11 of the Convention, the 'p' in brackets symbol, accompanied by the year of first publication and name of the owner of the rights in the sound recording, on a published sound recording, satisfies any formalities with respect to the recognition of the rights of producers of sound recordings. The artwork will also set out the owners and the publishers of the copyrights in the lyrics and music of the songs recorded.

When records started to become commercially viable at the start of the twentieth century it was obvious that a collection regime was required in relation to the public performance and/or broadcast of songs. Otherwise there was no way a songwriter could keep track of, and obtain payment for such uses.

The Performing Rights Society was established in the UK in 1914 for that purpose. APRA was established in Australia in 1925. APRA administers public performance, broadcasting and diffusion rights in musical works. APRA issues licences for musical works to be performed or broadcast in public, that is on radio, television, in venues, nightclubs, shops, offices and/or 'on hold' over the telephone. The licences are issued to the venue, broadcaster or user who pays the licence fee.

APRA distributes the licence fees to the appropriate songwriters and/or publishers. At least 50% of monies collected must be paid to the songwriter. The balance can be paid to the publisher. The publisher's share is then divided between the songwriter and publisher in accordance with their publishing agreement. The practical implication of this is that the portion of the "publisher's share" which is payable to the songwriter can be used by the publisher to recoup any unrecouped advances.

Registering a work with APRA is a prerequisite to receiving 'performance income'. This has nothing to do with performers as such. It is publishing income which accrues to the songwriter/publisher. Nor does registering a song with APRA confer any actual ownership of that song as is the case when a transfer of land is registered with a Registrar of Titles. It is, nevertheless, very strong evidence of ownership. Once registered there is a presumption that the person registered is the owner.

The Phonographic Performance Company of Australia Limited (PPCA) grants licences to publicly perform sound recordings and music videos. PPCA distributes the fees collected to the record companies who own the copyright in the masters of the records being played or broadcast.

These companies may or may not have a contractual obligation to pay part of those monies on to the artist concerned. If that obligation does exist under the recording contract the likelihood is that the income will be used to recoup outstanding advances.

Finally, there is the Australasian Mechanical Copyright Owners Society (AMCOS) which administers rights to reproduce musical works in a material form, that is, to record a song. These rights generate mechanical royalties which flow from record companies to publishers and songwriters who licence the rights to AMCOS. Mechanical royalties are paid on records sold, although when dealing with small pressings, for example 1000 units, they are usually paid on records manufactured.

There is no collection society for performers. This is because there is no copyright in a performance. For that reason, Frank Sinatra, whose records have been played in cocktail bars around the world for the past fifty years or more has been paid nothing for those uses. At the same time, the composers of the songs he has been singing and the owners of the copyrights in the masters have made a fortune. Frank might have had a contractual right to receive a share of public performance monies from records but that is unlikely. Frank has now been replaced by Norah Jones. Some performers have tried to gain access to a share of publishing income by claiming a part of a song or insisting on rewriting some lyrics before they agree to record it. Very few performers would have the 'clout' to get away with that. Elvis Presley did. This was known as the Colonel Parker Clause.

There are some rights which come under the heading of 'intellectual property' but which are not copyrights as such. They include moral rights which were developed in Europe and particularly in France. These rights exist in most of the countries which have signed the Berne Copyright Convention. Moral rights enable an author or creator of a work, which is protected by copyright, to stop someone debasing the work and to ensure that the author is properly credited. They are personal, not proprietary rights. They can only be owned by an individual and cannot be sold or assigned. Generally they only last for the duration of the copyright in the work. They apply to the traditional works and films.

After prolonged discussion, debate and consultation in Australia the *Copyright Amendment (Moral Rights) Act 2000* (Cth) came into effect on

21 December 2000. It establishes a right of attribution of authorship, a right not to have authorship falsely attributed and a right of integrity which is a right to prevent the derogatory treatment of a work to the extent that it diminishes the author's honour or reputation.

Over recent years (yes, years not months) I have been involved in a case based on moral rights which has been litigated in Paris.[3] The action was commenced by the beneficiaries of the Rachmaninoff's estate. The defendants were the producer of the film *Shine* and David Hirschfelder who composed, arranged, recorded and produced the music in the film and for whom I acted. David's arrangements were based on Rachmaninoff's works and were widely acclaimed. Indeed, David was nominated for an Oscar. The plaintiff argued that there had been a breach of moral rights in that the arrangements brought the original works into disrepute. It was also claimed that there had been a failure to properly credit Rachmaninoff in the film.

Civil actions in France are based on the material and affidavits submitted, that is there is no oral evidence given and no right to cross-examine. Perhaps not unreasonably the affidavits are in French. The process is very expensive. David took the allegations as a personal and professional insult. The decision at first instance was in favour of David and the producer. Unfortunately, in France, costs awarded are nominal. There is no real downside for the claimant.

The decision was appealed. Appeals in France are virtually a rehearing of the original application. The appeal was rejected on all counts and the court commended David for his work. Again, nominal costs were awarded. In July 2002 the decision was this time appealed to the High Court of France. That appeal was withdrawn in February 2003. David was not prepared to accept the allegations which had no factual basis and he had the courage of his convictions. Of course, he would have preferred to have been doing what he does best – composing music.

The other rights conferred by statute are trademarks, patents and designs. A trademark distinguishes the products and/or services of a business or company rather than the business or company itself. It identifies the source of a product or service and protects the goodwill and reputation of a business. A trademark can be registered or it can exist at common law without registration. Any misappropriation of an unregistered mark can be protected by an action known as passing off. This requires proof that there is goodwill and a reputation associated with the mark. Registration of a mark is sufficient proof and as such registration is preferable. Marks can be registered in relation to various categories of goods and services. Once registered a mark is a valuable asset which supports the goodwill and reputation of a business. It protects the 'brand'.

Patents protect industrial ideas and techniques which are new, inventive and useful and which are commonly referred to as inventions. They are the antithesis of copyrights in that they protect new ideas. Once registered the owner is given a monopoly over the use of that invention for a limited period (usually twenty years) in return for which people have access to that invention. If an invention is made public before registration it is no longer new and cannot be registered.

A registered design protects the features, shape or appearance of a manufactured product. Registration is only available for new designs. Again, as with inventions, if a design is disclosed to the public it will not be capable of registration.

Finally, there are the 'quasi' rights which complement the intellectual property regime. There are rights which arise under Trade Practices legislation, passing off, confidential information and the common law.

A few examples can best illustrate how this all comes together in practice. What if:

A retailer wants to make a jeans commercial using the original recording of 'Eagle Rock' by Daddy Cool. This is a song which is very close to the heart of Ross Wilson. Can he stop that use? Presumably, as was usually the case in the seventies, Ross owns neither the song nor the master. All the advertiser would require is the consent of those who do, probably a record company (for the use of the record) and a publishing company (for the use of the song). These days there would normally be a clause in the recording and publishing contracts giving Ross a right of veto. One might think about at action under Trade Practices legislation arguing that such a use amounts to an endorsement of the jeans by Ross and is misleading and deceptive. Getting evidence to support that contention would not be easy.

A composer is contracted to compose music for a series of milk commercials. Although the initial campaign is for Australia there is no discussion about a territorial restriction. The campaign is so successful it is to be launched in North America. The composer is offered a cheque for $50 as a sign of thanks. What can he do? He can stop the campaign because being a contractor he owns the copyright in the music. This is a contract for services not a contract of service (employment relationship). That is unless there is a clause in a contract to the contrary. If he did stop the campaign, he would probably be black-banned from the advertising industry for life.

An advertiser wants to use the recording of a hit song in a commercial. Can any one member of the group which recorded the song stop that use? The agency would seek the permission of the record company which owns the master, not the artists. The aggrieved artist may perhaps have a right in his or her recording contract to stop the use of the record. This in itself might not give the artist a right to restrain the use by the advertising company. The artist might just be left with an action in damages against the record company which authorised the use. Damages, in these circumstances, are very hard to prove. If the artist has an interest in the song, provided those rights have not been assigned to a publisher without reserving a right of veto, which would be unusual, he or she could stop the song being used. Provided the composer/publisher has consented the problem at least as far as the record is concerned can be solved by not using the original recording, that is by re-recording the song.

A songwriter wants to know what fee should be charged for the use of a song in a commercial? There is no short answer to this. It depends on the budget, the campaign, its duration and territory and the product. If the song is a signature song and is to become part of the brand e.g. Absolutely Everything/Ansett, We Are Australian/Telstra or I Still Call Australia Home/Qantas, the fee could be over a million dollars. The fee would increase as the term is extended usually on a year-by-year basis. APRA monies would also be payable.

A film producer wants to use a song in a film production. What is a reasonable fee? Again, it depends on many things including the budget and the use, e.g. in the credits or only as background and the amount of the song to be used. In television it is customary to charge for 30-second units. Of course fees are payable for both the song and the master. APRA monies are payable in Australia. In America no public performance fees are payable in relation to films exhibited in theatres.

A DJ in a nightclub plays Roy Orbison's recording of 'Pretty Woman'. What consents does he need? The venue would require a licence from APRA to publicly perform the song and from PPCA to play the record. What if he decides to produce a musical and to use Roy's record in it. He would need a dramatic context performance licence from APRA. It would also be necessary to contact PPCA to ascertain what rights they control in relation to the record. If they do not control the rights then the record company would have to be contacted.

A school music teacher decides to present the school's version of 'Phantom of the Opera'. Would it be appropriate to approach APRA? No. APRA does not control grand rights which apply to music specifically written for a show. The publisher who controls the works would have to be contacted direct.

A television producer wants to parody a hit song in a comedy special. This might debase the song and it would be prudent in Australia for the producer to seek the consent of the songwriter or publisher of the song. One solution might be to re-record the song in the same style and with different lyrics such that it is a new work. The parody might lose its impact if this is done.

A group wants to record and perform their own version of 'Yesterday'. What consents do they need? None. Mechanical royalties would be paid to the publisher of the song by the record company. If the group is distributing via an independent release, payment would be made to AMCOS which would collect the mechanical royalties at the time the records are manufactured and pay them through to the publisher/composer. Public performance/broadcast income would be collected by APRA and PPCA in the usual manner in relation to the song and record respectively.

A group moves from one record company to another. Can it immediately re-record songs recorded by the first record company for release in a 'Best Of' or 'Live' album? There are no copyright restrictions. However most record contracts include a restriction on re-recording for one or two years.

The members of a group work together and compose music to lyrics written by one member of the band. Who owns the copyrights in the song? The song consists of 50% lyrics and 50% music. Unless there is an agreement between the group to the contrary, the person who wrote the lyrics would own the copyright in them. Because the group has collaborated on the music, the copyright in the music would be owned equally. The song would be registered with APRA accordingly. Whilst the song is registered with APRA only the public performance rights are actually assigned to it, that is the copyright is retained by the songwriter/publisher.

What if, in the above example, one member of the group composed the melody? Often the melody constitutes a large portion of the music. It would not be unreasonable for that member to claim thirty or forty of the fifty percent of the song which makes up the music. This could be registered as a separate entitlement just like the lyrics. It does of course depend on the agreement between the members of the group. If there was a collaboration it would be registered equally or otherwise as agreed.

A member of the group composes the melody and gives this to an arranger to arrange. Should the arranger be given a copyright interest in the music? No.

One member of the group has an idea for a riff or melody for a song. This is worked up in a session and then recorded on a demo or written down in musical notation by another member of the group. The latter owns the copyright. Only when the melody is expressed in material form is it capable of protection. Copyright protects the person who expresses the idea in a material form, not the person who conceives the melody. Again there might be an agreement which overrides this. If not, the group will have a short career. As a matter of practice the group would have to agree on who wrote the melody to register the song with APRA.

Paul McCartney changes the credits of certain songs from Lennon/McCartney to McCartney/Lennon. Has the Lennon estate any redress? Probably not. This is not a copyright issue. Fans might be upset about the change but they are unlikely to be misled. Nor is this likely to be a breach of any moral rights. It is also improbable that there would be any enforceable contract between Lennon and McCartney as to how their songs are to be credited, although past practice might be evidence of an agreement.

An advertisement uses a song recorded in The Beatles' style and singers who sound like The Beatles. There is no action in copyright. The use of a similar vocal technique might amount to misleading and deceptive conduct but even that is unlikely, particularly if the original vocalist is dead. When does music in a similar style become an infringement of the original music? That is a question of fact and degree which guarantees an appropriate lifestyle for lawyers.

Four young men decide to call themselves 'The Beatalls', dress like The Beatles and sing Beatles' songs. Is this acceptable? Singing the songs is permitted. APRA will collect performance fees from the venues and distribute them to the publisher/songwriter. They can even record the songs provided mechanical royalties are paid. There is unlikely to be anyone misled or deceived into thinking that John or George is performing. There could be a problem with the name however. It might be said to be deceptively similar to the trademark 'The Beatles' if there is one.

A young student develops an idea for a television quiz show based on a certain format. She has discussions with a television company and submits a short paper setting out how the show will work. The network passes on the show but six months later a show with a similar name and not dissimilar format appears. Has the student any remedy? There may be an action for breach of copyright if the instructions, artwork or set designs, have been replicated. A more likely outcome would be an action for breach of confidence. Because of a 'balance of convenience' argument, it's unlikely that an injunction would be granted and the student would have to rely on a claim for damages. This would be expensive and damages awarded in these circumstances are always problematical. Whilst there is no 'format' right at law it is possible to register a format with the Format Recognition and Protection Association (FRAPA).[4]

Another television station decides to produce a satire of a rival network's current affairs program.[5] In so doing small excerpts of the rival network's program (some of which are only seconds in duration) are used. Does this constitute an infringement? More than likely this would not be held to be an infringement because there is no substantial use. There might also be a defence based on fair dealing. It could be argued that this is a criticism or a review and that humour and parody is just another method of expressing a view. The courts might not accept that argument if the main purpose of the production is to entertain people.

A group wants to use a montage of newspaper cuttings as the artwork for its CD cover. The copyright in these cuttings is owned by various newspaper proprietors who would have an action. The journalists would also have a right to restrain publication of their work if it is being used otherwise than in a newspaper, magazine or a similar periodical. If the journalist was a freelance journalist other than an employee, that journalist might own the copyright. The use of a montage in this way might amount to an infringement of these copyrights. The question will be whether this constitutes a substantial use. What is and is not substantial is a question of fact which would have to be determined in the particular circumstances. The quality of what has been used in relation to a work is more important than the quantity. For that reason the montage should only use brief extracts of the articles and portions which do not include a by-line.

A record company records a 'techno' dance music adaptation of the 'O Fortuna' chorus from *Carmina Burana*.[6] Does this require the consent of the publisher of the work? The short answer is no. Provided the adaptation does not debase the original work, the Copyright Act entitles a record producer to make a record of a work previously made in, or imported into, Australia. This does not amount to an infringement of copyright. Mechanical royalties will have to be paid to the songwriter/publisher, unless of course the music is in the public domain.

Three members of a group collaborate in composing a song and recording it in a 'demo' form. The costs of recording the 'demo' are incurred by a friend who has a home studio. One sends a copy of the 'demo' to himself by registered mail. Another sends it to his lawyer with a request that it be logged and retained. The other does nothing. Who owns what and who is the best protected? As far as the song is concerned, each of the members of the group is in the same position. Once an original work has been reproduced in a material form copyright protection is automatic. When it is published there will be a presumption under the Copyright Act that the person named on the work is the author. The onus of proving anything to the contrary is on the person seeking to challenge that ownership. The copyright in the master recording is owned by the friend who paid for it or who provided the recording facilities. Because the work has not been published he would require the consent of the members of the group before he can release the record. Once records are manufactured, mechanical royalties would have to be paid. All of this is subject to any overriding agreement between the people involved.

A lady wants to open a school of dance for local children. To make it interesting she wants to get the kids to dance to current hits of Killing Heidi, Regurgitator and Massive Attack. Does she need the consent of those groups? The answer is no. She would have to obtain a licence from APRA and PPCA to enable her to publicly perform the songs and the records respectively. The same would apply if she decided to play some music on hold on a telephone. At the end of the year she wants to make a compilation record of parts of the various tracks so that the children can perform a particular dance routine at the annual examinations. She would need the consent of the publisher/songwriter in relation to the songs and of the record companies in relation to the masters.

The lady involved in the previous example choreographs some dance routines for use in the annual concert. Are those routines protected? Because the lady is self-employed the complications that often arise in relation to choreographers employed by major dance companies, which claim ownership of the product of their work, does not arise. Under the Copyright Act a dramatic work is defined to include a 'choreographic show'. Hence, on the face of it, protection is contemplated. Nevertheless there are many difficulties in relation to the reduction of an ephemeral performance to a material form.[7] This is one of the areas where lawyers might actually serve a useful purpose.

A producer uses a sample of a particular Midnight Oil drum sound whilst producing a record for a young group. Only a very small portion is used. Are any permissions necessary? Yes. The permission of the owner of the copyright in the master is required. If the use is substantial, permission of the owner of the musical work would also be required.

A telephone company wants to install some music 'on hold'. A licence from APRA to publicly perform the music would be required. So too would a licence from PPCA in relation to the master. If the master is to be replicated on software a licence from AMCOS might also be required.

Finally, a teenager is lent a CD and decides to 'burn' a copy at home solely for his own private use. Is this legal? No. The Copyright Act does not allow copyright material to be reproduced without the consent of the copyright owner.

The industry has come full circle. Copyright is again facing the challenge of technology. On 1 April 2003 under the heading 'Copyright – The Devil and the Detail' it was reported in *The Age* that:

> 'Screenrights, the Australian Audiovisual Copyright Society, has opened up a new front in the battle over digital content and rights management here in Australia. Together with APRA, the royalty collecting agency has put a proposal to Canberra for the introduction of a levy on blank recording media as a way of securing compensation for its members for private copying'.[8]

This is just another way of taxing the consumer.

On 2 May 2003 in *The Australian Financial Review* under the heading 'Pirates Rule The Cyber Waves' it was announced that the music industry is waging a war against online pirates that it cannot win.[9] Paul Nemeth from Fish Records was quoted as saying, 'My biggest fear is that there is a generation of 9-year-olds to 14-year-olds who have never been into a music store and just file swap'.[10]

A lawyer from Baker & McKenzie, Mr Patrick Fair, referred to the Californian decision in April 2003[11] which concerns two internet sites, Grokster and Streamcast.[12] These sites hosted free software which locates whatever music file the user wants from anywhere in the world. It simply involves swapping. The material swapped can be legal or illegal. According to Rachel Osman, 'Just as Universal failed to stop Sony producing video cassette recorders in the 1980s, the record companies failed to stop those who provide "peer-to-peer" software'.[13] As Mr Fair pointed out, 'the music industry has to accept the solution lies elsewhere'.[14]

A little belatedly perhaps *The Australian Financial Review* on 7 May 2003 proclaimed, 'Entertainers Lose Battle with Virtual Bandits'.[15] Michael Wolf, who is the managing partner of the media and entertainment practice, McKenzie & Co, commented that new partnerships are needed 'with the equipment makers, fans, retailers and even the spooky fileswappers'.[16] He noted that suing the people you hope will be your customers is always a dubious approach, and further that 'The music industry squandered a great opportunity to get a handle on digital music when it shuttered Napster without figuring out a way to turn its powerful brand and 70 million users into a business'.[17]

Things really moved up a notch on 14 May 2003 when it was reported in *The Australian Financial Review* that three university students had appeared in a Sydney court charged with online music piracy.[18] ARIA unsuccessfully applied for leave to make a victim impact statement. Sentencing was adjourned until the students finished their exams.

That was followed on 25 May 2003 by an article in *The Sunday Age* headed 'Record Industry Backs Napster's Return'.[19] The article reported that 'Napster, the technology that launched mass music piracy on the internet, is about to be revived by the record companies that killed it'.[20] Music experts hoped that it would 'be used to open a legal worldwide, online music selling system similar to the new webstore opened this month in the US by Apple Computer'.[21] Universal and Sony are part of the joint venture with Roxio, a Californian software company.[22] Finally on 28 May 2003 *The Australian Financial Review* reported that the all-powerful 'analysts have applauded Apple's music venture'.[23] In Australia Michael Browning of 301 Records announced it intends to sell music on the internet file-swapping system Kazaa.[24]

The only consistent element throughout all this is copyright. It still protects the master and the song. What it can't stop is the rapid development of technology designed to replicate and distribute recorded music. Ironically much of the capital used to develop that technology has been provided by companies affiliated with the major record companies. They developed the video players which could duplicate videos, the tape recorders that could replicate tapes and the technology to allow people to 'burn' CDs. Perhaps it should not be too difficult for the record companies to recognise that this technology exists and to work with it.

If young people cannot afford to buy recorded music, they will access it elsewhere. Music has to be both affordable and accessible. For that to occur there needs to be a recognition that the existing methods of distribution are redundant. Rather than trying to hold back a raging elephant with a thousand pieces of string, the music industry should climb aboard. The creators are there, the product is there in the form of catalogues, so too is the demand. All that is required is to find an efficient method of supplying that demand at an affordable price.

It is time to accept that young people have the necessary expertise to access music whatever the technological or legal constraints. The kids will always be streets ahead of the executives who run record companies and the politicians and lawyers who are responsible for copyright legislation. The young people who enjoy contemporary music should be respected, not arrested. It is the mindset of the record industry which is the problem, not any perceived inadequacies of copyright law.

The most glaring inadequacy of copyright law is its failure to protect performers. They do have some rights under the Copyright Act but these fall far short of a copyright. Their consent is required before an unauthorised recording of a performance can be used or an authorised recording of a performance can be used on a soundtrack to a film. That limited protection should be contrasted with the rights of songwriters and record companies. This is obviously neither equitable nor sustainable in the long-term. Before the intellectual property cabal can have any real credibility, this will have to be redressed.

CHAPTER 10 – OUT OF THE CLOSET

In 1990 the Prices Surveillance Authority (PSA) began an inquiry into the prices of sound recordings. Of necessity this involved a review of the Australian recording industry and the laws which legitimise it.

The so-called parallel import provisions (the provisions) of the Copyright Act are sections 37, 38, 102 and 103. These sections and their foreign equivalents had been used by the predominantly American and European copyright owners to divide the world into exclusive territorial markets. One of those markets was Australia. In effect, multinational record companies decided what records could or could not be sold in Australia. The provisions acted as an absolute trade barrier. Section 102 applied to records. Musical works or songs were covered by section 37. Sections 103 and 38 concerned infringements within Australia. The combined effect of these sections was to prevent the importation into Australia of records for certain commercial purposes. These included the reproduction or sale of records where the importer knew, or should reasonably have known, that it would have been an infringement of copyright to make that article in Australia.

The multinational record companies had provided their Australian affiliates with the exclusive licence to import records, which were part of their catalogues, into Australia. The six major recording companies at that time, namely BMG, CBS, EMI, Festival, PolyGram and WEA controlled approximately 95% of all recorded product sold in Australia. It should be understood that the provisions related to legal product, that is product manufactured by, or under licence from, the copyright owner. They had no application to illegal product including pirated material which was covered by other sections of the Copyright Act.

For many years the recording industry, in particular Jim White during his time at Festival, was very vigilant in enforcing the provisions.

The record companies used the courts to injunct and obtain damages from any independent distributor who had the temerity to purchase records outside Australia and import them into Australia for resale. Often these people were small businesses with no substantial assets, certainly not enough to defend an action by a major record company. More often than not judgement would be entered without a formal defence being filed. It was the proverbial sledgehammer and the snail.

Occasionally the imported records were limited release records of no real commercial value and those which the major record companies had no intention of making available for sale in Australia. Nevertheless, the full weight of the law was used against the importers. Clearly, aside from any arguments in relation to price maintenance, this situation was not in the best interests of Australian consumers. Anyone functioning outside the ivory tower of the Sydney 'copyright club' would have known this was not sustainable in the long-term.

The inquiry was preceded by the 1988 Copyright Law Review Committee's report.[1] That was followed by an inquiry conducted by the PSA into book prices. The final report was published on 19 December 1989.[2] It resulted in the *Copyright Amendment Act 1991* (Cth) which came into force on 23 December 1991. This went some way towards opening the market in that it allowed books first published outside Australia after 23 December 1991 and not published in Australia within thirty days, to be imported without restriction. Restrictions still applied to books first published in Australia or published in Australia within thirty days of being published elsewhere provided supply was maintained. This pleased neither the copyright owners nor the free marketeers.

In this climate there was lobbying by the Australian Record Sellers Association (a group of independent record distributors who were long on lobbying but some of whom were short on credibility). Their activities were successful and resulted in the Labor government on 15 February 1990 announcing that the PSA had been requested to conduct an inquiry into the prices of recorded music in Australia. Even then the executives who controlled the club didn't see the writing on the wall. The inquiry was to be all-embracing and was to cover the industry structure, pricing practices, profitability, employment and new technology.

I was first instructed in August 1990 to assist the ACTU in preparing and presenting a submission to the inquiry. At that time my sympathies were with retaining the provisions. The ACTU was not really interested in the intricacies of copyright law and was open-minded about the provisions. They and their member unions were, however, very concerned about prices. Price regulation was a fundamental part of the accord which, broadly speaking, was an agreement between the unions and the government to restrain wage demands. The flip side was price restraint. That was why the PSA existed.

The ACTU recognised that for an industry to survive and prosper it is important that those who invest capital derive a fair return. It is also important that those who provide their skills and labour, in this instance, composers and performers, are properly remunerated. Many of these people were members of the Musicians' Union and Actors' Equity which also became involved. Then there were the consumers. They should not be compelled to subsidise the inefficiencies or greed of industry participants.

Several million Australian consumers are union members. Many of these are young people with limited resources. The providers of capital just happened to be multinational companies with considerable resources. My brief was to ensure that the industry participants represented by the union movement were protected in their work environment and at the same time consumers were not exploited. I thought these instructions were perfectly compatible with the aspirations of the Australian recording industry. They were not.

I took my instructions from Peter Duncan who was the Arts Officer of the ACTU. The then President, Martin Ferguson, also took an active interest. Duncan and Ferguson both have industrial backgrounds and are skilled at identifying an issue and attempting to reach a pragmatic and practical compromise. This comes from their training. They conduct their activities in a cost-effective and productive way because of the lack of resources in the union movement. They have no money to play with and tend to be frugal. No one could ever accuse record companies or their offshoots of acting in that way.

The first hearing day was 1 November 1990 – All Saints Day. We presented a purely factual submission[3] because our strategy was to wait and see. We would make a final submission with our recommendations later. That gave us a bargaining position. We assumed there would be some room for negotiation after the initial hearing. At that point the ACTU and the unions wanted to adopt a passive role.

The record companies, the publishers and ARIA, AMPAL, APRA, AMCOS, and PPCA all appeared and were represented directly or indirectly. On that day there was more 'silk' in that room than could be found in a Bangkok bazaar. The lawyers did what they had to do. The record company executives approached the whole process with a sense of indignation. Their initial submissions reflected that. They only briefly touched on the central issue which was price. This was a risky strategy. Lawyers know that if you fail to address an issue it might be taken as a given.

Their primary arguments were based on piracy and altruism. These themes were one step away from motherhood. It was thought that they would be so popular with the masses that no regulator or politician would dare challenge the status quo. For an industry which relied on its skill in identifying and exploiting popular trends they failed to realise that high prices for consumers are not terribly popular. It was suggested that if the provisions were removed, Australia would be swamped with illegal product manufactured in Indonesia. Not only was this argument essentially racist in its implications but it ignored the fact that the provisions only relate to legally manufactured product. We were forced to respond.

The piracy provisions of the Copyright Act were not relevant. Nevertheless, we pointed out that because of the ease of manufacturing pirated product, no one would go to the trouble of manufacturing that product in Indonesia. It would be easier to rent a shed in Box Hill or Strathfield and manufacture the product than go to all the trouble of importing it. If someone wants to get into the illegal importing business there are much more profitable things to import than pirated records.

As to altruism, no one had ever before imagined that the record companies were an offshoot of the Order of Mother Theresa. We submitted that the record industry is about mutual exploitation. It's about risk and return. We also went to considerable trouble to detail the amount of money record companies had made from the commercial exploitation of Australian groups: The Seekers, Air Supply, AC/DC, Men at Work, Little River Band and Midnight Oil to name a few.

If it could be demonstrated that the prices of records in Australia were indeed competitive with international prices, there would be no justification for removing the provisions. The point was not taken. Indeed, the argument that the provisions had to be retained to generate sufficient resources to continue to subsidise the local industry and to buttress the fight against piracy implied that Australian prices were not competitive. Professor Fels and his advisers, Jill Walker and David Couzens, might not look very bright, but they could work that out.

Pete Steedman, the Executive Director of Ausmusic, an industry funded and controlled body, made the somewhat presumptuous submission that he and his organisation represented workers in the industry. That made the unions sit up. Pete wears a leather jacket and has long hair. What more could workers want? He went on to support ARIA's argument with a submission about the evils of international drug barons. He held up two tapes and challenged the Tribunal members to 'pick the pirate'. Not unlike the 'pick the wine in the cleanskin' competition and equally useful as evidence.

Things were not helped when rumours circulated that Michael Gudinski was prepared to enter into an agreement where he could 'wear a price reduction of $2 per unit'. Had that been true (and I'm sure it wasn't because Michael would have been able to put much more than that on the table) it would have been an admission of the industry's ability and willingness to fix prices (an illegal activity).

The industry was still presenting a uniform position. But already there were divisions appearing and it couldn't be said that CBS, EMI and PolyGram were a happy and united troop of boy scouts. At the same time, the union movement itself was going through a period of reform and change. Bill Kelty, the then ACTU Secretary, had long ago recognised that if small unions did not merge and give themselves access to the resources and skills necessary to represent their members, they would wither and die. There was pressure for the unions representing musicians, journalists and actors to merge – understandably actors and musicians were not pleased about being associated with journalists. That environment engenders short-term insecurity and at that time the unions were at their most vulnerable.

The ACTU's resolve was strengthened when Pete Steedman and Ausmusic put up posters around Melbourne proclaiming that performers and composers were being ripped off and advising them to seek the assistance of Ausmusic. This goaded Peter Duncan into action. We began to formulate an industry package for performers and musicians which would be the price the industry would have to pay to retain their exclusive market. Even that was predicated on the industry being able to demonstrate that their prices were in fact competitive. Our package included a performer's copyright, a levy on record sales and an Industry Council. The problem with a levy is that it causes an increase not a decrease in the price of records. We put that in our list of demands to have something we could concede.

Peter and I travelled to Sydney on 8 November 1990 to meet Paul Turner, the MD of WEA, who was overseeing the case for ARIA at director level. This was the time to 'cut a deal'. Paul was his usual friendly self and apologised for his inability to spend time with us. He explained that he was busy with the PSA Inquiry into the price of records. This was a reality check for Peter who had presumed that the ACTU had some role to play.

We made our final submission on 19 November 1990.[4] We formalised the industry package. We left the issue of removing the provisions open to retain a bargaining position. At the same time we made it clear that the onus was on the recording industry to show good reasons why the provisions should be retained.

From the beginning we took the apparently radical view that a reduction in prices would not disadvantage the industry. We dismissed out of hand the proposition that a reduction in price would result in less money being available to nurture and develop acts, if that is what record companies do. Record companies paying advances to artists was nothing more or less than an investment decision based on the profit motive. Knowing the amount of money record companies had made from exploiting Australian artists, clearly that investment would continue despite a price reduction.

We argued that a reduction in the price of records would lead to more records being sold. The price of records was too high. Money was being diverted into other entertainment options including computer games. Our submission was that a reduction in the price of records would lead to a revitalisation of the industry. If more records are sold more people would go to live 'gigs', more people would buy merchandise and the industry would become vibrant. To us it was a simple application of supply and demand. Reduce the price and sell more. That could only benefit everyone including consumers. The industry opposed that out of hand.

Naively, I could not understand why the industry would not welcome a price reduction. Three or four years later, when the heat had gone out of the debate, one of the senior record company executives explained to me why they were so determined to maintain the provisions. By definition contemporary music is ephemeral. It is also price inelastic. If a record is being released by a popular artist such as Michael Jackson in 1993 or Powderfinger in 2004, young consumers will pay any price to purchase that record at that time. If a situation can be created whereby an exclusive market is maintained, the record company can charge whatever it chooses for that product during a three month window of opportunity and the kids will pay.

That same record company executive also said their whole strategy was based on delaying the legislation. Technological advances were such that it was only a matter of time before recording companies would be unable to protect their markets anyway. There would come a time when there would be no record as such to import. It would simply be downloaded. Perhaps they weren't so silly after all.

The mindset of the members of the PSA was probably not helped by an article which appeared in *The Australian Financial Review* on Wednesday 12 December 1990.[5] It reported, a little prematurely perhaps, that industry leaders had launched a counterattack. John Farnham was reported as having visited Canberra to argue the merits of maintaining the status quo in the recording industry. The members of the PSA were based in Melbourne. Obviously the political lobbying had begun!

Manny Candi, who was arguing the case as the CEO of ARIA, was quoted as saying, 'Furthermore, the PSA has yet to demonstrate that it understands how copyright works. This so-called Authority cannot hope to understand how the industry works'.[6] Fels, Couzens and Walker were not used to being dismissed in such a patronising manner. Furthermore, this was a prices not a copyright inquiry. Ominously, it was also reported that the preliminary report published by Price Waterhouse and commissioned by ARIA actually showed that the price of recorded music in Australia was considerably higher than in the major overseas markets. I was quoted as having said that the ARIA arguments consisted of the three Ps, 'piracy, patronage and imports'.

The PSA brought down its final report on 18 December 1990.[7] The PSA recommendations included the removal of the provisions to the extent they impacted on sound recordings. They accepted all of the recommendations of the ACTU and unions including tougher laws on piracy, extension of copyright protection to include a performer's copyright, and creation of a tripartite Australian Music Industry Council. An ACTU media release dated 18 December 1990[8] noted that ARIA had avoided the central issue throughout the Inquiry and rather had preferred to attack the PSA and to confuse and trivialise the issues.

My inclination was that it was time to move on. However, it is easier to get on a freeway than to get off. The next phase after a report of that kind is that submissions are made to Cabinet. This involves various inter-departmental committees. It is also the phase when lobbying becomes all important. I thought this is where the record companies would excel. After all, they are in the 'shmooze' business. Politicians are acutely aware of public opinion. Obviously newspapers are crucial to this. Never at any stage did the record companies receive any sympathy or support from the main financial newspapers, particularly *The Australian Financial Review* and *The Australian*, both of which are national publications and read by every federal politician. Support from the other media was also token to say the least. Even journalists could see through their arguments.

The rhetoric was turned up. Professor Fels suggested that the industry was in a backwater and that the recording companies had been running a racket. Manny Candi was of the view that there should be an inquiry into the PSA. On 12 January 1991 Michael Gudinski was quoted as saying that he had met with Simon Crean, the then Federal Minister for Science and Technology, and advised him that 'you let this go through and I'm selling Mushroom Records – I'm out'.[9]

Peter and I did the rounds of all the ministers in Canberra. Some ministers in the Labor government still thought the ACTU and the unions had some influence. We could always tell those who had been visited by ARIA and their lobbyist. They were the ones with a gold album on the wall.

Then things started to get nasty. The Victorian Rock Foundation, which was closely associated with Steedman's Ausmusic, decided to have a radio and records conference as part of the Melbourne Music Festival in February 1991. Kim Beazley was the principal speaker. Other speakers included Manny Candi, Brett Cottle from APRA, Michael Crosby from Actors' Equity and myself. Provocatively an invitation to Professor Fels was cancelled. At that conference I was referred to publicly by Pete Steedman as 'the ACTU's whore for hire'. I wasn't particularly shocked by that, indeed I took it as a mild compliment. Peter Duncan wasn't so accommodating and that led to what could be called a deterioration in their relationship.

Henceforth there was ongoing controversy about Pete's generous salary package at Ausmusic. He thought he was worth four or five times what he was paid for his 'role in promoting local music'. The disputation over his role continued through to August 1996 when the funding necessary to pay his package was cut.

By mid 1991 Federal Cabinet had agreed in principle to adopt the recommendations of the PSA. A final decision was deferred to allow a group of ministers including the then Treasurer Mr Kerin and Attorney General, Mr Duffy, to consult with the industry. The meeting took place on 6 August 1991. 'The industry' was a select group of artists which was supposed to include John Farnham, Neil Finn, Jimmy Barnes, Peter Farnan, Diesel and others, but over time came to focus on that great defender of the working class and trees, Peter Garrett.

I knew from experience that artists would be unlikely to get involved. Their instinctive reaction is to avoid politics and politicians. After all, they are in the image business. Politicians are their natural enemies. Renée Geyer has always regretted her decision to sing the Liberal Party's campaign song for the 1974 election.[10] John Farnham has also been careful in this regard. After his initial trip to Canberra he had gone quiet.

Garrett has distinguished himself as one of the few Australian recording artists to be financially successful. That is commendable. The great bulk of Australian artists get a day job or stay on the dole. Garrett is part of that elite group of artists who reach a point where they have the bargaining position to control their own recordings and songs. In short, they are as much a member of the 'copyright club' as any record company or their offshoot. I wonder what Che Guevara would have made of Peter.

In August 1991 'the biggest names in Australian music . . . announced they had united to take on the Hawke government'.[11] According to these musicians, the changes – designed to lower the prices of records, tapes and CDs – would decimate the local music business.[12] According to Garrett, it was 'crazy . . . blind, bureaucratic rationalism'.[13] It was hard to comprehend how someone who had done so much to fight the cultural cringe would so easily accept the right of multinational companies to dictate to Australians what music they could buy. Peter also seemed to miss the point that lower prices might benefit his fans. Certainly that point was not missed by the press. One headline screamed 'Rich Rock Stars Fighting to Retain the Consumer Rip Off'.[14] That was typical. Soon after, even ARIA started distancing itself from Garrett. One of my clients who should have known better was quoted as saying that the Musicians' Union only represented ukulele players. That only served to emphasise the point that we were trying to make.

At last the managers began to voice their opinion. They were led by Jeremy Fabinyi, who is one of the more rational and sensible people in the music industry. That is why he now lives in France. Jeremy's brother is also active in the music/film industry. Their late father was a legendary figure in book publishing. The managers actually began to address the real issues. They identified potential problems and argued against removing the provisions. They raised the deletions argument. This is that where records have been deleted from a catalogue in a foreign territory they can be sold to wholesalers, imported into Australia and sold into the local market, in other words dumped in Australia. Our response was that the commercial exploitation of the catalogues is the legal responsibility of the catalogue owners who are represented by ARIA. It is their obligation to ensure that sales of this kind do not occur. It was a contractual matter to be addressed in a contractual context. All that was necessary was to ensure that deletions could not take place until a reasonable time had elapsed after the release in Australia or, ideally, not at all. In my experience none of the majors has ever agreed to artists being able to control or restrict deletions.

They put forward an argument based on cross-collateralisation. If a record is successfully released in Australia by an Australian artist and at the same time is unsuccessfully released in America, the record company might ship the unsold American product into Australia. This would enable the profits in Australia to be diverted to America and recouped against any unrecouped balance in that territory. That argument still has me confused. It implies that the American parent would act in a conspiratorial way with its Australian subsidiary.

Then there was the suggestion that records would be manufactured in a foreign territory which has little or no copyright protection and in relation to which minimal or no mechanical royalties would be paid. This would disadvantage songwriters. Again, this assumes that the copyright owners would licence someone in such a territory to manufacture their product with no territorial limits on distribution. Remember the provisions only relate to legally manufactured product. Nevertheless, this was an argument which had some substance.

Finally, there was the 'piggyback' or 'free-riding' argument. This applies when a simultaneous worldwide release takes place, for example of a Michael Jackson album. The record company might organise a major promotional 'spend' to support the release by having giant statues of Michael and his noses floating down the Yarra. Someone could then import the product into Australia and sell off the back of that promotion. This argument also had merit. However it could only occur if the price of the records sold in Australia is not competitive internationally.

I knew that the successful Australian managers had been around long enough not to tie their futures to record companies and their causes. There was never any likelihood that well-managed artists would be marching on Parliament House. In our discussions with them it was suggested that the provisions be retained in relation to Australian product. That appealed to me. It was never going to be acceptable to multinational record companies.

During 1991 and 1992 frequent meetings took place around Australia between the various participants. Some of these were memorable for the wrong reasons. The most important was a very late night meeting at the Hyatt Hotel in Canberra when we came very close to a compromise which might have retained the provisions. There was also a memorable meeting at Percy's Hotel in Carlton between Peter, myself and a representative from one of the collection societies (not Brett Cottle). He left the hotel determined to walk the twenty kilometres to the airport. He was heading towards Port Phillip Bay.

On one occasion Peter and I were driving to a meeting in Melbourne with Michael Smellie from PolyGram. I was driving slowly because we were early. I was pulled over by a zealous police officer who assumed I must be drunk. When, to his disappointment, he found I wasn't, he justified his actions by charging me with various offences. These included 'impersonating a P-plate driver' – the P-plate was laying flat on the rear shelf of the car. When asked in court by my lawyer, 'Bernie the Attorney' Balmer if it was visible, I replied 'yes, to anyone who happened to be flying by in a helicopter'. All charges were dismissed.

The tried and true practice of having the big six and their various acolytes cross-funding, supporting and validating each other was not working in this very public environment. A split which should have been clear from the start took place between ARIA, which was representing owners of the copyrights of records covered by sections 101 and 102, and APRA and AMCOS which were representing owners of copyrights in musical works covered by sections 37 and 38. They all became suspicious of each other and for good reason.

It became obvious that it didn't necessarily follow that all four sections had to be repealed. There was a good argument, which was put forward forcefully and articulately by Brett Cottle from APRA, that sections 37 and 38 should be retained. His argument was that these sections underpinned the Australian music publishing industry and, in particular, one of the primary sources of publishing income, mechanical royalties. It would be a relatively simple matter to arrange for records to be manufactured in a country with minimal protection or remuneration for song-writers. By then it was a little late for rational thought.

Throughout this period the matter kept falling off the agenda for Cabinet discussion. This had more to do with the fact that Federal Cabinet had an ongoing obligation to run the country than any hidden agenda. Finally, on 10 June 1992 John Dawkins (the Treasurer) and Michael Duffy (the Attorney-General) announced that the government had ratified all but the recommendation covering a performer's copyright which would be formulated by the Music Industry Council. The changes were to be phased in after two years.

That is not the end but rather is the beginning of the political phase. Cabinet recommendations are not law until they become legislation. That never happened under Labor. The *Copyright Amendment Bill 1992* (Cth) was introduced on 16 December 1992 but lapsed on the dissolution of parliament prior to the election. Not surprisingly in 1993 the Labor government was preoccupied with the election (which they won). The next few years saw the development of a warm and friendly relationship between Labor and the Arts Lobby which was rewarded with a $250 million commitment via the Creative Nation package.[15]

On 2 March 1996 a new Federal Coalition government was elected. On 8 October 1997 it announced its intention to remove the provisions. A bill to this end was introduced into the House of Representatives on 20 November 1997. That was followed by the Senate Legal and Constitutional Legislation Committee Inquiry to which I made a submission on 13 February 1998. Phil Tripp missed all this and in May 1998 was still exhorting politicians to 'stop this madness before it becomes law and kills our industry'.[16] It did in fact become law on 30 July 1998.[17] Legislation was also passed to ensure that labels and packaging and other accessory material could not be used to frustrate the importation and commercial exploitation of the substantive goods.[18]

The record companies finally learnt that Professor Fels was not a good person to have as an enemy. He moved from the PSA to head up the vastly more powerful Australian Competition and Consumer Commission (ACCC). On 6 March 2002, penalties of more than one million dollars were imposed on Universal Music Australia Pty Ltd (formerly PolyGram), Warner Music Australia Pty Ltd and senior company executives.[19] The Court found that the companies and executives had breached the *Trade*

Practices Act 1974 (Cth) by threatening to refuse, and refusing, to supply CDs to Australian retailers who stocked parallel imported CDs. This amounted to both an abuse of market power and exclusive dealing. Universal Music Australia Pty Ltd and Warner Music Australia Pty Ltd were both permanently restrained from refusing or threatening to refuse supply of recorded music CDs to Australian retailers.

Professor Fels in his capacity as Chairman of the ACCC was quoted as saying 'This is an important precedent, as well as an important win for Australian consumers as it means that retailers will be able to freely access cheaper, legal, imported CDs without fear that they will lose supply of other stock'.[20] The record companies had argued that competition from cheaper imported CDs would affect their profits. Justice Hill rejected the argument that their conduct was to prevent 'free riding' and rejected 'any attempt on the part of Universal to suggest that the action taken by it was taken to prevent piracy'.[21] They really are slow learners.

On 22 August 2003 an appeal by the record companies and their executives was partially successful. The court agreed that their conduct did not amount to an abuse of market power. However, the finding in relation to exclusive dealing was upheld. The appeal by the ACCC against the penalty was also upheld and the fines were effectively doubled.

The upshot of all this is that the Australian music industry has not collapsed. It is true that it is under great stress but this has been caused by the inability of copyright legislation to insulate copyright owners against the advances of technology. There are reputedly more CDs burnt at home than purchased in the shops. CDs can be downloaded at will and the internet has made territorial boundaries redundant. There is also much increased competition for the entertainment dollar.

Finally, has the price of records come down? With current discounting and retailing practices it's hard to say. Prices have not increased to any degree in the five years since the provisions were removed. In the eight years prior to that, price increases were also contained because of the threat of removing the provisions. This in itself represents a very considerable benefit to consumers and the recording industry generally.

Ultimately, technology will change the industry to the point where there is no 'article' to be imported. Nevertheless that will be a slow process and the sale of a record is still central to the industry. Today the music industry is more competitive. More importantly, foreign-owned record companies no longer control what music will or will not be available to Australians in Australia.

The legislation was followed by various reports and meetings, none of which advanced the industry. The performer's copyright was abandoned. Had we had the support of the Garretts of the world it was there for the taking. Never again would the 'industry' as a matter of holy writ speak with one voice. The club and the exclusivity and privileges of membership would never quite be the same. Peter Duncan now resides in Indonesia. I keep away from Canberra. Martin Ferguson is there permanently. Professor Fels has retired. The Federal government's attempt to totally remove the provisions relating to books was blocked in the Senate by the Democrats in April 2003.

CHAPTER 11 – WIPEOUT

My first trip to the Northern Territory in 1994 was organised by Gillian Harrison who worked at the Northern Territory Trades and Labour Council in Darwin. The principal sponsors were Ausmusic and the Northern Territory Arts Council. It was in the nature of a music industry road show stretching from Alice Springs in central Australia to Darwin in the north and included several Aboriginal communities along the way.

One of the participants was Neil Murray. He wrote the evocative novel '*Sing For Me, Countryman*',[1] and has had considerable experience with Aboriginal people, having lived in their communities. For many years, he was part of the successful Aboriginal group Warumpi Band. He co-wrote the song 'My Island Home' which, for many people both black and white, is an Australian anthem. He was to provide workshops in musical composition.

Andrew McMillan was also on the tour. Andrew is a professional writer based in Darwin. He wrote *Strict Rules*,[2] a book about a Midnight Oil tour to the Northern Territory. They were supported by Warumpi Band. The realities (at least for the Aboriginal people on the tour) didn't quite live up to the imagery. But they are used to that. Andrew was going to provide workshops in creative writing. I was there to assist with copyright.

We rehearsed our act in Alice Springs. Unusually for me, I put quite a lot of work into my presentation. I was looking forward to the opportunity to bring some light into the lives of the less fortunate. Clearly, these workshops were going to be a defining moment for people who can genuinely claim to be members of one of the oldest civilisations on earth.

One workshop was to take place in Tennant Creek. With due respect to the residents of Tennant Creek, this is without doubt the most depressing town in Australia. It has all the debris, human and otherwise, left behind in mining towns when the miners move on. Rather than replace broken windows in the hotels they are simply boarded up. There is an ongoing problem with alcohol. The public bar in the main hotel has a concrete floor so it can be hosed clean. They remove the patrons after the dousing. My introduction to the town was to be told that if I had the misfortune to run over someone (this was considered more of a misfortune for me than the person run over) I was not to stop at the scene of the accident but was to drive to the local police station. To stop and render assistance would risk serious assault.

Our local co-ordinator, was experienced in the music industry, having managed the successful Aboriginal group Coloured Stone. Unfortunately, he had been in an accident when his car hit a kangaroo at Barrow Creek. A friend had become a little enthusiastic whilst towing his vehicle back to town and managed to overturn both vehicles. That could only happen in the Northern Territory.

We were set up in a large, corrugated-iron shed with several hundred chairs for the audience. We had generously agreed that if there were too many people for the first sitting we would repeat the workshop. We knew about Kylie Minogue and John Farnham who never announce the eighth concert until the other seven are sold out. An hour after starting time the seats were still empty. Our co-ordinator kindly said this was probably because there had been a death in the area and everybody was still preoccupied with 'sorry business'. Just then a young man dressed in a North Melbourne football jumper came walking past the hall on his way to buy milk for his mother. He was pounced upon and subjected to a three-hour intensive workshop on musical composition, creative writing and the intricacies of copyright. His mother drank her latté that day without milk.

It took me a few days to realise that on tours of this kind a per diem or daily allowance is paid for meals and accommodation. The trick is not to eat and to find cheaper accommodation. In, or under, your car is ideal. Andrew had organised a 'contra deal' for us at the Larrimah 'Hilton'. In return for Andrew giving a reading of his latest poetry and Neil singing some of his songs, we were to be provided with free accommodation consisting of some matresses in an outhouse.

We arrived at the hotel at approximately 7.00pm and went straight to the bar. We were served a beautiful meal of barramundi. The hotel is very popular with burly truck drivers. Three of them were there that evening. Indeed, they were the only people in the bar, which was decorated with posters declaring that the dingo was innocent. Their uniform consisted of brown boots, short black socks, shorts and blue singlets. Their stomachs rested comfortably on the bar.

After a short introduction Andrew began to read a deeply moving and introspective poem which drew on the subtle similarities between the female menopause and the rainy season in the far north of Australia. He was just starting his next poem about the sensuality of mangoes when one of the truck drivers turned to Neil and said, 'You better get a new f...ing PR man mate'.

Neil picked up his guitar and courageously began to perform songs which reflected his experiences with, and obvious empathy for, the Aboriginal people. After two or three songs Kev, the more sensitive member of the three, entered into a conversation with Neil which went like this:

Kev: 'Mate, do you play any Slim Dusty songs?'
Neil: 'No'.
Kev: 'Why not mate?'
Neil: 'Because he doesn't play mine'.
Kev: 'OK mate'.

Gillian, myself and Andrew broke out in cold sweats of anxiety and apprehension. We were emotionally drained. Andrew and I were endeavouring to keep Gillian between us and the terrible three but she kept going to the toilet. It is amazing how raw fear can increase a person's capacity to consume large quantities of white wine. By about 2.00am I wandered off into the bush and never did quite find my hotel suite.

Next morning the locals, in appreciation of our endeavours, took us on a train ride. We were placed in an open carriage and transported to an old American Second World War army base. It was beautifully decorated with hundreds of broken beer bottles buried upside down as a garden edge. There was no garden. Australians do have a sense of history.

After that first trip I made several visits to the Territory. There is a clear difference culturally and in many other respects including language between the desert people of the centre and the people in the north. One striking example is their art. In the centre the technique, colour and texture of dot paintings reflect the colours of the desert and the paucity of desert life. In the north the art features brightly coloured stick figures, birds and animals. There are strict cultural and territorial restrictions in relation to art and music. The Macassans from Indonesia had regular contact with the people in East Arnhem Land and the islands to the north. Whites are referred to as 'Balandas' which is thought to be a distortion of 'Hollanders'. The Macassans also had contact with Dutch traders.

In the centre, life seems to be predicated on survival. In 1996, courtesy of Ken Hutton of Kakadu Records, I visited Yuendumu. This community is situated on the fringe of the Tanami Desert, three hours' drive north-west of Alice Springs. The landscape reflects the determination of its inhabitants. Wind is the dominant factor and the scrub is festooned with plastic bags – a testament to modern marketing techniques. On the main street, graffiti – 'f . . . me' – acknowledges the realities of life and the innate politeness of Aboriginal people.

The first night the town was alive with a festival of 'moosik'. Festivals of this kind are common and usually include sport. Yuendumu, with a fixed population of about seven hundred or so people, has three Australian Rules football ovals. The music played was community rock with some 'retro'. Community spirit is alive and well.

Due to the egalitarian nature of Aboriginal society, the idea of a headline act preceded by support acts is not acceptable. Community bands from a thousand-kilometre radius, who use means of transport which takes optimism to a new level, perform at these festivals. Two Toyotas can very quickly become one. The line-up is decided by ballot and the choice of songs is left to each group. Prizes are also awarded by consensus. Because of the popularity of the surfing classic 'Wipeout' with the kids, who dance wildly and do backflips when it is performed, each group plays their own version. Like a bad red wine 'Wipeout' begins to grow on you after the fifteenth rendition.

Particularly in the north, in remote communities such as Gulin Gulin, Millingimbi and Elcho Island, traditional music, culture, language and beliefs have survived and are pre-eminent. This is not one's first impression when driving into these communities. The visitor is confronted by car wrecks and packs of scruffy dogs. There is a school of thought that the dogs are the source of many of the health problems which persist. Poor diet and alcohol, not to mention petrol sniffing and domestic violence, play a part. That warrior of the NSW Labor Right, Graham 'Swiss Bank Account' Richardson, once flew into Gulin Gulin. He was overwhelmed and flew out. For the locals it is a sixteen hour round trip to Darwin.

It is necessary to travel to the outstations to begin to experience and appreciate the antiquity and majesty of the culture. A hill, a tree or a bend in the river will symbolise 'the Dreaming'. Access is restricted. The bush is a natural barrier. Once after driving for two hours through scrub with no apparent track or road, I asked the driver how he knew where he was going. He said he was following the shadows of the trees. I am reluctant to use that technique in Glen Iris.

Sitting under a tree in the township of Galiwinku it soon becomes clear that there are several influences musically. Simultaneously one can hear strains of 'gospel, country crossover' from the local church (yes, the new religions have arrived) and pub rock from the basketball court where the community bands are doing sound checks. Traditional music can also be heard in the distance after a prolonged period of 'sorry business' and the new kids on the block are belting away on empty paint tins.

The kids are kicking a worn Australian Rules football around. This is a twenty-four-hour a day activity although things seem to peak at about 4.00am. In the north, unlike the centre, where the desert gets very cold, it can remain hot at night. The choice is to stay inside and not sleep because of the heat or sleep outside and get eaten by mosquitoes. I once took a nap on a beach on one of the islands. Two days later hundreds of sandfly bites started to appear. The Aboriginals have worked out that it is better to rest in the heat of the day and play at night. White people think that is strange.

There is a well-worn circuit throughout the Northern Territory for people like me who always look and feel out of place. On an island like Elcho, things are fairly relaxed. You just occupy a seat under a tree and local people come and go at their leisure. There is a genuine interest in contemporary music and time passes in a spirit of goodwill and mutual co-operation. The BRACS (Broadcasting for Remote Aboriginal

Community Scheme) radio network links the communities across an area almost as large as Europe. CAAMA, the Central Australian Aboriginal Music Association, helps mitigate the sense of isolation.

Community concerts are a regular occurrence. One night on Millingimbi the concert started at 9.00pm. By 2.00am my back was starting to give out. Sitting on the ground is not my preferred position. Then it was announced that the kids' rap competition was about to start. We had two hours of truly spectacular dancing. That was followed by a special presentation. Someone had been admitted as a full member of APRA. It was 4.00am. All those nasty things I have said about APRA came home to haunt me.

At 6.00am we started to pack the gear which was to be loaded onto a boat to cross to the mainland. We were due to leave at 8.00am. Our boat arrived at 4.00pm. Timelessness is one of the determining factors of Aboriginal life. The small boat was perilously overloaded and close to the waterline. Fortunately we survived the crossing and transferred the equipment to a truck to begin the fourteen hour drive to Darwin. Patience is also a significant factor in Aboriginal life.

We started picking up cousins along the track and soon there were fourteen people plus the gear on board. We then lost a part of the vehicle which was apparently a condition necessary for forward motion. Fortunately we managed to get to the nearest town – about three houses. The occupant of one kindly invited us all in for the night. My white companions being experienced travellers, all had their 'swags', which provide all the comforts of a double bed. I was a little less prepared with a leaking, pink, plastic lilo designed for a Glen Iris swimming pool, and a blanket. I failed the boy scouts' entrance exam. Our Aboriginal friends had nothing. It can get very cold at night even in those areas. This was indeed a three-dog night. Next morning I found them all huddled together wrapped in our host's curtains. Everyone seemed to agree this was better than going cold.

Aboriginal traditional music has been handed down through the clans (mobs) and communities under the control of songmen and elders over thousands of years. It is part of the 'language' and is not written down or reduced to a material form in a conventional sense. It is used for special ceremonial occasions colloquially referred to as 'business'. This can include death, initiation, weddings and other ceremonies which have special significance including procreation, rainmaking and regeneration of important species. Much of the music by its very nature is restricted. There is music and dance that can only be performed or observed by initiated men. Other music and dance is restricted to women.

The music is held in sacred trust by the elders and any breach of the law can, and almost certainly will, result in prompt remedial action. The music cannot be commercialised or trivialised. The lyrics tell ancient stories about the Dreamtime. By 'ancient', I mean ten thousand years or more before Christ. There is a distinctive rhythm. The beat is controlled by knocking sticks together in a regular but more or less spontaneous manner. Aboriginal music is harmonious. It is hard to identify the melody. The music to the ear is very similar to the mantra of Indian music.

It is almost impossible to reconcile traditional Aboriginal music with modern concepts of copyright. Copyright is based on the principle that creative endeavours should be encouraged and rewarded by some degree of creative control and financial reward. The public interest is served by the public having access to the product of those endeavours. There is the requirement for an original work, a composer and protection is for a period of time based on the life of that composer. The work must be reduced to a material form before it can be protected. All this assumes that the rights are owned by an individual.

Individuals in Aboriginal communities do have rights. There are as many disputes about rights, entitlements and personal property as in any other society. However, art, music, language, ceremonies and food brought by visiting lawyers are community based. This maintains a sense of communal responsibility which is essential for survival. At its worst it can degenerate into what is colloquially known as 'humbugging'. This is a 'what is yours is mine' mentality but without the community the traditional lifestyle would be long gone.

Aboriginal culture is complex and sophisticated. It has stood the test of time. This is overlooked by well-meaning people who try to over-simplify it in the name of reconciliation and reform. The missionaries tried that. This attitude is patronising and unhelpful. Aboriginal communities are very open and welcoming places. Nevertheless, it is good manners when invited into someone's home to wait a few minutes before rearranging the furniture.

The 'Western' notions of copyright do not fit well with Aboriginal life. Traditional Aboriginal music and art has more to do with the culture and belief system of the people than it does with popular entertainment or commercial exploitation. For example, if an Aboriginal artist dies, that person's name image or performances cannot be used in public until a period of mourning has taken place. Out of respect anyone in the community with the same name as the deceased will use another name during this period.

Aboriginal music is based on the principle that there is no single owner or author of traditional music and certain members of the community have no access to it. Even if there was a known author, the fact that these works have existed for thousands of years would deny any protection. The very nature of these works is that they are not reduced to a material form. The concept that they are held in sacred trust by the elders or songmen for the community negates any idea that these works are an original creation by a contemporary. From a technical copyright point of view traditional Aboriginal music is no different to the folk song 'Click go the Shears'. There is no recognised composer and even if there was the work has long been in the public domain, that is, outside the period of fifty years after the death of that composer. It can be exploited at will.

This problem has been identified and confronted by several Aboriginal musicians who have recorded traditional music in conjunction with contemporary music. If the traditional work is simply recorded without anything being done to obtain copyright protection, there will be no control over the subsequent reproduction of that work. For example, if a traditional work was recorded by Yothu Yindi and it could be shown that it was not protected by copyright (which it obviously is not) there would be no publishing royalties paid in relation to that work and no restriction on further use of it. A car dealer could record another version of the work and use it in a commercial to sell cars without the consent of, or any remuneration to, the traditional owners. The car dealer could not use the actual Yothu Yindi recording.

One approach has been to treat the music and lyrics as a rearrangement of a traditional work and to claim copyright in it as a new work. This has received some support from the copyright collection and licensing societies. It is yet to obtain the universal acceptance of traditional owners, some of whom regard this as usurping their communal rights. In some parts of the 'top end', this can result in spears being thrown – hopefully not at the lawyers. Nevertheless, for the moment, that is the only way in which traditional works can be protected.

A prerequisite of any such proposal is to meet with, and obtain the approval of, the traditional owners. The work can then be held by nominated trustees on behalf of the community. They would exercise control over the work and the distribution of any money derived from its commercial exploitation. A practical difficulty is that the decision-making process in Aboriginal communities is based on the assumption that any decision made in haste is a bad decision. Of course 'in haste' needs to be understood in the context of thousands of years.

White Australians can meet someone in the morning, know their life story by lunchtime and be lifelong friends by mid-afternoon. Aboriginal people are a little more circumspect. There are young Aboriginal leaders, Peter Miller of Blekbala Mujik is an example, who can live with one foot in Western society and the other in a traditional community. However, even with them, the decision-making process is long, protracted and bureaucratic. It can take several meetings before you get to talk to someone who actually makes decisions, if you ever do.

A musical work is protected until it is recorded and released. After that it can be re-recorded under the compulsory licence system subject to the payment of mechanical royalties. This process is inappropriate in the context of traditional works. At least it is no longer possible for someone to go into an Aboriginal community, surreptitiously record a performance and commercially release and exploit that recording. This had been done in the past. This is now prohibited under the provisions of the Copyright Act.

Existing copyright legislation doesn't solve the problems of reconciling individual with communal ownership, unrestricted access with cultural integrity, the ownership of traditional works being linked to a particular author and that author's life and the requirement that a work be reduced to a material form. These conflicts will only be solved by legislation applying specifically to traditional works. This may cause some difficulties with international obligations and copyright principles, but so be it.

These issues have been confronted to some extent in the context of Aboriginal artworks. In one case, there was a recognition by the trial judge that the relationship between the individual artist, Mr Bulun Bulun, and his Clan, the Ganalbingu people, involved a special fiduciary obligation.[3] The ritual knowledge of the artist had been acquired in the context of the law and customs of that community and was predicated on the trust and confidence those giving permission had in the artist. This stopped short of recognising a concept of communal ownership. All the judge was saying was that the individual was the author but the products of his endeavours were held in trust pursuant to an enforceable fiduciary obligation. Hence, 'collective' rather than 'individual' damages were awarded.

In 1994 the Galpu Clan sued the Reserve Bank of Australia claiming communal ownership in certain sacred images and in particular the design of a morning-star pole on a special bicentennial $10 banknote.[4] The artist (Mr Yumbulul) had been authorised by the Clan to paint the pole. According to customary law he had an obligation to prevent any unauthorised use of the design. The Clan retained ownership of the pole. This not only illustrates the ongoing conflict between individual and communal ownership but also highlights the difficulty of reconciling copyright law with Aboriginal customary law.

The *Copyright Amendment (Moral Rights) Act 2000* (Cth) was an attempt to extend protection to creative individuals beyond mere economic rights. It provides that an author should be properly credited and a work should not be treated in a derogatory way. These rights only apply to individuals and do not recognise any concept of community ownership. They are personal by nature. In May 2003 the then Communications Minister, Senator Richard Alston, announced new legislation which will attempt to address the problems associated with communal ownership. The Copyright Act is to be amended to create a 'class of collective rights for Aboriginal communities, enabling them to assume moral rights on behalf of an artist'.[5]

After all the hours spent sitting under trees in the Northern Territory not much progress has been made. Aboriginal people have learnt over the years not to expect too much too soon. There has been discussion about setting up publishing companies for each community. These publishing companies would enter into agreements with a mainstream publisher or a dedicated Aboriginal publisher to ensure their works are administered in accordance with Aboriginal law and custom. The extent of that protection will be limited to the protection provided by copyright legislation and conventions and this is inadequate. It will still be necessary to confront the problems associated with authorship, ownership, original works reduced to a material form and access to those works.

Traditional works have been handed down for thousands of years. Aboriginal law and custom requires that these works be protected for the rest of time and not just until Collingwood wins a premiership, which hopefully will be a little sooner. The concept of a global market has yet to be acknowledged, let alone confronted. The economic and utilitarian principles which form the basis of copyright law simply have no application to Aboriginal concepts of traditional music, dance and art.

In the short term there is probably as much chance of solving these problems as the composer of 'Wipeout' has of collecting public performance royalties for the multiple uses of the work throughout outback Australia. Specific legislation will be necessary to address these difficulties. Perhaps if legislation can be passed to protect the name Don Bradman, the Olympic rings and Crown Casino, measures to protect Aboriginal culture, which is uniquely Australian, are worth the effort.

CHAPTER 12 – THE FILUM

The Australian film industry was reborn in the early seventies when the South Australian Film Corporation was established. The Corporation produced films for government and provided facilities for feature films and television series. Films successful both commercially and artistically, including *Sunday Too Far Away* and *Picnic at Hanging Rock*, were produced.

Belatedly the Commonwealth and the other State governments became aware of the economic and cultural potential of the film industry. The Australian Film Commission was established on 5 May 1975 and by the early eighties there were film corporations in Western Australia, Victoria, Tasmania, NSW and Queensland. The Australian Film & Television School operated parallel to the Australian Film Commission which included Film Australia.

It was obvious that without access to investment capital the Australian industry would have little hope of competing internationally. Hence, it was decided that taxation incentives should be provided to encourage investment in the industry. The mother of all incentives became law with the enactment of Division 10BA of the *Income Tax Assessment Act* (Cth) ('the Act'). This provided for a 150% tax deduction for monies invested after 28 May 1981. Income from the film to an amount equal to 50% of the initial qualifying investment was exempt from taxation. From that date the 'foxes were in the chookhouse'.

To qualify, the investment had to relate to the capital cost of acquiring an interest in the initial copyright in an Australian film. An 'Australian film' was one which was wholly or substantially produced in Australia or, where produced in an external territory, had a significant Australian content. The monies had to be actually invested in the production of the film and had to be at risk. Money would not be at risk if for example the investment was funded by a non-recourse loan, that is one where the borrower is not personally liable on default. It was also necessary for the film to generate income within a stated period. For this to occur it had to be completed within certain time constraints.

It soon became clear that the Commissioner of Taxation was going to take a narrow view of the legislation. The Commissioner limited the deduction to expenses relating to the production process and excluded costs associated with raising money or marketing the film. For a film to qualify for a 150% tax deduction it had to be certified as an eligible film by the then Minister for Home Affairs & Environment – the Cultural Commissar. He or she took advice from anyone in Adelaide wearing a dark green, velvet, sportsjacket with patches on the elbows.

It didn't take long for the accountants to work out that, provided there was a minimum pre-sale, a film was a gilt-edged investment irrespective of its creative content or commercial potential. Given the then maximum personal tax rate of 60 cents in the dollar, an investment of $100,000 would generate a tax deduction of $150,000 which would represent an immediate tax saving of $90,000. With a pre-sale of 15% of the budget, the investor would be in front from day one and still retain the upside potential (blue sky) of having an investment in the film and the right to receive tax-free income.

Mad Max, *The Man from Snowy River, Crocodile Dundee* and a few other films were commercially successful in this environment. They were a rare commodity. The figures bandied around indicated that only one film in thirty actually recouped its budget. The tax deduction and pre-sale became the only priorities.

I was personally involved as executive producer in several films which were structured on small budgets and guaranteed distribution arrangements. One was provisionally entitled *The Cricketer*. It was about a retired cricketer who makes a comeback and we all hoped it would star Robert Redford. When it was released in 1987 it had a new title, *As Time Goes By*, and was a quirky science-fiction story about the Australian outback and time travel. It starred Nique Needles. Nique's real name was Con Delaney. His father Bernie had worked in the Homicide Squad in

Melbourne. No one was concerned about these subtle creative changes, least of all the executive producer and the investors; the film was released and the investments were tax deductible.

Tax lawyers and accountants became pre-eminent. They were the stars. They received everything except an above-the-title credit. The cost of funding a film became disproportionate to the budget. Films with large budgets required a prospectus to seek funds from the public. It was possible to get an exemption from the prospectus requirements. The alternative, which was called an 'offer document', itself became one of the major items of expenditure. As an expense which had to be incurred before the film was funded, this involved high risk seed capital.

One of the unfortunate consequences of all this was that it compelled producers to enter into pre-sale agreements with distributors. This put the distributor in a prime bargaining position, at the cost ultimately of the producers and the investors. It also resulted in the distributor having an input in the screenplay, choice of cast and principal crew. The one advantage was that distribution was guaranteed, that is the film would get a 'shot'. That was, of course, if the distributor actually had the capacity to distribute the film. One widely touted distributor turned out to be a dog sitting on his tuckerbox in West Hollywood.

The copyright in the film was central to securing the tax benefits. Copyright in the context of a film includes the copyrights subsisting in the film. Like record companies, film distributors are in the business of acquiring catalogues, which in the film industry are called libraries. The maker of a film, i.e. the producer, is the owner of the copyright unless there is an agreement to the contrary. Copyright protection does not extend to the original idea for the screenplay or film. For an idea to be protected it must be reproduced in a material form. Even then it is the person who reduced the idea to a material form, not the person who conceived it, who owns the copyright.

There is no copyright in a title although there may be some right of action based on misleading and deceptive conduct or passing off. There are underlying copyrights in relation to a literary work upon which a film is based and there is a copyright in the screenplay itself as a dramatic work.

It is an infringement of copyright in a literary or dramatic work to reproduce that work in a film.

Often the first contract is an agreement with the owner of the copyright in a book or screenplay. Usually an option is taken. The option agreement should be clear in relation to what rights are being acquired and on what terms if, and when, the option is exercised. If royalties are to be paid there should be clear definitions of 'gross receipts', 'net profits' and 'producer's net profits', all of which are different and can lead to much confusion.

An agreement will also be required with the owner of the rights to any music and the person who is contracted to produce the soundtrack. If required the film producer will commission someone to compose, arrange and/or record the necessary music, lyrics and score for the film. A record producer might be contracted to produce a recording for commercial release. Sometimes one person fulfils all these functions.

Most record producers are well advised and know about points, advances, credits, gross, net and direct accounting. This should never be assumed in the case of film producers. I became involved in protracted and expensive litigation concerning the film *Shine* because there was not a clear understanding in this regard. A record producer regards a point as a percentage point of all income derived from the exploitation of the copyright in the record. There may be some argument whether it is of gross or net but no one would suggest that it is a percentage of the points payable to the film producer. For example, if the film producer negotiates an agreement with a record company to get 18 percentage points, the music producer would get 2 of 18, not 2 percent of 18. Only a film producer would not understand that.

Never presume that film producers have any knowledge of, or even experience in, the film industry. They are often better acquainted with arts politics and menus in French restaurants. Many are producers because they can access the money or have an 'in' with one of the film-funding organisations. The music industry is more inclusive and collaborative and actually values and respects experience. Capital is also consistently available from record companies and publishers. For that reason the music industry is more stable than the film industry which is reliant on subsidies, the arts bureaucracy and the sad collection of sycophants that go with it.

There are several distinct stages in the production of a film. There is the development phase which includes acquiring the rights, organising seed funding, entering into pre-sales or distribution agreements if necessary, obtaining funding and finalising agreements with the investors, producer and executive producer. Then there is pre-production which involves formalising agreements with the principal participants, actors and director, finalising locations, building sets and making costumes.

Principal photography is when the caterers, technical staff, the director, camera operators, make-up people, art and costume departments, hairdressers and production accountant take charge. This is when ordinary, well-adjusted people become rude, arrogant megalomaniacs. They tramp through houses with muddy boots and butt their cigarettes on the carpet. They close off main roads and divert emergency vehicles. They erect catering tents in the middle of manicured gardens and park semitrailers on footpaths. Filming does funny things to people.

Then follows post-production which encompasses editing, composing, recording and synchronising music. Finally, there is the marketing, distribution and exhibition phase. That's usually followed by the rationalisation and recrimination that precedes the auditors being brought in.

The first major 'filum' with which I became involved in the context of the 10BA madness, was *The Pirate Movie*. The investors were from Queensland. It was co-produced by David Joseph who had previously produced music-industry television shows, and Ted Hamilton who has had a very successful career as an actor and performer both in Australia and America. David had employed Glenn Wheatley in England when David managed The New Seekers.

I first acted for Ted and David in 1980 when they were suing Channel Ten over the demise of the Ted Hamilton Show. This was a late-night chat show which fell victim to Channel Ten's unique production style. The backdrop was grey, ensuring that Ted's grey hair was invisible. The top of the desk was made of foam rubber, giving Ted that sinking feeling. The seats, one of which was borrowed from reception, were aligned such that the final guest was out of camera – the proverbial mystery guest. The commercial breaks were filled with Ted and the production crew screaming profanities at each other. The research department was based in the hotel opposite the studios in Melbourne. Ted would ask questions like, 'How is your wife Marlene?' – only to get the response, 'Pauline died three years ago'. It was a disaster. We settled that one. We probably should have run it. In 1987 Mike Walsh's company successfully sued Channel Nine and was awarded a million dollars plus for the demise of *The Mike Walsh Show*.[1] Granted it had been running a little longer than Ted's show.

The Pirate Movie was intended to be a musical comedy film loosely based on *The Pirates of Penzance*. The Gilbert & Sullivan works had recently come into the public domain, that is they were out of copyright. As has been noted, a circuitous method of funding films prevailed. A budget had to be prepared and a certificate obtained as a prerequisite to the investments in the film being tax deductible. This was based on certain criteria of 'Australianness' in relation to the content, locations, producers, director and actors. Ted had to throw a tantrum in Canberra to finally secure this.

A pre-sale was necessary so the accountants could prepare the financial calculations to justify investment by the private sector. This is not necessarily an orderly process. Step three often precedes step one and is predicated on complying with step two. Chaos reigns. Ted and David were aware of the potential of a commercial movie of this genre and were able to obtain major distribution through Twentieth Century Fox. That involved a large pre-sale advance payable on delivery of the master print and a first release in almost 1500 theatres throughout North America.

Twentieth Century Fox insisted on certain creative controls and their financial commitment was based on securing two then very marketable young American actors, Christopher Atkins (*Blue Lagoon*) and Kristy McNichol (*Little Darlings*). Their agents realised that their clients were a prerequisite to the pre-sale and their fees and everything associated with them, including their entourages, escalated accordingly.

Funding had not yet been finalised but contracts were being entered into in relation to the writer, director and everything else that goes into pre-production. In other words, the ship was launched before the keel was sealed and with no destination in sight. Along the way Trevor Farrant, the writer, resigned. The director also left. Everyone realised that the original budget had no relevance to the film and the day of commencing principal photography moved ever closer.

Initially I only had a passive involvement. Phil Gerlach of G & S Management Services in Sydney and his solicitor Greg Stevens were active in the early stages. David Joseph's lawyer in Los Angeles looked after the contracts with the principal artists and Twentieth Century Fox. In Australian Rules football terms I was 'keeping out of the pack and waiting for the odd handball'. Sometimes the pack can move and unless you are quick enough, you find yourself in the middle of it. That happened.

In September 1981, Ted rang to let me know that a 'serious problem has arisen'. The film was well into pre-production, the stars were in Australia and there was a shortfall in the budget. Budgets in the film industry don't really mean that much. However, it is usually considered a good idea to pay the wages.

In a major movie like *The Pirate Movie* there is always a completion guarantor, that is, an underwriter who receives a large fee and is thereafter responsible for ensuring that the film is completed within budget. If it is not the guarantor has an obligation to step in and complete it. This also means very little because of the complex nature of the contractual terms. It is not difficult for a completion guarantor to avoid its obligations.

The Pirate Movie commenced with a budget of three million dollars and by the time it was finished, had a budget of close to eight million dollars. The increase was not only tolerated by the investors but, to some extent, welcomed. This was one of the rare occasions when sending good money after bad seemed like a good investment. As the film progressed, despite the confusion, everyone including Twentieth Century Fox became excited about its chances of success. Then, of course, there was the tax deduction.

Some of the budget increases were to secure the services of the principal actors. That usually involves payment of large amounts of money and some points out of the gross. Well-advised actors in the film industry have no interest in net receipts. They know that means nothing. The same applies to successful directors and to American attorneys who are never backward in coming forward.

There were some budget increases we could have done without. The film was to be shot in Queensland and there was a contract to use a large sailing ship and its crew. Several days after the producers had decided not to film in Queensland or even to use this particular ship, the ship's owner was advised by the work-experience girl in the Art Department, at great cost and inconvenience, to change the sails on the ship to make it more authentic. She was a true professional.

The decision not to film in Queensland was not welcomed by one of the initial investors, the Queensland Film Commission. Actors who are told that they have cameo roles and negotiate fees accordingly, only to find they have a major role in the film, are also not overly enthusiastic. Garry McDonald started with a very small role and became one of the stars of the film. While this was all going on, minor matters in the context of a musical, like the music, are put on the back burner.

I was feeling decidedly out of my depth. After one emergency meeting in Melbourne Phil Gerlach left to return to Sydney and in his haste took my suit coat with him. In it was a wallet befitting a lawyer. He left me with one befitting an accountant.

One way of solving a cash-flow problem is to convince a bank to advance monies secured by the monies due under a pre-sale agreement. This, in effect, means that the pre-sale advance used by the investors' accountants to justify their initial investment is no more. It has become part of the budget. Obviously, this requires the consent not only of the distributor but also of the investors. Ted and I flew to Surfers Paradise on New Year's Day 1982 and imposed ourselves on the investors who were holidaying with their families. Who could resist Ted in his G-string and me in my boxer shorts? They surrendered. This all had a bearing on legal entitlements and contractual obligations which were also put in the 'too hard' basket.

At the last possible moment a new director, Ken Annakin, was contracted. Ken had considerable experience having directed major films including *The Longest Day*. He immediately decided there was no need to construct expensive sets on the beach at Port Douglas opposite a resort. The film could be made at a mansion at Werribee Park just out of

Melbourne, opposite a sewerage farm. He also decided that the beach scenes could be done at a particularly beautiful part of the Victorian coastline near Warrnambool. It was 'beautiful' in an aesthetic sense but also notorious for its weather. Indeed, the site chosen was the place where a sailing ship, the Loch Ard, had been wrecked with great loss of life.

Midway through principal photography it was apparent that David was having a personality conflict with the online producer. It came to a head on the set. After a yelling match David screamed 'I hate f . . .ing tall people'.

This was followed by a crisis board meeting of the production company JHI Productions at Werribee Park that evening. Ten minutes into the meeting the director's assistant banged on the door. He complained that the lights in the room were clearly visible in the night shoot which was taking place. We were rudely ordered to turn the lights off. The meeting continued for another two hours with expletives echoing around the room. Fortunately given the pitch darkness there was always some doubt as to who was insulting whom. The minutes of the meeting were a little sketchy.

Finally, some thought had to be given to a soundtrack. As is usually the case there was a last-minute rush. Peter Cupples and several other conscripts assisted in the last weeks. There was some suggestion that it would be good to have the group Idle Minds record a track. This all became too difficult and Ian Mason from The Music Farm 'did it for them'. His suggestion was that the 'group' should be called 'Freddie Fairlight & The Fuse'. Under great pressure Roger Savage and David put the music together. Ted, Garry and the music carried the film.

A meeting in Hong Kong took place to decide what could be done about US withholding tax on payments from Twentieth Century Fox which were imminent. The meeting was addressed by an intense, young LA lawyer, Scott, who tabled a long, written advice which was preceded by a very large account. I have never yet met an Australian client or lawyer who reads advices from American lawyers. Fortunately Ted managed to locate a spelling error! That justified us all refusing to read such an unprofessional document. The next day Ted directed Scott to carry my luggage to a waiting taxi. He did. I returned to Melbourne for Glenn Wheatley's wedding. Scott went off to sit on a mountain in Tibet.

The film was a commercial success in that the investors received their money back either from the film or the Australian taxpayer. More importantly there was enough money to fund the activities of the lawyers and accountants for the next few years. When a film opens in 1500 cinemas in North America simultaneously there is a substantial budget for print and advertising. A print is required for each cinema. Much of the advertising paid for was either never delivered or was shown on late-night television in Alaska. It is a relatively simple matter to re-allocate advertising spots to other films. It is also almost impossible to track.

Theoretically, on a gross of 27 million dollars a budget of seven million dollars should be recouped. The gross box office is divided by four. The rest goes to the exhibitors and the distributor with the investors last in line to recoup their investment. American studios have developed a sophisticated system to ensure that this never quite happens. The general rule is whatever a production company gets on the pre-sale is probably all it will get. American studios think they are being generous by paying that. If a film is lucky enough to recoup its budget, future net income is usually shared equally between the producer and the investors, pro rata to their investment. That is after the exhibitors and distributor have taken their share and anyone with 'points' has been paid.

If a budget is recouped the investors should be very happy because they have recouped their investment for which they received a tax deduction anyway. They do have to pay tax on the monies received but they have deferred any tax that was payable. The producers are also satisfied because they have been paid the producer's fee included in the budget. They have also lived a lifestyle fit for French royalty before the revolution. It is always a little depressing at the end of a film project when the five-star hotel and 'limo' is replaced by the little flat in South Yarra and a Volkswagen.

One of the problems with continually changing budgets and securing new investors is that recoupment priorities begin to change. There are different stages of recoupment for investors who put in seed money or initial capital and distributors who provide monies either by way of investment in the production or as an advance. An 'investment in' must be distinguished from 'income to' the production. Then there are the royalty participants to be considered. The situation is further complicated when loans are made and interest is payable. None of this is usually factored into the budget. The same problem occurs when an advance against a soundtrack by a record company is treated as part of the budget rather than income.

Income from the film and income from merchandising and record sales (ancillaries) should be accounted separately. This is because different entitlements might apply. Similarly the competing rights of royalty participants must be determined. They might have a royalty against gross, net or producer's gross or net.

When income is being generated from a foreign source there is a likelihood of withholding tax being charged. This also impacts on the various recoupments and entitlements. Ultimately this necessitated meetings in Los Angeles, New York and Hong Kong. The problem with *The Pirate Movie* was that it did actually succeed at the box office. It grossed something in the vicinity of 27 million dollars which was just enough to cover the costs of the exhibitors, print and advertising, repay Twentieth Century Fox and recoup most of the budget. Because of this there was money to distribute. With the great majority of Australian films this problem never arises and contractual entitlements don't really become an issue.

On one of my post-production trips to Los Angeles I spent most of my time with Ted in various coffee shops and lunching at the Westwood Marquis Hotel. Ted was convinced the hotel was occupied by 'vagrants and vagabonds'. I'm not sure this was consistent with the self-image of most of the wealthy and genteel Beverley Hills ladies who frequented it. By that stage Ted and I had been frozen out of the process. There was still general optimism about the film and Twentieth Century Fox were actively marketing it. Certainly they were accounting for large expenditure on advertising, although where and when that was actually spent was still a mystery.

Because of the anticipated success, credits became an issue. To establish the 'Australianness' of the film, it was necessary and perhaps not unreasonable that the Australian participants be credited. Contractually only the American principals could be credited above the title, which is really all that anyone cares about. The unofficial compromise was to credit

Australian performers above the title in advertising material in Australia and the American principals above the title in America. It didn't take long after release for credits to no longer be an issue.

After the movie, David progressed to bigger and better things. He produced what has been described as Australia's worst movie, *Bullamakanka*. This was funded on the drip feed. Much to their embarrassment it featured cameo performances from almost everybody who was anyone at that time in the Australian contemporary music industry. It was a sensitive story about boy scouts on camp who discover sex, drugs and rock 'n' roll.

I was summoned to Camden in NSW when there was a small problem about paying the motel bill. Coincidentally I flew to Sydney with Glenn Wheatley who, having been born in Queensland and lived in Melbourne, thinks he is an expert on Sydney suburbs. He advised me that Camden was just down the road and to get a taxi. Two hours later I arrived. I knew I was in trouble when I noticed the key production staff were dressed in army fatigues, dark sunglasses and caps on backwards, and had vague looks in their eyes.

Largely as a result of David's determination, the film was made. To secure the tax deduction the film had to be released and generate income. Its world premiere took place at a Sydney drive-in which was hired particularly for the occasion. There were two people in attendance and they had other priorities. We put the lack of interest down to the stormy weather that night. David was annoyed that it was not nominated for an AFI award.

David went on to have considerable success with the film *Navigator* which had a major international release. Ted is still a much sought-after performer, now working in Australia. America had its revenge. In January 2003, Ted fell and broke both arms while walking in Los Angeles. I was commiserating with him and enquired who would be assisting him with the necessities of life. He said people were queuing up.

In 1992 the revival of *The Norman Gunston Show* closed after three or four shows due to the nervous breakdown of its star, Garry McDonald.[2] The writer, Trevor Farrant, who was also acting as producer for the first time, left the show. The executive producer was Phil Gerlach. Perhaps this is a modern version of Tutankhamen's curse.

It quickly became clear that the 150% tax deduction and 50% tax exemption were not sustainable. The deduction was progressively reduced to 100% by May 1988 and the tax exemption was phased out. This concerned potential investors because it meant that unless there was a guaranteed release commitment, there was a real risk of losing money. Commercial films had to be made. This was unacceptable.

Again, the accountants came to the rescue. Forget the film. Create a cash-flow, discount it and fund the exercise from borrowed money and the Australian taxpayer. It went like this. A producer arranges for a financier to lend an investor $10,000. The investor gives that to the producer to be used in the production and gets an immediate tax deduction of $10,000. By immediate, I mean the investment would be made on 30 June of a particular financial year and the deduction would apply in that year. The film would be certified as an eligible film by the (now) Minister for the Arts, Sports, the Environment, Tourism and the Territories. The distributor would agree to pay for non-deductible expenditure in the film and the deduction would then be 100% of monies invested. A distribution guarantee would be put into place whereby 3.5% of the investment would be returned to the investor in each year over an eleven year period. In the twelfth year the balance, 61.5% would be paid. The repayments would be secured by a bank guarantee. This meant that the investor was able to defer income tax over a twelve-year period. It worked because the Australian taxpayer subsidised the whole exercise.

Even this didn't satisfy the accountants. The deduction still only applied if the film was certified by the Minister. It had to have a certain element of Australianness. The accountants realised that the 10BA regime could easily be circumvented by using the general provisions of the Act which allowed revenue expenses necessarily incurred in gaining assessable income to be deducted. The film could be a totally foreign production, the return on the investment could be secured by bank guarantee (supported by the American distributor) and the investment could be massively geared. For instance, every actual cash contribution of $1 by the investor could be supported by a loan of $19 thereby providing a tax deduction of $20 for every $1 which came out of the investor's pocket. The cash-flow benefits are obvious.

One particular production group, Kamisha Corporation Pty Ltd, and its associates used this to great advantage. They acted as production contractors and their role was to provide funding and production services. Hence any monies invested with them were said to be totally deductible under Section 51(1) of the Act. The return on the monies invested was secured by a letter of credit from a bank. Of the monies invested 105% was repayable as to 4% in year five, 6% in year six and 95% in year seven. The funds were used for American productions. That group alone raised ten million dollars for *Night of the Leopard* in 1990, ten million dollars for *Alamagordo* in 1991, 20 million dollars for *Carlito's Way* in 1992, 20 million dollars for *The War* in 1993 and 38 million dollars for *Clockers* in 1994. Other "Kamisha" films included Liar Liar, Hard Target and Mercury Rising.

This amounted to a direct subsidy by the Australian taxpayer of the American film industry. None of this could have occurred had the Tax Commissioner not allowed it to happen by his inactivity. There was a much-delayed reaction some years later but, by then, it was probably all too late for the Australian film industry. The good news is that the Australian art film bureaucracy is alive and well. The Australian Film Finance Corporation spent the whole of 2002 arguing about who would be its CEO.[3]

Looking back it's fair to say that the 10BA scheme in its original format and as modified, was a scandalous waste of taxpayers' money. The deferment, gearing and Section 51 schemes which followed were a great fillip to the American film industry but deprived the Australian industry of whatever investment funds were available to sustain it. Today the Australian film industry is little more than a backlot for the American studios, one of which is owned by a sort of Australian.

CHAPTER 13 – EIGHT SHOWS A WEEK

Professional theatre is the entertainment industry equivalent of owning a yacht or a racehorse. Again, it is a question of risk and return. At one end of the scale there are the low-risk productions which include *Sound of Music*, *Chicago*, *A Chorus Line, Carousel*, any Gilbert & Sullivan musical and the usual standards. At the other end are new productions. They are very high-risk but because a new 'property' is being created the potential returns are great.

Over the years there have been many valiant attempts to create new Australian productions. By this I don't mean successful Australian productions of overseas shows of which there have been many. *La Cage Aux Folles*, *Nine*, *Man of La Mancha* and *Cabaret* are examples. Rather, I mean new shows like *Rasputin*, *Manning Clark's History of Australia – The Musical, Bad Boy Johnny and the Prophets of Doom* and *Better Known as Bee*. These were all commercial failures.

Hot Shoe Shuffle and *Boy from Oz* were successful but these are the exceptions. Not only is it difficult to get investors for new shows but the producers find themselves competing with highly subsidised cut-down productions which have more to do with self-indulgence than artistic excellence. They also have to compete with packaged versions of new, foreign productions like *Mamma Mia*.

As distinct from records and to a lesser extent films, theatre is highly capitalised and labour intensive. A record and/or a film once released can be replicated, exhibited and exploited around the world without the ongoing involvement of the singers, actors and production crew. A theatrical production can cost as much or more than a film to acquire the rights, rehearse and get to opening night. It's not uncommon for an Australian production to cost five to eight million dollars to get to that point. Thereafter the show still requires a cast, director, musical director, musicians and production crew. The initial investment must be amortised over a long period and can only be recouped after payment of recurring weekly expenses. A budget of five million dollars after payment of current expenses can take from six to twelve months or longer to recoup depending on the tickets sold – as to both the number and average ticket price.

Some producers operate on the false assumption that they can access the box office to fund their show or other activities. In 1982 Harry M. Miller was given some free board and keep for doing just that in relation to Computicket. These monies are held in trust and are not available until the particular performance has been completed. The funds can sometimes be made available provided a bank guarantee is given to the agency holding the box-office monies.

It is possible to 'pencil in' a booking. This will minimise the problems of 'spot bookings', such as the local school booking the venue on a Saturday for their speech night in the middle of a run. Ultimately firm commitments do have to be made. Theatres around Australia have to be booked on a continuous and long-running basis when there is no guarantee that the show will succeed.

Not only is there a need to secure theatres, but also the principal production staff and artists have to be contracted. They can be contracted on a 'run of the show' basis but some minimum commitment is required. They have to be paid during downtime periods which occur when moving from theatre to theatre. Because of Australia's large size and relatively small population, this occurs frequently.

For some reason musicals have not attracted the government support directed towards the film industry. Investments are made in a musical purely for commercial purposes, that is on the basis that the budget will be recouped and profits made. For that reason the production companies which survive in the long-term are those which have their own sources of funding. Sports & Entertainment Ltd (SEL) and International Management Group (IMG) are probably the best examples. Successful individual producers are soon acquired by the larger organisations with access to funding. Or, like Stewart Macpherson, Bill Marshall and Ian Crawford, they come and go.

Once the budget, which includes a production fee to the producer, is recouped, profits are usually divided 50/50 between the producer and the investors. A budget will include the capital cost of getting the production to opening night. It should also allow for ongoing advertising and any shortfalls in box office in the initial weeks to provide sufficient time for the advertising and word of mouth to take effect. Optimism and artistic integrity do not pay the bills.

The copyrights associated with musicals are straightforward. There are the copyrights in the music and lyrics, the book, choreography, artwork, costume designs and any master recorded. To use a song it is necessary to obtain a licence from the copyright owner. The licence which allows works to be performed in public (subject to payment of a public performance fee) would normally come from APRA in relation to musical works and from PPCA for sound recordings (where the copyright owner is a PPCA member). However, 'grand rights', as they are called, are not controlled by APRA and it is necessary to negotiate these licences direct with the publisher or rights owner. 'Grand rights' are the rights to publicly perform or broadcast music with words in a dramatic context, for example musicals, operas, ballets and stage plays. Grand rights apply when a song has been specifically written for a show. This should be distinguished from performances of a song which is already a hit such as 'I Still Call Australia Home' being used in the *Boy from Oz*. Then there are 'small rights' which apply when a performance takes place neither in a dramatic context nor where there is an exercise of a grand right. The Main Event is an example.

My first professional experience with theatre was in 1984, acting for Anthony Warlow, who starred in *The Phantom of the Opera* in Australia. No one in the world has ever come close to Anthony in this role. The producer of that show was Cameron Mackintosh and it had already been very successful internationally. Mackintosh is 'star' averse. He develops his shows around the show and all advertising and promotion is directed to that end. The best or perhaps worst example of this is *Cats* where not only are the actors not featured but they are not even recognisable. There is no person behind the character. Cameron is credited above the title. He is the star. This facilitates shows being franchised around the world and obviously restricts the bargaining position of performers. It also helps his self-esteem. This is consistent with the concept of the Cameron Mackintosh 'family'. Sometimes families, like walls, are concerned just as much with keeping people in as they are with keeping people out.

Several productions can be playing around the world at the same time. The norm is eight shows a week, i.e. Monday through Saturday with a matinee on Wednesday and Saturday. In *The Phantom of the Opera* the time required to apply and remove makeup for each performance was almost longer than the show itself. With someone like Anthony who treats each performance as his first and last, there is little time left for self or family. Anthony paid a price for that when his involvement in the show ended. He was contracted to star in the arena version of *Jesus Christ Super Star* but was unable to take the role because of serious health problems. Fortunately they have now been put behind him.

John Diedrich introduced me to Colin Devine in 1987. Colin was a very successful life-insurance agent. He had crystallised that success by taking advantage of a race to be 'number one' between the AMP and the then National Mutual (now AXA). These companies were providing what were euphemistically called 'development loans' to seduce and secure successful agents to sell their products. This was also the beginning of the end for two of Australia's oldest financial icons. Those who were responsible for this fiasco were rewarded handsomely and left the companies. Thousands of loyal employees who were not responsible were given very small cheques and made redundant. Colin took advantage of one of these 'loans'. From the day he received his 'loan' he only sold one insurance policy. That was to me.

Colin became the major investor and co-producer in the Australian production of *Nine*. It was co-produced, directed by and starred John. It was based on Fellini's movie *8 1/2* and concerned the adventures of Guido and twenty-one lovely women. Theatre had been part of John's life since childhood and the show was produced creatively and economically with the investors in view. It ran more than twelve months around Australia and covered its running costs.

Nine had the usual problems of securing theatres and added costs associated with moving from theatre to theatre. The holding costs while no income was being generated had to be covered. Obviously not all of the twenty-one ladies were interested in moving interstate with the show. Whilst most performers are generally signed for the run of the show, personal considerations are respected and if someone doesn't want to stay they are replaced. This can cause problems with a production like *Nine* which had three costume changes, each very expensive. Three new costumes would be required for each replacement. This was overcome by John ensuring that before prospective performers were auditioned they had first to fit the costume.

Colin applied his experience as a marketer with enthusiasm and élan. There were moments. One of these concerned the opening night in Adelaide. Colin organised for me and my guest (Unity, the wife of my friend Mario, my plumber) to be collected at Adelaide airport. We were met by a very tall, thin lady carrying a whip and dressed in a black, leather uniform who drove a Rolls Royce. Because of time constraints, I directed her to take us straight to the theatre, rather than via the hotel. I noticed that there were two vacant seats beside us. This was also noticed by John who can count an audience even during his most dramatic performances. We soon became aware that the seats should have been occupied by Colin and his wife. They were at the hotel waiting to be collected by a lady dressed in black leather.

Colin moved on to finance and produce a new show called *Better Known as Bee*. He put on a spectacular opening-night party at the Southern Cross Hotel. It was better than the show and lasted longer. After that the hotel had to be demolished. The production which was based on the story of a Sydney 'bag lady', opened in Melbourne. It had the wrong audience. It didn't make the next weekend. Paul Dainty, who owned the Comedy Theatre at the time, was not pleased.

Then Colin decided to produce and sponsor *The Great Overland Cattle Drive*! In years gone by cattle were driven from central Queensland to Sydney along the old stock routes. Colin's idea was that this should be re-enacted, only this time wealthy American tourists would be given the opportunity of a lifetime. They would be swept away by the idea of eating campfire food with a dust entrée.

Colin was convinced that a suitable advertising campaign would have Americans flocking to the 'Great Drive'. He organised for a film crew to travel to a country property west of Newcastle to film the all-important commercial. Our director had won awards for music videos. There were several buses which were going to be contracted to pick up and deliver the tourists at various intervals throughout the drive, as well as tent displays and campfires. I was given a starring role as an American tourist, dressed in pink pyjamas, coming out of a tent at sunrise and stretching seductively. Everything was ready to go. I was well rehearsed.

At dawn on the day of shooting, we realised that the farmer who was to provide the cattle had only delivered six rather sad-looking cows of the milking variety. By the end of the day, having been shot in single file coming over the ridge, through the valley and crossing the creek twenty times to the sound of whips being cracked by the nine drovers on horseback, they were considerably sadder. The production values in that commercial are of Academy Award standard. It is regrettable that it was supposed to have something to do with cattle. For some reason the Americans didn't rush to the drive and it is still in the planning stage.

I was also involved in various capacities (after a while, as a defensive mechanism, one forgets what) in the Bicentennial production of *Manning Clark's History of Australia – The Musical*. The production company was Avenue of the Americas Pty Ltd – one of the streets of New York. I thought that was worth a smile. There were the usual budgetary and funding problems. The budget was approximately one and a half million dollars. A very, some would say too, cheap production by modern standards. The writers were committed to the production and worked on a 'she'll be right mate' basis. So did I. There was only nominal government investment. I raised approximately $700,000 from my contacts. They invested for purely commercial reasons believing the show had genuine potential.

Since it was the official Bicentennial musical, every politician in Australia wanted to get involved. That does not mean they wanted to make a financial commitment. Politicians wanted the private sector to fund the musical which was to be a vehicle for their self-aggrandisement.

It is an axiom of the entertainment industry that those who pay the least expect, and usually get, the best seats. The 'A' list never pay. For my part I have always considered it a professional obligation to pay for tickets to shows. Rarely do people for whom I have bought tickets have the courtesy to express their appreciation. There have been several times when 'guests' have not taken the trouble to turn up at all. Performers and producers really love empty seats in the middle of the tenth row.

I once bought tickets for a union official to attend *The Phantom of the Opera* only to be told that he left at 'half time'. That is what important non-payers do. Whilst there were no meaningful financial contributions from government, the program included messages from eight prominent politicians from the then Prime Minister, Bob Hawke, down (or perhaps up).

One of the major investors was the then PolyGram Records. Its managing director Michael Smellie and his wife travelled from Sydney to Melbourne for the opening night on 16 January 1988. Fortuitously, I happened to meet them outside the Princess Theatre. Michael said there seemed to be a problem in that there were no tickets for them at the box office. I handed two tickets to him. My wife and I spent the rest of the night having a pie and chips at a Café in Swanston Street.

After opening night it was immediately obvious that the production had great potential. It had well-motivated messages of hope, reconciliation and love to all. Because it had become the subject of creative input from just about everybody, it was self-indulgent and longwinded. Unlike *The Phantom of the Opera*, which had three great songs, or *Les Miserables*, which had six, this had thirty-two not-so-great songs.

There had been feathers ruffled in the establishment because of arguments over the rights to use the name 'Manning Clark's History of Australia'. Why we needed such a pretentious title I never quite understood. I have since learnt that it was on the insistence of John Bell the Director,[1] the same person who thought it was a good idea to rehearse the show in Sydney. Manning Clark personally supported the musical but the rights were controlled by the Melbourne University Press and their Mr Ryan was not so accommodating. In retrospect, the name was hopelessly non-commercial anyway and should have been dispensed with. At a restaurant in Carlton sometime after the show had closed, Max Gillies said we should have called it 'Australia'. I had another name entirely for it.

The cash flow forecasts were premised on novel mathematical principles of hope. They assumed that as of the first week there would be sufficient people attending the production to cover recurrent expenses, that is wages, rent and advertising. In the first week there were more people in the cast than in the audience. Things got better marginally. Because the music had been programmed on computer and John Bell was involved in another production in Sydney, there was no capacity or potential for making the many changes that were required immediately.

The cast had the unrealistic expectation that they would be paid on a weekly basis. Ultimately, the cast was incredibly supportive and agreed to work for nothing. Whilst this was generous, it involved the exploitation of labour. I think I was the only one who appreciated the irony of that. David Marriner, who owns the Princess Theatre and who is supposed to be a hard-headed businessman, offered to forego rent for the theatre.

I saw the show about ten times. One of the very small investors ($5000) went public and let everyone know he was so committed to the production that he had mortgaged his house and sent his mistress out to work in a sweatshop to support it. Finally, it collapsed in a sea of confusion and embarrassment.

Some of the credit for the demise of the show can be given to Clark Forbes, then critic for *The Sun*. He could never be accused of letting a few jobs get in the way of a good line. Forbes reviewed the production on Monday 18 January 1988.[2] He called it a 'tawdry and tacky affair' which 'is enough to give the Bicentennial a bad name'.[3] The musical was 'more lost than Burke and Wills'.[4] The thirty-two lyrical songs did not include 'one big production number, ballad or contemporary rocker among them'.[5] Obviously Forbes was expecting Céline Dion.

Leonard Radic of *The Age* probably had more negative impact on the box office than Forbes, but he did it in a more subtle way.[6] Radic's review appeared on the same day. He congratulated the entrepreneurs for their persistence and bravery. He lamented the fact that the production quickly dissolved into a 'comic parade of people and personalities'.[7] According to Radic, much had been made of the fact that the musical was light on both women and Aborigines. This was nonsense – made by who and when? The production 'ambles along from incident to incident and from scene to scene, propelled chiefly by the pastiche score which ranges from waltz to samba, from reel to rock'.[8] At least Radic had the decency to pretend to be constructive. The production was 'old fashioned' and the impression was one of 'patchiness and a failure of imagination'.[9] In short, 'the makings of something well worthwhile are there, but further work is needed'.[10] After that review there would be neither audience nor investors for whatever was 'worthwhile'.

Alan Attwood in *Time* (Australia) on 25 January 1998[11] was enthusiastic, supportive and constructive but by then it was all over. Unfortunately, not many women over thirty-five, who are the driving force behind audiences for musical theatre, read *Time*.

None of this was a great wealth-creation plan for me personally. I didn't get paid and did pay for a hundred or so tickets. It did have its bright side. Ben Hills, a journalist, then writing for *The Herald* (Melbourne), decided to have his own little bit of fun. He wrote a satirical article about the people involved, likening them all to members of the Mafia.[12] There was a Godfather, Capo etc. Many of the people behind the show were members of, or associated with, what used to be known as The Carlton Push. This was a group of mainly Labor or left-wing-minded people who went out of their way to support productions by Australians which added to Australian culture – not something which should be encouraged. Certain groups of the elite were delighted to see these people get what was due to them after the very public execution of the show.

Hills made the mistake of including me in the piece as the 'bag man'. I didn't mind so much being called a 'bag man'. In Labor circles that is something of a compliment. Nor did I mind the implication that I was associated with raising money for a failed production. None of my investors was a housewife. However, I did object to being depicted as a member of the Mafia and the geriatric Mafia at that. I issued proceedings and the settlement went some way towards balancing the ledger. My associates in the production were also aggrieved about the article but like all good left-wing activists they chose to air their angst at Percy's Bar in Carlton rather than in the courts.

There have been some attempts by creative producers to structure shows to minimise or offset the financial risk of productions by making investments tax effective. This usually involves gearing. This was particularly the case in shows like *Jolson* which was co-produced by Michael Brereton. Most such shows ended in disaster, not only at the box office but also at the Taxation Office.

David Marriner attempted to create a pool of investors to fund shows which had a particular interest to him. He was and still is the major theatre owner in Melbourne and was keen to counter competition from the over-capitalised Melbourne Casino. He produced *Show Boat* in 1998. Investors usually like a return and that exercise was not terribly rewarding. His next production, *Ragtime*, was cancelled.

Promoters more than anyone know that it is possible to lose money even when a tour or show is successful. Paul Dainty (*The Rolling Stones*) and Garry Van Egmond (*George Benson* and *Bad Boy Johnny and the Prophets of Doom*) learnt this lesson the hard way. Nevertheless, they are irrepressible and Paul has had his greatest successes with a production featuring TV wrestlers and his investment in *Mamma Mia*. He was not so successful with the proposed tour of Paul McCartney, which was cancelled. For some reason known only to the Victorian Government it chose to subsidise the tour with one million dollars of taxpayers' money. McCartney preferred to use the Bali bombing, rather than low ticket sales, as the reason for the cancellation. Steve Vizard, who is in charge of the Victorian Office of Very Small Projects, must be given some of the credit for this visionary attempt to transfer wealth from Victorians to one of the richest people in the world.

Producers realised that one way to make the investment work was to increase the capacity of the venue. This could be done by having an arena spectacular. Harry M. Miller first exploited this with his production of *Jesus Christ Superstar*. IMG had success with arena productions including *Carmen* and Kevin Jacobsen had some success with *Aida*. That success was despite the fact that the elephant became bogged in soggy ground at the Carlton football ground, half the sound system didn't function and when it came to send the sphinx to fulfil dates in Los Angeles and Tokyo, it didn't fit into the aeroplane.

Failure is not in Kevin's vocabulary. He has now floated a public company. Unfortunately it was less buoyant than his elephants. Eight million dollars was raised. Most of this was lost on the Witches of Eastwick and the Bruce Springsteen tour. Kevin was annoyed because Bruce wouldn't agree to reduce his fee to mitigate the losses.[13] I wonder if Bruce would have been requested to increase his fee had the tour been successful.

There have been some very successful arena productions with the resurrection of *Jesus Christ Superstar*, *Grease* and *The Main Event* featuring

John Farnham, Olivia Newton-John and Anthony Warlow. However, of late the arena spectacular seems to have run its race.

There are producers like Mario Maiolo in Adelaide and Casino Promotions (nothing to do with the Casino) in Melbourne who successfully produce shows on relatively small budgets year in and year out. Their success is based on their ability to control costs. They are more into promoting their shows than self-promotion.

There was a foray by superannuation funds into commercial theatre. One managed to lose a large amount of money by investing in spectacularly unsuccessful productions. These included a modern Romeo and Juliet musical based on Edward and Mrs Simpson. The good news was that so many important people travelled to the opening night in London. It lasted a week. For some reason people did not warm to a love story about an effete British royal who shirked his responsibilities and who, in the weeks before opening night, had been accused of being a Nazi sympathiser. Superannuation funds should keep away from the glitz and glam.

Some producers minimise the risk by government subsidy. This applies particularly in opera and ballet. It rarely works. Perhaps what is missing is the commercial entrepreneur or the super manager and agent of the past. Norman Lebrecht has chronicled these.[14] Personally I have always respected the talent and dedication of the singers, dancers and musicians in these disciplines. I have never quite been able to relate to the audiences.

Subsidies imply that the audience is not prepared to pay for a ticket costed on commercial principles, i.e. based on the production costs plus a reasonable return. That does not mean the audience is wrong. It simply means that the production costs cannot be justified. Why should that be redressed by taxpayers, the great majority of whom have no interest in the art form? The day arts councils, politicians or socialites start deciding what is best for 'the people' will be the day the music will surely die.

Finally, there are the rock 'n' roll promoters. Over the years things have lurched from one crisis to another. There was the concert to raise money for kids. Entrance was by donation in a barrel at the door. No one bothered to keep an eye on the barrel, which disappeared. There was the wunderkind who booked Rolf Harris on the same bill as The Angels at a

New Year's Eve concert at the Opera House. At the 'Australia Made' fiasco in January 1987 the cash ran out. Does an act refuse to go on in these circumstances and disappoint an audience? That is one of the reasons I am not a manager. Sadly on that tour Peter Trotter died after collapsing on stage during a performance by Mental as Anything. *The Great Concert for Life in 1992* featuring INXS didn't fare much better. In 2002 *Rhumba* managed to lose three or four million dollars.

Then along came the Jacobsen/Chugg production of *Long Way to the Top*. This production was commercially successful, at least initially, and proves that nostalgia and familiarity will beat originality and creativity every time. The participants had a great time. I read an e-mail which described the artistic preparations that went into the show. That description was as follows:

> '3.00am – G (with no hair) and B (with too much hair), both collapsed on the floor, drunk out of their minds with P running naked up and down the hallways of the hotel, with a black marker signature of N on his arse. People complaining and the management sending up bouncers to shut us up. This was the first night'.

In December 2002 the producers received a writ from us alleging that Brian de Courcy, a genuine rock 'n' roll legend, had been omitted from the credits and rewards of the show. That was settled.

Live entertainment in its various forms, from opera to wrestling, demonstrates that there is one absolutely essential ingredient without which nothing works. It is an audience and it is never wrong. People spend time and money. They know what they want and they make an informed choice. Most people simply want to be entertained. The audience should not be patronised, educated or subsidised. At the same time investors are not stupid. Their money and their support should be acknowledged and respected. Only then will a professional industry thrive and survive.

CHAPTER 14 – THE FIRM

This chapter has more to do with the legal profession than the music industry. Since lawyers seem to be a permanent fixture in the industry, it might be helpful to know how they think.

I fell into the law by accident. In 1966 as a 20-year-old I won the raffle of all raffles and was 'called up' into the Army. I was quite pleased about that. I was about to become engaged. Service in Vietnam, a war zone, carried with it automatic entitlements to a low-interest home loan and other benefits. My brother, who was in the Navy at the time, advised me that war service was too good an opportunity to miss.

I asked the Army for their assurance that I would be sent to Vietnam. Their response was that they would decide where and when I would serve. This could include spending eighteen months at Puckapunyal in Victoria where no benefits would accrue. From that point on I became a diligent, if not necessarily conscientious, objector. A deferment was available for students. I applied to study law based on four rather average passes in final year at school. The form didn't have provision for failures at tertiary institutions – three out of three subjects in accountancy, including commercial law. The engagement was deferred and the ring was left on 'lay-by'. It remained at the shop until the final payment was made – two years later.

I was accepted into the second ever annual intake of law students at Monash Law School which was then based in the Monash Engineering Faculty. I had never met a lawyer. I was part-time and continued to work in the Taxation Department. My archaic motorcycle helmet and perennially wet business suit were not really compatible with the law undergraduate uniform of check sports coat, school tie and green corduroys. Nor were they a great entrée into the Scotch College set who seemed to be dominant at the time. This was probably because entry into Monash usually implied failure to be admitted to Melbourne University. They were the type of people who never seem to leave school. Certainly their sense of self-importance was not diminished by their lack of worldly experience.

One of my first run-ins with the 'A' Team was when a tutor, who I had dubbed 'the French Prostitute', decided to combine my evening tutorial, which consisted of me, with her honours group. I wasn't happy about that and said so. Madam Lash had her retribution when, despite my protestations, she insisted that I had failed to produce a Torts exercise. Fortunately my (by then) wife had typed the essay and I had a carbon copy. It was marked D plus – just a pass. The same day my original essay turned up. It had been inadvertently marked by another lecturer – A plus. After a not-too-polite discussion with the Madam and threats of exposure in *Lot's Wife*, the student magazine, I walked away with an A plus. That was not a great long-term strategic victory and was the beginning of several years of D pluses.

I tended to gravitate to the few other part-time students including Bill Coady (a policeman) and students like Ian MacDonald and Ron McCallum, neither of whom seemed to realise they were disabled. I wasn't going to enlighten them. Ron is now the Dean of Sydney Law School. Ian has had successful careers in law, industry, horse breeding and aviation. Being part-time and a slow learner, I took eight years rather than the usual five. By then Bill and a mature-age Monash student Lou Rotman had established Coady Rotman & Associates in Melbourne.

Bill arranged for me to get Articles at a firm in Tatura, Dawes & Vary O'Toole & Macpherson (sometimes called Dawes Ovary Tool & Macpherson). One of my major achievements during Articles was to have a prisoner, who was charged with a serious offence in Rushworth (an old gold town in Victoria), plead 'guilty' rather than 'not guilty'. I was also contacted one day by the secretary of the local building society, the firm's biggest client, wanting to know the status of a particular mortgage which had recently been finalised. I was advised to look out the front window. I observed the house, our primary security, heading out of town on the back of a truck. Then there was the client who wanted to sue the owner of a dog which had allegedly savaged his sheep. I was the owner.

The day after I finished Articles I started as a partner in Coady Rotman & Associates. A month later I was instructed in a distressing case. A father collected his two-year-old daughter for access on a Sunday and departed that evening on a plane for Lebanon. I tried unsuccessfully to have the man arrested by Australian Consular officials along the route. On his arrival he sent me an autographed photo of the 'beautiful plane' which had transported him to Lebanon. I appeared on television to complain about this obvious defect in the immigration system. The interviewer referred to a provision in the legislation whereby people could notify the authorities should they suspect a person might abscond in this way. I had several reasons to suspect that the abduction might occur and my embarrassment was obvious. The client wasn't ecstatic either. She was prevented from entering Lebanon to see her child because of her failure to live up to her responsibilities as a wife and mother. For my part, it taught me that lawyers should stay out of the media.

Eighteen months after I joined the practice, Lou, who had another life as a chemist, left to pursue his many successful interests. On 25 July 1975 the firm changed its name to Coady Dwyer & Associates. By then it had a momentum of its own. It had very few outgoings and good cash flow. Our success was due in no small part to the fact that we worked in separate areas. Bill had many contacts with serving policemen and specialised in Magistrates Court appearances – a profitable area when you have the co-operation of the clerks of court who can list several cases on a particular day and with priority. I looked after taxation and commercial matters – commonsense really having failed commercial law!

I had developed five or six 'A' centres of influence, that is people who for whatever reason are proactive referrers of business. Because of their social and business contacts they always manage to refer 'A' type clients. Most of these were accountants I had known in the Taxation Department. Then there was Glenn Wheatley, who was probably the best of them all. I also had my share of 'B' centres of influence. These are equally enthusiastic and active but the people they refer tend to be of the 'bleeding heart' or 'lost dog' variety. Because neither Bill nor I had any real interest in, or need for, the trappings of wealth, our outgoings and personal drawings were kept to a minimum and the first ten years were good for everyone including our clients.

In the early eighties typists were still using carbon paper, there was no fax or internet and electronic communication was by way of telex. These machines were expensive and cumbersome to operate and words were used sparingly. For that reason international and interstate travel was an accepted and necessary part of the working environment. To me, with my public service background, this was like being paid to take annual holidays. It was also a great learning experience.

There were moments of course. I once stayed at a very sophisticated hotel situated in the centre of Amsterdam. A waiter was displaying cheeses when he was called to the phone. In his absence I assisted him by slicing a piece from the large cheese ball which had been offered. How was I to know it was his 60-year-old, virgin, display model?

I once flew to New York and checked into an up-market hotel. To try and relax I went to the restaurant and ordered a cup of coffee. On requesting milk, the not very friendly waiter produced a white, curdled substance. On dropping it into my coffee I immediately realised it was their excuse for butter. On requesting a replacement cup of coffee the waiter took it upon himself to make a sarcastic remark about people who put butter in their coffee. The injustice was that I was the one ejected from the restaurant.

Then there was the bus in Santa Monica. I found myself dressed in my three-piece suit sitting in a bus full of students on the way back to Westwood. It had been impossible to get a taxi. The large, black, female driver stopped the bus and in a loud and aggressive voice demanded to know why I had not paid the fare. When I replied that I thought payment would be made on leaving the bus, she pointed to a receptacle and insisted that I immediately deposit the exact money. I didn't have change and remarked that it was a strange system which required people to get onto a bus, ascertain the fare and then get off the bus to get the correct change. I was removed from the bus to the clapping and cheering of the students.

I once flew to Sydney with Ted Hamilton. Ted was asked by a person who was then known as a 'hostess' if he would like a roll. He responded (not impolitely) 'with you, any time'. That resulted in both of us being blackballed for the rest of the flight. Luckily we weren't flying to Europe.

Humour has always been a rare commodity. I needed plenty of it on the last flight from Sydney to Melbourne one Friday night. It was during the air traffic controllers' 'go slow' which preceded the pilots' strike. Whilst over Albury the pilot announced that they had closed Melbourne Airport. He said that a traffic controller at Melbourne Airport had suffered a 'period pain' and we were returning to Sydney. On arrival after midnight the flight attendant welcomed us to Sydney and thanked us for flying Ansett. Then they all disappeared and left us on the tarmac. The Airport was closed. There was neither transport nor accommodation. Next day I had trouble re-booking a flight because I had already used my ticket. Despite all that I am an Ansett orphan and I miss them dearly.

In Australia there are few lawyers who are active in the entertainment industry. Those who are act for many clients and their relationship, with some exceptions, is more professional than personal. In America the situation is quite different. In Los Angeles alone there are hundreds of so-called entertainment lawyers. They attach themselves to a successful group or artist and become twenty-four hours a day quasi manager/agents. This is a reflection of the difference in size between the Australian and American markets. It also results in American lawyers being somewhat paranoid and insecure. They live in fear of losing their client. An Australian lawyer can lose a client with few long-term repercussions for his or her practice. We know that we will usually get them back anyway.

There is also a difference in approach and attitude between lawyers on the east and west coasts of America. Those in the west are more relaxed and approachable. Those in the east seem to be in a permanent state of neurosis. In the late seventies many of the Australian artists who made forays into the American market were represented in Los Angeles by Owen Sloane who was initially supported by John McDonald of Image Music and Glenn Wheatley. Owen typifies the west-coast lawyer.

In the early eighties, because of mergers and takeovers, much of the American contemporary music industry moved to New York. The firm of Grubman Schindler & Indursky was pre-eminent at that time. This was largely due to their close relationships with the then CBS Records and, in the Australian context, support from Michael Gudinski and the Mushroom Group. They feature in the book *Hit Men*.

During that time I organised two seminars in Melbourne and Sydney under the auspices of the Victorian Law Institute. The first featured Owen Sloane and the second Paul Schindler – first-class return tickets, great exposure, the lot. I was returning from Owen's office in Santa Monica when I was thrown off the bus. Ask yourself why I was on it?

Schindler also returned the favour. I was visiting his office in New York late one cold December afternoon. I thought I might get taken out for a drink. I wasn't impressed when he took a call from a manager ringing from Melbourne in my presence and without disclosing that fact to the manager. He told me how busy he was and that he would have to pass that evening. I went back to my cell in the hotel. Fortunately the red light on the phone was flashing. I rang Fred Bestall. He took me to Madison Square Garden. After walking through a labyrinth of passageways (very Spinal Tap) we arrived backstage with John Mellencamp. Halfway through his concert the power failed. It could not continue and the box-office monies had to be refunded. At the rather solemn after party who should turn up – Schindler!

There is also a difference between American lawyers who work in the music industry and those who work in the film industry. As noted, the former tend to have a one-on-one relationship with their client. The latter operate very much like the average Australian commercial top-tier firm. My experiences with these lawyers gave me my first insight into modern principles of managing a law firm. There is the almost obsessive use of yellow stickers. One lawyer had a habit of writing on these in pencil. I was severely rebuked when I took to one with a biro. The reason for his concern became clear when at the end of a contractual negotiation he carefully removed each yellow sticker and erased the pencil marks for re-use.

Reusing stickers was an incredibly profitable activity since the time taken to erase the pencil marks was then billed to the client as part of the billing system invented by the Americans called 'time costing'. This was a system whereby firstly the expenses of the office were calculated. To that was added the profit that the partners (or their spouses) required. The total was divided by what was called 'the number of billable hours in the day'. The profit could be increased simply by increasing the charge-out rate of particular operators or the number of operators. That is why large firms always have more than one 'operator' at a meeting. I once asked a solicitor from a large firm if he ever had any difficulty accounting for his time each day. He said no. Any shortfall was simply allocated to the ANZ Bank. To me that seemed very reasonable.

American film attorneys take themselves very seriously. I was representing an Australian film producer at a meeting in the boardroom of a large Los Angeles law firm. A Sydney lawyer (Bob Barraket of Lebanese extract) was representing the Australian investors. American lawyers were representing the distributor and completion guarantor. There were approximately fifteen lawyers present and it didn't take long for Barraket to make a disparaging remark about Melbourne lawyers generally and me in particular. This led to a heated debate about Sydney's history as a penal settlement and Melbourne's glorious tradition based on gold and free enterprise. Barraket resorted to the gutter language often adopted by Sydney lawyers and I responded in a professional way. The American self-appointed chairman of the meeting tried to inject some mid-west Christian principles into the debate and was told by me to 'shut up'. American lawyers aren't very good when the gloves are off. Several of them had to take toilet breaks and not for what is usually expected in the entertainment industry. Finally the chairman, fearing violence, declared that the meeting was counter-productive. He adjourned it to the next morning by which time he said he hoped that Barraket and I would be able to conduct our discussions with each other in a civil way. Bob turned to me and asked where we were going for dinner.

On that same trip Bob and I and a couple of other Australians needed some relaxation. I suggested a madrigal recital. Bob preferred interactive, lady wrestling. I was dragged along. The next day he told a journalist friend in Sydney that I was seen mud-wrestling. It was reported in a Sydney paper that I was a champion competitor in that particular event.

In the early eighties the Americans started to use word processors. The benefits these would bring to a legal practice were manifest. It wasn't just the technology which was impressive. The Americans used word processing to totally change the way legal practice was conducted. It was the new religion. At that time, because of the difficulties with retyping documents like Wills and Trust Deeds, clients would be encouraged to make their instructions fit the precedent rather than the lawyer make the precedent fit their instructions. Word processing would change all that. It was hoped that it would also free lawyers from the burden of overheads.

The standard configuration before word processing was that each solicitor was supported by a secretary who would not only attend to his or her calls but would also do all that solicitor's typing. At the top of the tree were the stenographers who would sit with the solicitor and take shorthand. They would then type the letters. I used that system although often my method of dictating a letter would be to say, 'here's the file – send a letter to . . .'. A solicitor in those days would be considered profitable if the fees generated were three times the total wages associated with that solicitor including any back-up staff. That formula has not changed much over the years. including any back-up staff. That formula has not changed much over the years.

In the late seventies I started using dictaphones and typists would type from the tape. I have always been fortunate to have secretaries who are particularly skilled. They require both accuracy and speed. The Americans by the early eighties had modified the accepted configuration to accommodate the use of word processors. They developed the word-processing pool which would handle all the typing. Each solicitor or operator would then have access to, or a share of, a personal assistant. The role of the personal assistant was not to take shorthand or to type but to assist the solicitor with phone calls and appointments. The irony was that this system managed to defeat the purpose of word processing which was to reduce, not to increase, overheads.

I accepted the new developments with an open mind. The firm adopted them with religious zeal just as my interest was on the wane. One of our first purchases was a Daro accounting machine which was supposed to look after our trust account. It cost in today's currency the equivalent of $100,000, took up half a room and increased our accounting staff from one to three. We also purchased three word-processing machines at great cost. They were so noisy they had to be encased in large boxes. We installed central dictation, that is dictation being fed directly into the word-processing area rather than to a secretary. Really all it involved was a longer cord. That was the beginning of the end of the person formerly known as a 'stenographer'.

Around that time, on a trip to Hong Kong, I was advised by an accountant Warren Duncan that he and his partners had managed to achieve a tax-free capital gain by introducing young partners into the firm. The amount paid for their entry into the partnership reflected the appropriate share of work-in-progress and debtors less liabilities and amounted to a capital tax-free receipt in the hands of the existing partners. That was attractive to me. My years in the Taxation Department had given me a particular ability to ignore personal tax matters to my detriment. New partners were introduced.

From that point on the direction of the firm changed. We had to be a commercial firm which embraced technology and modern administrative principles. That necessitated certain innovations which are a necessary precursor to any successful law firm self-destructing.
These include:

- taking one of the firm's most successful fee earners and turning him into a quasi office manager;
- expanding the accounting section to ensure there are more bookkeepers than fee earners;
- upgrading the premises and keeping a vast vacant area for future expansion;
- replacing one competent typist per operator with two personal assistants and access to a word-processing pool;
- devoting much time and energy to the development of a new logo and letterhead;
- sponsoring a marquee at the races and a box at the football and filling that marquee and box with relatives and friends;
- having many lunches and meetings with firms with similar cash flow and structural problems in anticipation of a merger which never takes place;
- funding the firm by borrowing against optimistic work-in-progress estimates and debtors which are uncollectable;

- paying drawings to partners based on the expectations and needs of their spouses rather than the profit generated by the firm. I have never yet met a partner's spouse who did not consider that they were not deserving of the latest Mercedes and that their children shouldn't attend the best private schools;
- calculating work-in-progress and debtors on a time-costing system based on the profit required rather than a client's ability or desire to pay relative to the dispute in hand;
- opening an office in Sydney so the firm has an office in Sydney;
- developing a relationship with a client such that the firm needs the client more than the client needs the firm; and
- continuing in business when there is more money going out than coming in.

The answer to all of these problems is called 'diversification'. This assumes that if a firm is unsuccessful in a field in which it has experience and expertise it will be successful in a field where it has no experience or expertise. Our solution was to develop a litigation-support system.

The infamous Mr Barraket referred a client to me who had been charged with a white-collar crime and who was to be subjected to a long, complicated and expensive trial. Bill Coady was convinced that, given enough resources, he could develop a litigation-support system. It would utilise computer technology to co-ordinate complex documentation and facilitate those documents being presented as evidence in the trial. The system was developed and this was the first trial in Australia where computer technology was used to this extent. Our client was acquitted. Bill proposed that we should set up our own litigation-support company to exploit the expertise he had acquired and I agreed.

The move to a commercially based firm was prompted to some extent by our experience in a case involving custody of children. We were acting for a Jewish mother and the father was a Rabbi. At first instance the wife was successful. The case was reversed on appeal. It became quite a celebrated case because one of the reasons for the success of the appeal was that insufficient weight had allegedly been given to the impact of Jewish culture and religious law.

A sad consequence was that the children were shunted from one parent to another. This caused considerable trauma in the office and one of our female solicitors was distraught. I advised her that she was a professional lawyer, not a social worker, and suggested she find another occupation. She did the right thing and took a position at the Law Institute advising lawyers how to conduct their professional activities. Our client refused to pay the bill and threatened to sue for negligence. From that point on the firm rarely handled family-law cases. That also received my total support.

The reality that we were losing money on a weekly basis had not impacted. In the mid-eighties banks were more than happy to advance whatever funds were necessary to meet a particular lifestyle. It was also masked by optimistic estimates of work-in-progress. When the overdraft went up this was rationalised by the false assumption that work-in-progress or debtors must also have increased. In reality it is probably more indicative of an increase in creditors. Nor was it of any real concern that the changes we were making were not client based.

Nevertheless our friendship was still strong. On short notice I was told that I had to accompany Bill to a fund-raising function for a then Labor member of parliament, Bob Miller. I accompanied Bill to the function only to find that everyone else in the room was accompanied by their spouse. Bill's invitation was addressed 'Bill Coady and Partner'.

From then on it became like a bad marriage. Bad marriages aren't like football matches or title fights which have a quick and clean ending. They are dragged out over two or three years. Whilst it is correct that love has something to do with a successful marriage and mutual respect has something to do with a successful business partnership, both those relationships are underpinned by an ability to pay the bills as and when they fall due. This was not happening.

The final act commenced when I was having lunch with a friend who told me he had just organised the insurance for 'Bill's litigation-support company'. I was neither a director of, nor a shareholder in, the company. Soon after, on returning from a trip to Sydney, I was informed that the partners had held a partnership meeting in my absence. They had decided that the personal assistant I then shared with Bill and my personal secretary who did all my typing were to be allocated to other duties. I was to be given access to the word-processing pool. I should upgrade my computer skills (I had none) and use time costing like everybody else.

When the firm dissolved six months later both the personal assistant and the secretary went with me. So too did one of the principal securities for the overdraft of the firm, my house. On Christmas Eve, 1988, I was told that I could not take my desk, chair and an old lounge suite which were of no value and which I had used for fifteen years. Suffice it to say they went with me.

My small team of Annie the secretary, Gabrielle the personal assistant and Rodney the solicitor launched into the new firm, Dwyer & Co. in January 1989 with enthusiasm. We had boxes everywhere and shared premises with another solicitor located a hundred metres from our former offices. The firm focused on entertainment, taxation and superannuation, all areas in which we had some claim to expertise. The main centres of influence and client base supported us. So did the receptionist at the old firm. Suddenly income exceeded outgoings and life was good again.

The realities of life began to dawn on the former partners of Coady Dwyer & Associates now trading as Coadys. The goodwill of the firm which we all liked to think was of considerable value was worth nothing. The work-in-progress which supported the overdraft was also of minimal value. Indeed, because of the tendency for lawyers to get pre-payments for costs and the ongoing servicing obligations, work-in-progress is more a liability than an asset. Most debtors beyond ninety days at the dissolution date were never recovered.

With this background and because of some lingering bitterness which I never quite understood, my former partners issued proceedings against me in the County Court. The hearing occupied December 1989. By then I had moved on and relied on my barrister, Dr Robert Dean. Two days before the trial was due to commence he decided to extend his overseas holiday. I ended up at the last moment with a barrister who had no understanding of the case or enthusiasm for the fight. Dr Dean is the same person who, as Shadow Victorian Treasurer in November 2002, forgot to register to vote in the electorate in which he was the sitting member which meant that he became the not-so-sitting member. This caused the Liberals much embarrassment in the middle of an election campaign.

For no good reason, I failed to attend the first day of the hearing and appeared under threat of arrest. I spent the next two weeks writing out Christmas cards in the back of the court. I subsequently learnt that the judge in the case had recently experienced a personal tragedy involving his son (a barrister) and I still regret the way I conducted myself during that trial.

Their barrister showed his expertise by cross-examining me over a long period of time in relation to my Diners Club expenditure. The point of all this was to establish to the court that I had spent the six months prior to the break-up entertaining clients with a view to setting up my own firm. Of course, I had. What amazed me was his assumption that the only lunches I had were those which were paid for by me. I would say for every meal I paid for there were probably another three where a client paid. At one time I was asked in cross-examination what I proposed to do when I made my decision to leave Coady Dwyer & Associates. My response was that I had thought seriously about getting out of the law and going to the bar. Despite my best efforts, the decision in the case was a very fair and favourable one which allowed me to move forward.

Dwyer & Co. progressed and managed to secure a niche for itself in relation to the targeted areas, namely, entertainment and superannuation. Taxation dropped by the wayside. It is an area which is probably best left to the larger firms with the necessary resources. In reality I became bored with it. The firm uses technology, but it is used as a tool of trade, not a reason for being. I still nurture and maintain my 'A' class centres of influence. No time costing is used in the firm. Work-in-progress is not a factor in that it is billed regularly and most debtors outstanding beyond ninety days are written off.

The main administrative tool is the overdraft. If it goes up there has been less coming in than going out and this needs to be rectified immediately. If it goes down, provided all creditors including counsel fees are paid within thirty days, something right must be happening. There is no firm logo. Other than Friday night drinks, there have been no meetings of the firm since its inception. Hopefully the services provided add value to the client and as long as this continues, the firm will prosper.

Clients often forget that solicitors and some barristers are people too. They have their good and bad days. I once had lunch with a solicitor who drank a bottle of red wine. I said I wouldn't be able to work after that. He said he couldn't work without it. Most solicitors would work for nothing. They are invariably poor businesspeople. They all work on the false assumption that they have personal goodwill which is of great value. The irony is that the more successful a solicitor is, the less is the value of that solicitor's goodwill because of the personal nature of it. Most lawyers have no superannuation and no concept of an exit strategy. They tend to expire rather than retire.

The previous comments relate to small firms. Lawyers in large firms are members of a bureaucracy and other than their scale of pay are very similar to career public servants. At the upper level these lawyers are more administrators and/or co-ordinators than lawyers. The person who fails the lawyer test is made managing partner. He or she will go on to be a politician or start up a dot com. The real lawyers have superannuation and all the insecurities that go with it. They have no personal goodwill. An upstairs downstairs mentality prevails in larger firms just as it does in public service departments. My experience is that this is driven more by downstairs than upstairs.

Trying to compare small and large firms is like comparing apples with oranges. The small firm is appropriate when a client wants personal attention from someone with specialist knowledge. A large firm can provide immediate access to large resources. The small firm should be used for a commando attack; the large for a landing in Europe on D-Day.

Over the years I have been involved in many negotiations and there are some general principles and techniques which might be helpful to young lawyers or managers.

The solicitor must know what the client is trying to achieve but be prepared to give a little along the way. One of the only things I remember from university was a story told by the then Dean, David Derham, at the first lecture I attended. It was about two boys who bought a chocolate frog. They were having difficulty breaking it in two. The wiser of the two broke the head off the frog and threw it away. They then divided what was left equally and remained friends for years after.

Whoever has the numbers will usually win. If a client doesn't have the numbers that situation is unlikely to be improved by a speech from the heart. I once accompanied a client to a meeting of shareholders in Bellingen, a small, seaside town in NSW. My client was a minority shareholder. My speech was truly magnificent. Within five minutes of completing it, the vote was taken. We lost. We spent the rest of the day fully suited sitting on the beach in Coffs Harbour waiting for a flight back to Melbourne.

It is wise to control the agenda. What is not on it is often more important than what is. Agenda items can become the subject of long and protracted negotiation whereas matters of consequence which are not on it are taken as a given or never raised. This is particularly the case when dealing with large firms. They all have lawyers who love to be chairpersons. They almost never look beyond the agenda or their checklist. As long as everything on the list is ticked they are happy. They have a tick fetish.

When I was in the Taxation Department we had a clocking-on system. If I was one minute late I would be clocked on in red rather than black ink. If I accumulated more than five red marks in a month I would receive a 'please explain'. I was at the point when I was on my fourth 'please explain'. My friend, who arrived an hour late and clocked on in red every day, never received a query! In desperation I asked his secret. He explained in confidence that he had worked in the staffroom where it was his job to collate the red marks. He did this by collecting all the cards every Thursday and separating them into two piles – cards with red marks and cards with no red marks. He would throw the cards with only black marks in the bin and dutifully record those with red marks. Since leaving the staffroom he had simply continued the practice of removing his card every Thursday and throwing it in the bin. Two months later I received a letter of commendation from the staffroom.

Beware of the hidden agenda. I once acted for the cast in a high-rating comedy television show. I was advised by a client in the advertising business that because of the show's ratings, if they negotiated as one, they could move the show from one channel to another and improve their deal substantially. He would provide the introduction. After several meetings with the cast it was agreed that this should be done. On going back to my advertising person with the good news, I was told that this might breach the 'KOG' (keep off the grass) understanding between the major broadcasters. Rather than leave the clients with nowhere to go I executed a discreet yet still humbling retreat.

Remember that most lawyers are poor communicators. One of my solicitors once settled a very complicated conveyance in Ballarat involving 'old law' title. We all celebrated. Five days later the client rang. He was still sitting in rented accommodation surrounded by boxes. No one had told him it had settled. Never assume that silence is evidence of some cunning strategy. It usually means the file is lost.

Of course clients are not always great communicators either. I took instructions on a weekend from a policeman. His marriage was over and he wanted a divorce as a matter of absolute urgency. I heard later via another source that the warring couple had been reconciled. When I was next contacted by the client, twelve months later, I gave him the good news. His divorce had come through.

Clients can also be unreasonable in their expectations. I was instructed by a client at 5.00pm on a Friday to prepare recording and publishing contracts. I explained that my wife was pregnant, I was going into hospital the next day and my dog was dying but said I would have them done next week. He called Monday morning to collect them.

It is a good technique not to take any notes in a meeting. This makes people relax. There should be five or six key words remembered and detailed notes dictated or prepared soon after the meeting ends. Certainly carrying a tape recording or a video camera into a meeting should be avoided. It is always good to get cards from the various participants.

If arranging a meeting for a client who has no real case or does not have the numbers, it is preferable to have that meeting in the office of the opposition. This is because it is very difficult to walk out of your own office. On the other hand, arranging meetings interstate or in another country always puts you at a disadvantage and should be avoided if possible.

Where a party is spending someone else's money, ego, timing or convenience might prevail. I was once going through the humiliating exercise of trying to get a small advance from the ABC for one of Australia's most talented authors. In frustration, I told the secretary to remove the just-delivered cups of decaf and said the meeting was over. That was the turning point.

Entertainers, by their very nature, are susceptible to the views of the next person who happens to walk up to them in a bar and make complimentary remarks and wild promises. They will also often judge a lawyer on the outcome rather than the lawyer's contribution to that outcome. This is understandable when looked at from the perspective of the client. There are clients who are impossible to satisfy and it is necessary to identify them at the outset and refer them to the opposition.

I have often struggled with the 'corporates'. I had the misfortune to travel to the Grand Prix in Adelaide in a Lear Jet chartered by a 'would be' mogul. He had made a temporary fortune in a company which made compact discs. On arrival in Adelaide he accused a porter of stealing his wallet. It was in the mogul's pocket. He then 'collapsed' onto a large rock. On the return flight to Melbourne he, his accountant and corporate lawyer started throwing beer at each other. The floor was awash. When I said what I thought of them, the lawyer, a partner from a large firm in Melbourne, suggested that I should learn to relax and 'when in Rome do as the Romans do'. I reminded him that we had been to Adelaide and that he was a member of a profession. He cleaned the floor.

Never let a client's problems become your problems. This can occur by letting a case go too long before it is billed. It might also arise if promises to fund a film or project are made without any firm commitment from a financier. Next thing you will find yourself funding pre-production of a film on your Diners Club card. Whatever you do you will not get any thanks for it.

No one is ever quite as important as they think they are. I thought I had some influence in Melbourne. The Victorian government commissioned the painting of several Melbourne trams. One was painted by Mental as Anything. It featured many of the Mambo designs and was very popular with Melburnians. After a few years the responsible Minister decided it would be good to over-paint the tram with a series of paintings depicting the achievements of Labor Women. It was a very small tram. I was approached by Jeremy Fabinyi, who managed the group, to stop this vandalism. The Mentals were prepared to come to Melbourne free of charge to 'touch up' the tram. I had a meeting with the Minister at 3.00 o'clock on a Friday afternoon. The meeting went well. By 9.00am the next Monday the tram had been sandblasted back to the metal.

Never take yourself too seriously. I once left a high-powered and successful meeting at 6:30 pm and drove to Olympic Park to see one of my kids compete. I parked and walked across the bridge over the river. It was a hot summer evening and there were several people using the BBQs along the river. Halfway across the bridge I rested my foot on the iron railing to tie my shoelace. As I adjusted my foot the shoe dislodged and fell into the river with a loud splash. People thought I was committing suicide bit by bit. As I walked back to my car wearing only one shoe, the revellers gave me a wide berth. I left before the police arrived.

When dealing with public servants remember they are omnipotent. They exercise discretionary power. They can accept or reject a proposal or simply lose the file. This can make life for your client impossible. A little humility and courtesy will go a long way. One of my kids managed to get me blackballed by the all-powerful probate office for a month because of his failure to recognise this reality.

Never assume that lawyers know what they are talking about. A venerable colleague of mine of Greek extraction once stated that he had a friend who spent seven years in Changi Prisoner of War Camp in Singapore during the Second World War. Orm Thomas, who knows his history, remarked, 'he must have liked it so much that he decided to stay on a while'.

When dealing with older lawyers try to understand that they have different priorities. If you lose a case that costs the firm $100,000 they will soon get over it. If you leave the lights on overnight, get a parking fine, leave an empty cup on your desk, send a letter by mail rather than DX or catch a taxi rather than a tram, your future is at risk. The same Orm Thomas asked a junior solicitor to research the law of genetics. A learned opinion duly arrived. When asked for the source of some data there came the reply: *A Current Affair*. A second opinion was commissioned from Naomi Robson.

Never ask for a wage rise on a Friday afternoon or fix a figure. You may be told the firm can't afford you. I once said that to an employee solicitor. He said he was prepared to negotiate. I pointed out a Mercedes Benz which I would love to own but couldn't afford either. I agreed that he was worth what he wanted but had to let him go because I wasn't in the exploitation-of-labour business.

Things always come in runs. If you win a case you will probably get a letter from the Tax Department enclosing a reimbursement of overpaid tax. If you lose a case you can expect a letter of complaint from the Ombudsman and the bank will return your wages cheques. Because of this it is important to stay in the game. That can be done by not opening the letter from the bank. Three weeks later when you pluck up enough courage to open it you could find it is an invitation to lunch.

Avoid the media. Any media appearance requires absolute trust in the editor and producer. It is usually misplaced. During the PSA enquiry I did an interview. I was left alone in a studio in Melbourne with a faulty earpiece being interviewed live by someone in Canberra and making a total fool of myself. During a recent inquest into the death of a child I advised the mother not to react to the press. On leaving the court we were set upon by cameras and thrusting microphones. A camera man knocked over a woman with a baby in a pram who just happened to be passing by. In the chaos a rugby scrum developed around the client and her solicitor, one of my daughters, neither of whom reacted. The entire episode was edited down to me reacting to the press. That is exactly what they wanted.

Finally, it takes time to develop the necessary skills as a lawyer to be of value to a client and to obtain the satisfaction and rewards that go with it. Sadly no one will become wealthy practising law. It contravenes the two fundamentals of wealth creation. Firstly, money cannot be made selling time. Secondly, anyone who knows what they are earning is not earning enough. My advice to young lawyers who want to be wealthy is to drive a truck.

CHAPTER 15 – NOTHING CHANGES

The technological advances at the start of the twentieth century allowed performers to transcend time and space. No longer were their performances ephemeral by nature. They could be recorded, retained and reproduced. They could be commercially exploited and marketed globally. Copyright facilitated the growth of international markets. The development of collection societies allowed the participants in the process to be rewarded for their efforts. This all came together in what is generally referred to as the 'music industry'. Whilst Australia was an important market for music it was neither a source of creative material nor part of the capital infrastructure of the industry. That was based in North America and Europe.

There was an increasing market for recorded music in the years before and after the Second World War, the swing era. This was followed by a tidal wave of American product in the fifties with the reincarnation of rhythm and blues as rock 'n' roll. The English charge in the sixties and early seventies was led by The Beatles. Still, Australia was not part of it.

It was not until the seventies that Australians started to buy music composed and recorded by Australians based in Australia. This occurred because the songs and the artists were Australian in character. There was never any ambivalence about Skyhooks, Sherbert, Australian Crawl, Cold Chisel, The Angels, Flowers/Icehouse, Midnight Oil, The Dingoes, Goanna Band or Men at Work. Australia was the source of their inspiration. It was also an important market. These groups found an Australian audience for their music.

The Australian contemporary music industry had ten great years and started to mark time. To some extent this reflects the nature of contemporary music. It is by definition, a part of the fashion industry. In the mid-eighties Australians tried to compete directly in what were foreign markets in every sense of the word. It's hard for Australians to compete with urban American rap – black or white. Why try? Australia did produce Jason and Kylie. At that time they were more to do with TV merchandising than contemporary music.

Australian artists began to treat their home market with contempt. It is true that artists such as Little River Band specifically targeted foreign markets. However, they always respected and worked their home market. Indeed, the irony is that Men at Work who had the greatest success internationally of any Australian-based group, created product which was essentially and unapologetically Australian in character. The same could be said about our most successful movie. Both Men at Work and *Crocodile Dundee* exploited the unique humour which characterises Australians. The main reason for the decline in the mid-eighties was the deliberate attempt by many record companies to emasculate, sanitise and deodorise the Australian character. Ask Peter Andre. It is no surprise that those who rejected this trend - Paul Kelly, John Farnham, Neil Finn (an Honorary Australian) and Midnight Oil - continued to have success in their home market.

There were other reasons for the gradual decline. Perhaps this is where I start to reveal my age. I talk about the good old days when Paul O'Gorman had hair and Graham Goble was old. With the focus on image and marketing it is easy to forget that one of the basic ingredients of the music industry is a performance. For a performer to be successful it is necessary for that person to connect with the audience. Renée Geyer called this 'channelling'.[1] A cover band might entertain an audience but they do not connect with it. Successful Australian groups all connected with their audience, both musically and personally, in a professional sense. They achieved that rapport by years of touring and performing.

Since the mid-eighties there have been very few Australian performers who can connect with an Australian, let alone an American, audience. Kylie comes close but she has been around a long time and has worked hard to build her audience. In the late seventies the environment existed for a group to develop an audience. There were venues where they could perform their own songs not interrupted by the seductive flow of five-cent pieces into plastic cups. There was also a receptive audience. Today the young audience has to be coerced away from a computer game.

Even in Melbourne there are very few venues left. Indeed, there is a concerted effort by inner city 'yuppies' to kill off those that remain.

Perhaps it is too easy and unhelpful to blame the venues and the audience. A good act will always find an audience and a venue. In the seventies there were people who nurtured and guided artists over the long-term. They were easily identified. Glenn Wheatley and his two kookaburras, Michael Gudinski and the Mushroom mafia, the touch of the old-world Fabinyi brothers, the New Zealand All Blacks led by the Thomas brothers, the 'work 'em till they're dead set', founded by John Blanchfield & Co., the Mt Eliza School Prefects featuring the Reyne brothers, the 'down and dirty ten-to-a-room in The Diplomat crowd' starring Woodruff, Hearn and Willis. Every artist could find a home of sorts and there was a genuine commitment to find an audience somewhere. By the mid-eighties most of these people had expended their enthusiasm and energy on successful acts. They had entered the comfort zone.

The 'pay for play' scandal in the early eighties didn't help. Not only did it corrupt the market, but cynicism replaced idealism. I was signing an artist to Mushroom at that time. I felt obliged to let the Business Affairs Manager, Simon Young, know the artist couldn't sing. He said, 'Does it matter?'. Groups like TISM, who reeked of hypocrisy, became popular. The performer, the performance and ultimately the audience were held in contempt.

Technology also played a part in the decline. Its upside has been the reduction in the cost of recording, better quality sound and infinitely more efficient methods of communication, promotion and distribution. The downside was that some of Australia's best studios were unable to fund the cost of keeping up with technological changes and disappeared. Then there have been the changes from vinyl to tape to compact disc and DVD. The record companies have used these changes to breathe life into moribund back catalogues at the cost of new material. This is the reason we have to endure The Rolling Stones, who have not had a creative idea for twenty years. They are the manifestation of the corporate establishment. How can there be a credible contemporary music industry which is Jurassic in its origins? Cliff Richard must be due for another tour. No wonder the kids are turning to video games.

The irony is that technology has created an environment where many more artists should have an opportunity to participate in the industry. They can record product for a fraction of the cost of twenty years ago. Artists are no longer totally dependent upon risk capital or distribution being provided by a major record company. The digital world allows information to be disseminated without territorial restraint. The market is global and accessible. It is also subject to minimal legal constraints. The challenge facing the industry is to ensure that the copyright licensing and collection regimes properly reward the providers of capital and creative input.

The same commercial principles still apply. For every return there is a risk. Artists have to make choices. In an industry where time is truly of the essence, when opportunities present they must be taken. People still want to be entertained. Markets have to be identified and targeted. There is merit in exploiting a foreign market. However, there is no shortage of Americans singing American songs. Furthermore, they do it very well. Keith Urban has done it better. He probably decided that the Australian 'country' audience is not worth the effort. It was smart for Tina Arena to record and release songs in France in the French language. But how many of those records sold in Australia and what happened to her Australian audience in the process?

John Farnham has proved it is possible to do very well in the Australian market. That is not an implicit criticism of Savage Garden. All it says is that any Australian who ignores their home market is indeed a high-stakes gambler. Australia has been a successful source of Australian songs and performers. The decline which started in the mid-eighties is a trend which can be reversed. For this to happen, songs and performers need to connect primarily with Australians. That is the key to success, not failure, in foreign markets.

The music industry could be contrasted with the film industry and the hundreds of millions of dollars which have been squandered in taxation subsidies. In the seventies it was still producing films set in the Australian Outback and starring Kamahl as an Aboriginal tracker. Since then there have been some commercial successes including *Crocodile Dundee* and *The Man from Snowy River* but the cost far outweighs any gains, culturally or commercially.

Commercial theatre has never been subsidised. There have been some brave attempts to create new product: *Manning Clark's History of Australia – The Musical*, *Bad Boy Johnny and the Prophets of Doom* and *Rasputin* fit into the 'Gallipoli' (glorious failure) category. In an international context these productions have always been on the margins of amateur theatre – the money simply hasn't been there. Nor, for that matter, has there been an audience – Australian or international. Whilst all this has been going on, opera and ballet have maintained their subsidised existence with the luxury of not having to care about an audience. In the process the art form, at least in Melbourne, is in need of urgent palliative care.

Australian comedy was pretty well still-born. Max Gillies, Rod Quantock and the people from 'Australia You're Standing In It', 'the D-Generation', 'Fast Forward', 'The Comedy Company' and Working Dog gave it a go. Comedy is like carving a masterpiece out of ice. It is geographic and immediate. It has no shelf life. This is the reason comedians are all so insecure. Australian comedy reached a low point when Steve Vizard decided it was easier simply to replicate American comedy in its totality. That is why he is now an adviser to the Victorian Government.

Then we have the Australian book publishing industry – or do we? There have been a handful of people who have tried to source and develop Australian product. Limiting myself to those with whom I have been involved, names such as O'Neil, Currey, Gribble, McPhee, Timlin, O'Donovan, Donovan, Hyde, Burgess and Gilder come to mind. Inevitably by the mid-eighties all roads led to Penguin and I don't mean Phillip Island. We have to find a new road.

My long battle with the Sydney establishment is all but lost. I was never going to outmanoeuvre APRA's General Licence and his foot soldiers. The corporate infrastructure of the industry is firmly fixed in Sydney. Everywhere else is an outpost. Melbourne is still hanging in there but only just. Melbourne won the consolation prize, Pete Steedman. Adelaide has surrendered. What can you say about a city where people write to the paper begging John Farnham not to make it his last tour? King Billy Coke Bottle is a headline act there. Perth and Brisbane were never contenders.

As has been said, an image can take on a life of its own. Cameron Mackintosh perfected this in *Cats*. TISM tried to turn the parody into reality.

That image can also date quickly. Fame is indeed a fickle thing. The saddest thing in the entertainment business is to see a former 'star' loitering around his or her manager's office when the manager is interviewing his new act. It is true that sometimes the imagery matches the reality. But always there is a living, breathing person hidden away somewhere. Lawyers in particular need to remember that.

Despite the desire of some record company executives to live in a musician-free environment, the industry is still a people business. By definition it is a young people's business. It is time some of the older brigade hung up their hats. That is not directed at Molly although the sentiment is probably applicable. Although no one does more behind the scenes for people in the industry than Molly's close relative Ian.

Things can't be all that bad. As of April 2003, Patrick Donovan in *The Age* was writing enthusiastically about the 'rock revival'.[1] I wonder if he was referring to John Farnham's 'It Might Be The Last Time I Don't Know Tour'? Probably not but I enjoyed it even though a concert like that can be a little depressing. I acted for most of those people when they were young. I looked at the people attending John's 'last' concert and convinced myself that I still have marginally more friends than enemies in the industry.

Taking instructions from young musicians today is no different than it was thirty years ago. With a bit of luck and timing they have just as much chance of succeeding as Men at Work. Hopefully, today, the infrastructure and experience is there to make the enjoyment of the spoils of their talent and toil a little less acrimonious.

For me nothing much has changed. I don't take a cut lunch or go by train to work anymore. In fact it's no longer 'work'. It is now 'the office'. I still deal with people. To me, dealing with Anthony Warlow or Glenn Wheatley is no different from dealing with a customer at the Taxation Department enquiries counter. They are all people with aspirations and stories to tell. I still enjoy what I do. For anyone who spent years assessing tax returns, practising law is a fun-filled experience.

And what happened to Pat Daly? Did he impale himself on his rusting ice pick? No! He realised that there are ways of making a living other than carting blocks of ice. He became a financial planner. He now delivers wealth-creation solutions to empty nesters!

ADDENDUM

1. PARTNERSHIP AGREEMENT

The partners agree to be partners in accordance with the provisions contained in the conditions of partnership.

Partners:	Name	of
	Name	of
	Name	of

Partnership Business:
[Clause 1]
Conducting the usual activities of a group of artists in the contemporary music industry including but not limited to performing, touring, recording, songwriting and merchandising.

Date of Commencement:
[Clause 2]

Professional Name:
[Clause 3]

Place of Business:
[Clause 4]

Exclusive Jurisdiction: State of
[Clause 24]

DATED the day of , 200 .

Conditions of partnership

Partnership Business

1. The partnership business shall be as specified above unless otherwise agreed by the partners in writing.

Commencement

2. The date of commencement of the partnership is as specified above and the partnership shall continue until dissolved in accordance with the terms of this agreement.

Professional Name

3. The partners shall carry on the partnership business under the professional name as specified above or any other name which the partners may agree upon.

Place of Business

4. The partners shall carry on the partnership business at the place of business as specified above or any other place which the partners may agree upon.

Bank Account

5.1 The partnership shall maintain a bank account at such bank as the partners may agree upon.

5.2 Any partnership bank account shall only be used in the ordinary course of business. Cheques drawn on any partnership bank account shall require the signature of at least two partners unless otherwise resolved by the partners and subject to clause 6.

Manager

6. If the partners have appointed a professional manager that manager is authorised to be a co-signatory for banking purposes in which case cheques will only require the signature of one partner and the manager.

Capital

7. The capital of the partnership shall be contributed by the partners equally.

Loans by Partners

8. If any partner advances money to the partnership, brings any assets into the partnership in excess of that partner's due contribution to capital or leaves any undrawn profits with the partnership, that money, or an amount equal to the agreed value of that asset, or the amount of those un-drawn profits, shall be deemed to be a loan by that partner to the partnership. Interest on any such loan shall be calculated monthly and shall accrue at the rate of 6% per annum on the monthly balance. The principal and interest shall be payable on ninety (90) days written notice from the partners.

Profits

9. The profits of the business shall be shared equally between the partners.

Losses

10. All expenses and losses incurred in carrying on the business (including losses of capital) shall be borne by the partners equally.

Drawings

11. Each partner may during the continuance of the partnership, be paid out of the partnership bank accounts such amounts as may from time to time be agreed upon on account of that partner's share of profits. However if it appears that a partner has been paid any sum in excess of that partner's share of profits, then that partner shall repay the excess to the partnership bank account immediately if the partners so resolve.

Partners' Salaries

12. Each partner shall be entitled to be paid a salary as and if fixed by a resolution of the partners. Any payment so fixed shall be treated as an expense before net profits are ascertained.

Books of Account

13. Appropriate books of account shall be kept in a proper manner and shall not be removed from their usual place without the consent of the partners. Each partner shall have free access to the books of account at all times and may, either personally or by an agent, make extracts from or copy them.

Annual Accounts

14. On 30 June each year or as soon after as is practicable, a balance sheet and profit and loss account making due allowance for depreciation and appropriate reserves and for recouping any lost capital, shall be prepared. Copies shall be furnished to all partners who shall be bound by them unless some manifest error is discovered in which case the error shall be rectified.

Partners' Duties

15. Each partner shall:

15.1 Devote such time and attention to the partnership business as the partners from time to time resolve and otherwise as is reasonably required in the circumstances and shall diligently and faithfully use his or her best endeavours for the benefit of the partnership;

15.2 Forthwith pay all moneys, cheques and negotiable instruments received by him or her on account of the partnership into the partnership bank account;

15.3 Be just and faithful to the other partners and at all times give them full disclosure and truthful explanations of all matters relating to the affairs of the partnership and afford the other partners every assistance in carrying on the business for their mutual advantage;

15.4 At all times conduct himself or herself in a professional manner such as to enhance the professional standing and reputation of the partners and to ensure the partners carry out their contractual obligations in a professional manner.

Restrictions

16. A partner shall not without the prior written consent of the other partners:

16.1 Use any money or assets of the partnership, or pledge the credit of the partnership, except in the ordinary course of business and for the benefit of the partnership and when authorised by the partners to do so;

16.2 Lend any money or other assets of the partnership;

16.3 Give any security or promise for the payment of money on account of the partnership except in the ordinary course of business;

16.4 Do, or permit to be done, anything which may put partnership property at risk;

16.5 Assign, mortgage or charge his or her share in the assets or profits of the partnership;

16.6 Draw, accept or endorse any cheque or negotiable instrument on account of the partnership except in the ordinary course of the partnership business; or

16.7 Directly or indirectly engage or have an interest in any business which is in competition with the partnership business without disclosing that involvement or interest to the other partners and obtaining their consent.

Defaulting Partner

17. If a partner ('the defaulting partner'):

17.1 Commits a breach of any of the provisions contained in clauses 15 and 16; or

17.2 Becomes bankrupt, enters into any form of administration or any other arrangement with his or her creditors; or

17.3 Has his or her share or interest in the partnership taken in execution under any legal process; or

17.4 Does anything which would be a ground for the dissolution of the partnership; or

17.5 Does anything which brings the partners or the partnership business into disrepute.

Then the other partners ('the continuing partners') within one month after becoming aware of the default may by notice in writing to the defaulting partner dissolve the partnership. In this event the other partners shall have the option to be exercised when giving the notice, of purchasing the defaulting partner's share in the partnership upon the same terms as are set out in clause 19 in relation to the purchase of the share of a retiring partner.

Option to Purchase Where A Partner Dies

18.1 If a partner dies the other partners ('the continuing partners') may, by notice in writing to the legal representative of the deceased partner, opt to carry on the partnership and the partnership business. Notice must be given within sixty (60) days of the date of death. If such notice is given the continuing partners shall pay to the estate of the deceased partner an amount equal to the deceased partner's share of the partnership as at the date of death. Goodwill and the irrevocable right to acquire the name, domain name and any trademarks used by the partnership, is agreed to be valued at 'Nil'. The amount payable shall be fixed by a valuation made by a qualified valuer agreed upon by the parties or, failing agreement within thirty (30) days of the giving of notice by the continuing partners, then by a valuer as appointed by the solicitor for the partnership.

18.2 The deceased partner's estate will be entitled to all additional entitlements (if any) that would apply if the deceased partner was a leaving member.

18.3 The valuer's fees shall be paid equally by the estate of the deceased partner on the one hand and the continuing partners on the other; and

18.4 The purchase money shall be paid within ninety (90) days of the valuation being finalised unless otherwise agreed by the parties.

Option to Purchase Where A Partner Retires

19.1 A partner can retire from the partnership by ninety (90) days written notice. On receipt of that notice the continuing partners ('the continuing partners') may, by ninety (90) days notice in writing to the retiring partner, opt to carry on the partnership and the partnership business. Such notice must be given within thirty (30) days of the effective date of the retirement. If such notice is given the continuing partners shall pay to the retiring partner an amount equal to the retiring partner's share of the partnership as at the date of retirement. Goodwill and the irrevocable right to acquire the name, domain name and any trademarks used by the partnership is agreed to be valued at 'Nil'. The amount payable shall be fixed by a valuation made by a qualified valuer agreed upon by the parties or, failing agreement within thirty (30) days of the giving of the notice by the continuing partners, then by a valuer as appointed by the solicitor for the partnership.

19.2 The retiring partner will be entitled to any and all additional entitlements (if any) that would apply if the retiring partner was a leaving member.

19.3 The valuer's fees shall be paid equally by the retiring partner on the one hand and the continuing partners on the other; and

19.4 The purchase money shall be paid within ninety (90) days of the valuation being finalised unless otherwise agreed between the parties.

Winding-up

20. The partnership shall continue until dissolved at any time by a resolution of more than 50% of the partners at a partnership meeting. On dissolution of the partnership the assets and the property of the partnership shall be realized and sold and the debts due to the partnership collected. The proceeds shall be applied first in discharge of the liabilities of the partnership and the expenses of realization and winding-up and secondly in payment to each partner of any money due or owing to him or her. They will then be applied in payment of any unpaid profits and finally in payment of the partners' shares of capital. Any residual surplus or deficit will be apportioned on the same basis that profits are shared in clause 9.

Service of Notices

21. Any notice given pursuant to this agreement may be given by or to a partner or by or to the solicitor for that partner and may be served personally or sent by certified mail, facsimile or email.

First Meeting

22. The partners agree to attend a first meeting of the partnership which will be held within seven days of signing this agreement. The Minutes of that meeting provided they are signed by all parties will be binding as if they were a clause of this agreement. If there is any misunderstanding the Minutes are to prevail. Copies of the Minutes are to be circulated within seven (7) days of the meeting.

Subsequent Meetings

23. Any resolutions taken at a meeting shall be passed by more than 50% of the partners at the meeting. A quorum of two partners is required. Seven (7) days written notice of meetings is necessary. Copies of Minutes are to be circulated to all partners within seven (7) days of the meeting.

Jurisdiction

24. The partnership is governed by the laws, and is subject to the exclusive jurisdiction of the Courts, of the State as specified above.

Signed by the partners

....date ....

....date ....

....date ....

2. MINUTES OF MEETING

The meeting took place at:

____

It commenced at: _._am/pm

on the ____ day of __________________200 .

It ended at: _._am/pm

on the ____ day of __________________200 .

The following people attended: [*insert*]

These resolutions were discussed and passed unanimously:

1. The formation of the group:
   A group has been formed to perform professionally and to conduct other related activities in the contemporary music industry.

2. The members of the group:
   The members of that group and their functions are as follows:

Name	Address	Function

3. <u>The group name</u>:

The name of the group is to be [*insert*]. Lawyers are to be instructed to carry out a search of that name. If it is not available for registration as a Business Name in Victoria or Domain Name, a new name is to be agreed upon. If the name is available it is to be registered as a Business Name, a Domain Name and, if possible, as a trademark. The Business Name, Domain Name and trademark are to be registered in the names of all members of the group.

4. <u>The group structure</u>:

The group is a partnership made up of the members of the group. It is regulated by a Partnership Agreement which is to be read as if it incorporates these Minutes and to which a copy of these Minutes is to be attached.

5. <u>Division of income Assets and Liabilities</u>:

All net income from the professional activities of the group including recording, performing, touring and merchandising but excluding songwriting is to be divided equally between the members of the group. 'Net income' is gross income less all expenses necessarily incurred in gaining that gross income. Liabilities are also to be apportioned equally. Band equipment, vehicles and any other partnership assets are owned equally by the group. If any partnership asset is held in the name of one member of the group that member holds that asset on trust for all members of the group equally.

6. <u>Publishing income:</u>

Either:

[*This applies when non-writers do not share in publishing income.*]

All publishing income derived from the commercial exploitation of musical works (songs) composed by a member of the group is to accrue to the songwriter/publisher. Those songs are to be registered with APRA in the name or names of the songwriter or songwriters as agreed by them.

Or:
[*This applies when non-writers share in mechanical royalties from records recorded by the group.*]

Publishing income derived from the commercial exploitation of musical works (songs) composed by a member of the group and recorded by the group, is to accrue to the songwriter/publisher. However of this income 15% of mechanical royalties is to be shared equally between all members of the group including the songwriter. The 15% entitlement only applies to songs on records recorded by the group and does not apply to mechanical royalties paid in relation to records recorded by other artists (cover records). Any publishing advances are to be paid to the songwriter. The percentage of mechanical royalties payable to non-writers is not available for recoupment purposes. Wherever possible any negotiations with publishers are to take this into consideration. If this is not practicable then an appropriate portion of the advance is to be paid to the members of the group. All songs are to be registered with APRA in the name of the songwriter or songwriters as agreed by them.

Or:
[*This applies when non-writers share all publishing income.*]

Publishing income derived from the commercial exploitation of musical works (songs) composed by a member of the group and recorded by the group is to accrue to the songwriter/publisher. However, of this income 10% is to be divided equally between all members of the group, including the songwriter. Any publishing advances are to be paid to the songwriter. Wherever possible negotiations with publishers are to take into consideration that the publishing income paid to non-writers is not available for recoupment purposes. If this is not practicable then an appropriate portion of the advance is to be paid to the members of the group. All songs are to be registered with APRA in the name of the songwriter or songwriters as agreed by them.

7. <u>Leaving member</u>:

At any time a member can give ninety (90) days written notice (or less if agreed) of that member's intention to leave the group and the partnership. At the same time any member can be requested to leave the group and the partnership by ninety (90) days written notice provided the notice is signed by least two-thirds of the members of the group. At the end of the ninety (90) day period the leaving member will then leave the group.

The continuing members will be entitled to continue to conduct the professional activities of the group and the partnership. The leaving member will retain that member's entitlement to share in income from all recordings on which that member participated and/ or any tours carried out prior to the end of the ninety (90) day period.

If the leaving member has participated on more than one album featuring the group the member will also be entitled to a share of artist royalties on the next album released by the group based on that member's percentage share of the previous album and subject to the provisions of the applicable Recording Agreement. The leaving member will also retain the member's entitlement to publishing income as agreed in paragraph 6 in relation to songs on recordings on which the leaving member performed.

Where the group is bound by a Recording Agreement the continuing members will, if possible, obtain a release from the recording company in favour of the leaving member or indemnify that member in relation to all future liabilities arising under the Recording Agreement. The group's accountant will be instructed to reconcile royalty statements to ensure wherever possible that any future recording advances are not recouped against royalty income which accrues to the leaving member in relation to previous recordings. The accountant will also prepare a balance sheet showing the assets and liabilities of the group at the end of the ninety (90) day period.

Goodwill will be valued at 'Nil'. The continuing members shall have the right to acquire the name of the group and any associated company, business and domain names or trademarks for no consideration.

If there is a surplus of assets over liabilities the leaving member will be paid out that member's share of the surplus by the continuing members within ninety (90) days of finalising the accounts. On the other hand if there is a deficit the leaving member will pay his or her share of that deficit into the group's bank account within ninety (90) days of finalising the accounts.

8. Manager:

Either:

At the present time a Manager is not required. If and when that need is recognised, it will be the subject of further discussion.

Or:

Discussions are to be entered into immediately with a view to appointing [*insert*] as Manager of the group. No agreement is to be entered into or be effective until all members of the group unanimously agree with the appointment and its terms.

9. Creative decisions:

All decisions concerning the group's professional activities are to be by consensus and, if no consensus can be reached, by majority vote. This includes choice of songs to be recorded, singles to be released, promotional material, professional attire and image and all other matters relating to the professional activities of the group. If there is a deadlock and a manager has been appointed, the manager will have a casting vote. Otherwise the manager will not have a vote.

10. <u>Group goals</u>:
The group has been established to perform original material professionally in the contemporary music industry. The longer term goal is to enter into a recording agreement with a major record company with a view to having records released in major territories throughout the world.

11. <u>Consents</u>:
The members collectively and each of them individually acknowledge, consent and agree as follows:

11.1 To perform in recording sessions and videos as members of the group. When performing in recording sessions and videos they irrevocably consent to their performances being recorded and commercially exploited by the group and any record company to which the group is contracted.

11.2 That their likenesses and professional names can be used in artwork and promotional material featuring the group associated with packaging and promoting recordings, videos, tours, merchandising and the group generally.

11.3 To make themselves available for, and to participate in, tours and any other professional and promotional appearances and to conduct themselves at all times such as not to bring the group or its members into disrepute.

11.4 Not to engage in activities in the entertainment industry either as a solo performer or with other artists without the consent of the members of the group which consent will not be unreasonably withheld.

11.5 To sign whatever documents are required to give effect to this Agreement.

12. <u>Solicitors:</u>
The firm of [*insert*] is appointed as solicitors for the group.

13. <u>Accountants</u>:
The firm of [*insert*] is appointed as accountants for the group.

14. Bank:

A bank account is to be opened at the [*insert Bank*] in the name of the group. Cheques are to require the signature of any two members of the group. If, and when, a manager has been appointed, one of the two signatories is to be the manager. All income of the group is to be paid into that account and all outgoings are to be paid out of that account by cheque.

15. Meetings of the group:

It is intended that group meetings be held not less than monthly. If a manager has been appointed the manager will act as Chairperson and will be responsible for preparing Minutes and circulating those Minutes to all members of the group no later than seven (7) days after the meeting. Minutes of future meetings can be signed by the manager if one is appointed. If not then a Chairperson will be appointed at each meeting and that Chairperson is authorised to sign the Minutes. At each meeting a date will be set for the next meeting.

16. Incorporation:

The group may be restructured at some time in the future such that the activities of the group are conducted via a company or a trust. The members and each of them agree to sign whatever documents, assignments, consents or shareholders' agreements which are reasonably necessary to formalise any such restructuring provided that the basic rights and entitlements as set out in these Minutes and the Partnership Agreement are retained.

17. Next meeting:

The next meeting of the group is to be at the same place at 11.00am on the ______ day of ______________________ 200 .

Signed by all members of the group as a true record of the meeting.

....date ....

....date ....

....date ....

3. MANAGEMENT AGREEMENT

This Agreement is made the day of , 200 .

Between: of (the 'Manager')

AND of (the 'Artist')

Whereas:

A. The Manager is engaged in the business of providing management services in the entertainment industry.

B. The Artist wishes to appoint the Manager to be the Artist's exclusive Manager in the entertainment industry.

The Parties Agree as follows:

1. TERM

1.1 The Manager will, throughout the world, for an initial period of three years from the date of the Agreement, serve the Artist as the Artist's exclusive Manager in the entertainment industry (the 'professional activities'). The Manager has an option to extend the initial period for a further two (2) years (the 'option period'), such option to be exercised by written notice at any time prior to the expiration of the initial period (the initial period and the option period, if exercised, is referred to as 'the term').

1.2 The 'entertainment industry' includes but is not limited to, media, sound recording, film, personal appearances, television, radio, motion pictures, theatre, merchandising, endorsements, testimonials, commercials and concerts. It also includes all appearances and activities as a performer, entertainer, recording artist, actor, composer, lyricist and in any way connected with the entertainment industry.

1.3 In the event that the Artist has not been signed to a major record label within eighteen (18) months from the date of this Agreement, the Artist shall have the right to terminate this Agreement. That right is to be exercised by written notice no later than ninety (90) days from the expiry of the eighteen (18) month period.

For the purposes of this clause 'a major record label' means the following companies and their subsidiaries and affiliates:

EMI, BMG, WARNER MUSIC, SONY, UNIVERSAL MUSIC, FESTIVAL MUSHROOM RECORDS and any other company the parties may agree upon.

2. <u>Artist's Obligations</u>

2.1 Throughout the term the Artist shall:

(1) Advise the Manager of all offers of employment and refer any enquiries concerning the Artist's services to the Manager. The Artist will instruct all agents, theatrical agencies, accountants and/or lawyers who may from time to time act on the Artist's behalf to remit all monies owing to the Artist as a result of the professional activities to the Manager.

(2) Provide all necessary equipment as is required for properly undertaking any performance.

(3) Carry out to the best of the Artist's ability all agreements, engagements, rehearsals, performances and bookings negotiated, procured or arranged by the Manager <u>PROVIDED THAT</u> the Manager shall have informed the Artist in sufficient time to comply with this provision.

(4) Fully consult with the Manager before communicating with the press, radio, television or other media.

(5) Keep the Manager fully informed of the Artist's whereabouts and availability.

3. <u>Agent & Attorney</u>

The Artist irrevocably appoints the Manager the Artist's agent and attorney for the purpose of executing documents including contracts relating to the professional activities during the term.

4. Non-Exclusivity

The Artist acknowledges that the services of the Manager are not exclusive to the Artist and the Manager is at all times free to perform the same or similar services for other artists.

5. Accounting / Expenses

5.1 The Manager shall keep or cause to be kept, such books of account as are necessary and proper. The books of account shall be kept in the usual office or place where the business is carried out. They must be accessible at all reasonable times to the Artist or any person the Artist appoints for the purpose of audit, inspection, examination and copying.

5.2 The Manager shall forward to the Artist within sixty (60) days after the expiration of 31 March, 30 June, 30 September and 31 December in every year during the term, a statement of all receipts and expenses in respect of the quarter ending on that date. The Manager shall forward to the Artist all monies which are due to be distributed within fourteen (14) days of receipt by the Manager PROVIDED HOWEVER the Manager in the Manager's discretion can withhold paying the Artist an amount equal to reasonably anticipated agreed expenses becoming due.

5.3 From the monies received on behalf of the Artist the Manager shall be entitled to pay all reasonable expenses incurred by the Manager in the conduct of the professional activities. These include but are not limited to, interstate and international telephone calls and facsimile charges, publicity, advertising and promotional, accounting and legal, postage and courier, travel and accommodation expenses which relate directly to work being carried out on the Artist's behalf but excluding general office expenses. No single expense in excess of $1000 is to be incurred without the prior approval of the Artist.

6. Manager's Remuneration

6.1 By way of remuneration the Manager shall retain and/or be paid 20% of gross earnings. This entitlement shall apply to all gross earnings received throughout the world during the term. It does not apply in relation to income accruing from agreements entered into prior to the date of this Agreement unless specifically agreed by the parties. It will also apply for a period of two (2) years after the end of the term in relation to income derived by the Artist from records recorded and/or compositions written during the term which are subject to recording and publishing agreements or extensions thereof entered into during the term. The remuneration in those two years is to be as follows:

First year - 15% of gross earnings
Second year - 10% of gross earnings

In the second year the Manager shall be entitled to commission recording and publishing royalties which are in 'the pipeline'. This means income relating to all records sold during that year and the previous year notwithstanding that such royalties may not have yet been accrued or paid to the Artist. Commission will be payable when the royalties are accrued or received and at the second-year rate of 10%.

6.2 In the event that the Artist is paid an advance, royalties or income in relation to records released on a label affiliated with the Manager, or compositions assigned or licensed to a publishing company affiliated with the Manager, there shall be no commissions payable on any such advances, royalties or income unless otherwise agreed between the parties. 'Affiliated' means having any direct or indirect interest in.

6.3 The Artist acknowledges that one of the Artist's primary objectives is to achieve international success and as a consequence the Manager at the Manager's discretion may deem it necessary to appoint an overseas Co-Manager. In the event that such appointment is made the commission paid to the overseas Co-Manager will be paid 50% by the Manager from the Manager's 20% entitlement and 50% by the Artist.

6.4 The expressions 'gross earnings' or 'income derived' mean the total of all money or other consideration exclusive of goods and services tax (GST) or similar taxes. This includes but is not limited to advances, salaries, earnings, wages, fees, royalties, bonuses, gifts, goods or benefits of any kind, shares, properties or profits directly or indirectly accrued to the account of, compromised or forgone or received by the Artist or any person company or trust on the Artist's behalf which relate to the professional activities but excludes any dividends, profits, wages or distributions to the Artist which are derived from income which has already been commissioned. All money or other consideration paid to the Artist's creditors pursuant to legal process or by virtue of an assignment by or at the direction of the Artist shall be deemed to be part of the Artist's gross earnings.

The following income is excluded from 'gross earnings':

(1) Agency fees;
(2) Recording, video, website and tour-support advances to the extent that the Artist does not receive any monies, that is, the monies are paid to a third party on the Artist's behalf;
(3) Royalties applied to recoup such advances, that is, which are credited to the Artist's recoupment account and not actually received by the Artist; and
(4) The following live production costs incurred by the Artist in relation to touring or performing, namely:
    (a) Advertising and promotion;
    (b) Transport and accommodation;
    (c) Direct venue and support act;
    (d) Sound, security, lighting, engineer and any other production expenses which are part of the production budget other than wages and profits to the Artist.

6.5 All payments to the Manager under this Agreement are exclusive of GST which is payable in addition on receipt of a GST invoice.

7. <u>Minutes of Meeting</u>

The Manager will convene a meeting within thirty (30) days of signing this Agreement. At that meeting all matters concerning the professional activities, career and aspirations of the Artist are to be openly discussed and minuted. Thereafter meetings will be called regularly as required by the Manager and/or the Artist.

8. <u>Manager's Responsibilities</u>

Throughout the term the Manager shall:

(1) Act in the best interests of the Artist. The Artist's professional reputation is to be paramount and the Manager agrees not to do anything which impacts on that reputation without prior consultation with the Artist.

(2) Use the Manager's best endeavours to procure engagements in the entertainment industry for the Artist and promptly attend to any and all offers of employment or engagements of the Artist which are submitted to, or come to the knowledge of, the Manager.

(3) Use the Manager's best endeavours to promote, publicise, develop and advance the professional career of the Artist and confer with and advise the Artist as required in relation to the entertainment industry including but not limited to the following:

(a) Selection of artistic and musical material to be performed by the Artist;

(b) All matters pertaining to publicity, public relations and advertising; and

(c) Act as general business manager of the Artist and to attend to matters in a businesslike manner <u>PROVIDED HOWEVER</u> that the Manager shall not be required to provide any specialist professional advice in relation to taxation or investment matters or legal and/or accounting advice other than of a general nature.

9. Artist's Responsibilities

The Artist undertakes and warrants that:

(1) There is no current agreement whether in writing, oral or implied with any person which could interfere with the rights and obligations of the Manager under this Agreement;
(2) The Artist will not question the authority of the Manager;
(3) The Artist will not engage any person other than the Manager to act as a manager, agent, representative or consultant or otherwise in relation to the Manager's functions;
(4) The Artist will not accept any employment or engagement in the entertainment industry of whatever nature without the prior consent of the Manager; and
(5) The Artist will not do anything which will have the effect of excluding the Manager from the Manager's responsibilities, remuneration and entitlements under this Agreement.

10. Non-Exclusive Licence

The Artist grants to the Manager for the duration of the term the non-exclusive right and licence to use and publish the Artist's name, approved photographs and approved biography and other materials in connection with advertising and promotion. The Manager shall consult with the Artist on any proposed use. The Artist shall provide the Manager with all information and material which is necessary for the Manager to perform these services.

11. Termination

11.1 The Artist upon giving thirty (30) days written notice to the Manager, can terminate this Agreement on the happening of any one of the following events:

(1) The Manager wilfully refuses or neglects to perform the Manager's obligations under this Agreement; or
(2) The Manager is unable to pay the Manager's debts as and when they fall due; or

(3) In the event that the Manager is a company should [*insert name of personal Manager*] cease to be involved personally in the day-to-day activities of the Artist or of the company.

11.2 This Agreement will only terminate if the Manager has not remedied any of the above breaches within thirty (30) days after service of the required notice.

11.3 The Manager shall be entitled to terminate this Agreement by thirty (30) days written notice to the Artist if the Artist is in material breach of this Agreement.

11.4 The Agreement will only terminate if the Artist has not rectified the specified breach within thirty (30) days after service of the required notice.

11.5 Termination by the Manager or the Artist is without prejudice to any other rights, remedies and entitlements under this Agreement.

12. <u>General</u>

12.1 This Agreement does not create a partnership or joint venture between the Manager and the Artist.

12.2 This Agreement shall be binding upon and enure to the benefit of the parties, their respective heirs, executors, administrators and assigns.

12.3 In the event any provision of this Agreement shall be unenforceable, this shall not affect the validity or enforceability of the remaining provisions.

12.4 No party shall have the power to assign this Agreement without the prior written consent of the other party or parties.

12.5 Any notice may be served personally or sent by certified mail, facsimile or email.

12.6 The Artist acknowledges that the Manager has no responsibility or obligation to negotiate, resolve, discharge or settle on behalf of the Artist any dispute, obligation or debt of the Artist arising directly or indirectly out of any act, matter or event occurring prior to the date of this Agreement.

12.7 This Agreement embodies the entire agreement between the parties.

12.8 If there is more than one Artist the obligations imposed under this Agreement are imposed jointly and severally.

12.9 This Agreement is subject to the exclusive jurisdiction of the Courts and the laws of the State of Victoria.

12.10 If the Artist, or any of them if more than one, is less than eighteen (18) years of age this Agreement is signed by that Artist's guardian who acknowledges that this Agreement is in the best interests of that Artist.

12.11 Both parties will comply with applicable privacy legislation but the Manager is entitled to retain, use and disseminate the Artist's name, likeness and promotional and professional material for the purposes of this Agreement.

13. Legal Advice

The Artist has been advised and given the opportunity to seek independent legal advice from a solicitor with experience in the entertainment industry before signing this Agreement.

Signed by the Manager ....

in the presence of: ....

Signed by the Artist ....

in the presence of: ....

Comments:

Clause 1: In the music industry management agreements are fairly standardised and should always be in writing. The agreement is straightforward in its content and documents a manager agreeing to provide his, her or its services as a manager to an artist for a certain period of time. Members of a group usually sign management contracts both individually and collectively. The artist is exclusively signed to the manager but not vice versa. Three years is the norm and the territory is the world.

The manager is often requested to set career goals for the group. Obtaining a recording contract with a major record company or releasing an album in a major territory would be typical. It is not uncommon to include a clause that if these goals are not achieved within a certain time the agreement can be terminated at the discretion of the artist.

Clause 5: The manager is required to provide appropriate office facilities. Expenses directly related to the artist such as interstate and international travel, telephone and communication expenses are reimbursed by the artist. Care needs to be taken when more than one artist is managed that expenses incurred are properly apportioned to avoid one artist funding other artists managed by the manager.

Clause 6: Commission is commonly charged at 20% of the gross income less agency fees (10%) that is 20% of 90%. The commission can apply not only to income earned during the period of the management agreement but also in relation to income from recording and publishing contracts entered into during the term but received after the term. This is referred to as 'post-term commission'. Sometimes this entitlement applies for a period of two years after the term and on a descending scale, say, from 15% to 10% in each or those two years. If an artist is unlucky enough to be a winner of finalist in Australian Idol post term commissions could apply for fifteen years at the rate of 20% for the first nine years and 10% for the next six that obviously is ridiculous.

It should be clear what income is commissionable. The norm is that all income and advances from recording, publishing, touring and merchandising are commissionable. This has some practical consequences. If a recording company advances $100,000 to make a record they expect that amount to be expended on the record not $80,000. This typically results in managers deferring their entitlement to commissioning an advance or agreeing not to charge commission on certain advances. The cashflow problems this can cause a manager are obvious.

The same applies to a tour-support advance. In relation to tours if, for example, a tour grosses $100,000 and only $10,000 net profit is left to be divided between five members of a group the fact that a manager is paid $20,000 might not go down very well. Again, some practical compromise is usually reached to maintain the relationship in the long-term. That might involve the manager being paid 20% of the net or some other reduced figure or being treated as a member of the group for this purpose.

Where the Artist is signed to a recording or publishing company in which the Manager has an interest, income from these sources should be non-commissionable. This is to avoid double dipping.

General: In NSW, under section 18 of the *Entertainment Industry Act 1989* (NSW), managers are required to be licensed.

4. RECORDING HEADS OF AGREEMENT (AGREEMENT)

1. Date of Agreement:

2. Record Company:

3. Artists:

4. Services:
The Artists are to provide their exclusive recording services to the record company (the company) throughout the term and the territory.

5. Territory:
The World.

6. Term:
The term shall comprise an initial period commencing on the date of this Agreement and ending twelve (12) months from the release of the recording commitment for that period.

The company shall have the option to extend the term for three (3) further periods each of twelve (12) months (subject to extension for late delivery) from the release of the recording commitment for that period.

Each option is exercisable by written notice no later than thirty (30) days prior to the expiry of the then current contract period.

If an option is not exercised within the stated period the Artists are required to give the record company thirty (30) days written notice during which time the option can be exercised. If it is not the option will lapse.

7. Recording Commitment:
Initial Period One (1) album.
Each option Period One (1) album.

8. Advance:
No advance will be paid on signing this Agreement.

9. Royalty:

9.1 Australia and New Zealand.
For net sales of full-priced records the following royalties shall apply:

(1) Singles and/or EPs: 16% of the royalty base price.
(2) Albums (in all formats including live and compilation albums): 20% of the royalty base price.
(3) Videos: 16% of the royalty base price.
(4) All other audio/visual formats: 16% of the royalty base price.
(5) Sundry uses: 60% of net receipts.
(6) Reduced rate: (50%) of royalties otherwise payable for TV, mid-price, budget, club and mail order sales, premiums, picture discs, third party licences and soundtrack albums.
(7) No royalties will be payable in respect of records or videos distributed for promotional purposes or on a no-charge, sample or free basis.
(8) Where records are sold as digital downloads the album rate for CD's will apply unless downloads are sold direct when the sundry rate in 9.1(5) will apply.

The royalty base price is the Published Price to Dealer less a packaging deduction of 25% of that price (35% for new technologies) and the royalty is inclusive of all and any royalties due to any third parties including a Producer.

All royalty rates and other terms of this Agreement shall be subject to the terms of any Third Party Licence Agreements (if applicable).

9.2 Rest of the World
70% of the royalties otherwise payable.

10. <u>Recording Fund:</u>
Budget to be agreed in good faith between the parties and paid for by the company. The recording fund will be fully recoupable from artist royalties but not returnable.

11. <u>Videos:</u>
Budget to be agreed in good faith between the parties and paid for by the company. The company will commit to a video per single released. The production of a DVD will be at the sole discretion of the company. Video production costs will be fully recoupable from artist royalties but not returnable.

12. <u>Rights:</u>
The company owns the copyrights in all audio and audiovisual recordings and artwork made under this Agreement throughout the world and for the full period of copyright. The Artists consent to the commercial exploitation of those copyrights at the discretion of the company.

13. <u>Label/Credit:</u>
The parties are to mutually agree on credits and good-faith use of logos and trademarks.

14. <u>Release Commitment:</u>
The company agrees to secure a commercial release of the minimum recording commitment in the territory within twelve (12) months after delivery to the company of the master recordings.

15. <u>Recording Restriction:</u>
The Artists are not to re-record any songs recorded under this Agreement for a period of two (2) years after the expiry of this Agreement.

16. Mechanical Royalties:
Mechanical royalties payable on controlled compositions, that is those composed or controlled by the Artists in the United States of America and Canada shall be 75% of the applicable statutory rate.

17. Creative Control:
The choice of producer, studios, tracks, singles, artwork, promotional materials, videos and any other matter which reflects on the professional image or career of the Artists is to be subject to mutual agreement. If agreement cannot be reached, the reasonable decision of the company will prevail.

18. Artwork:
All artwork commissioned and paid for by the company remains the property of the company.

19. Accounting:
Accounting and payment of royalties due is to occur within ninety (90) days following the end of June and December in each year. All usual and reasonable rights of audit will apply.

20. Assignment:
The company in its sole and absolute discretion shall have the right to licence or assign the rights accruing under this Agreement.

21. Joint & Several:
If there are two or more Artists they are jointly and severally (individually and collectively) liable under this Agreement.

22. Applicable Law:
The Agreement is subject to the laws and the sole jurisdiction of the State and Courts of Victoria.

23. Formal Agreement:
As soon as possible the parties will conduct good-faith and

expeditious negotiations to enter into a formal agreement which will be based on this Agreement. In the interim this Agreement will be binding on the parties.

Comments:

Clause 2 If the company is not a major a key-person clause might be appropriate. A clause allowing the Artists to terminate the Agreement if the company is in breach or unable to pay its debts on time could also be considered.

Clause 4 Because of this exclusivity the Artists might ask for the inclusion of a 'sideman' clause. This would allow the Artists to record as session players.

Clause 7 The recording commitment is one album per period. This applies to new albums and does not include Best Of, Greatest Hits and Live albums.

Clause 8 The Artists would want an advance on signing and also on exercising options. An allowance for legal costs is often included in the advance. Sometimes tour-support advances are also paid.

Clause 9 The royalty rates should be reduced to dollars and cents and an example given as to what royalty would apply in relation to say 1000 units sold in Australia. The example should indicate how producer's royalties are to be treated. It is then possible to calculate the number of records which have to be sold to recoup.

The royalty rates are too low and deductions too high particularly for packaging and new technology. There should also be a definition of 'net sales'. Royalties are not paid on 100% of sales but sales less returns. Sometimes there is a fixed percentage for returns and royalties are paid on, say, 90% of sales.

There should be some cap on records distributed for promotional purposes or at least some understanding in relation to what numbers are involved.

The 50% reduction for TV should only apply to sales during the TV campaign. The record company would argue it should include records 'bought in' by retailers in anticipation of the campaign. There should also be a clear understanding of what comprises a national TV campaign.

The paragraph relating to Third Party Licence Agreements should be modified or deleted. It is much too broad.

There is no justification for reducing royalties on soundtrack albums. The reduction for foreign sales is also unwarranted.

Clause 10 There should be some agreement in relation to the amount to be expended on the recording fund. This is the financial commitment by the recording company. There should be a definition of 'recording costs' which should not include costs associated with manufacturing, distributing or promoting the records. The recording fund is treated as an advance, that is, it is fully recoupable but not returnable. This means that it is recoupable against artist royalties but is not repayable by the Artists should there be insufficient royalties to recoup the advance.

Clause 11 The production costs of videos are recoupable. Sometimes 50% is recoupable from recording income and 50% from video income.

Clause 12 There should be some discussion about copyright ownership of masters, videos and artwork if and when advances are recouped. By then the Artists have in fact paid the production costs. Major record companies rarely, if ever, concede this point.

Clause 14 Twelve months should be reduced to three but at the most to six. The release commitment provides for a release in the territory which is described as the world. It would be preferable to nominate the country in relation to which the release is to take place, for example, Australia or the United States of America.

There is no provision as to what would happen should the release commitment not be fulfilled. The Artists should have a right to terminate the Agreement by reasonable notice. During this notice period the record company has an obligation to effect the release, failing which the Agreement would terminate. Further discussion would be required in relation to the status of any recorded but unreleased masters at the time of termination.

Clause 15 The recording restriction is an important clause because it prevents the artists from re-recording songs recorded during the term for a certain period. This prevents them from releasing a Greatest Hits or similar album without obtaining a licence of the tracks previously recorded by the former record company with all that entails. In any event the restriction should only apply to songs recorded and actually released.

Clause 16 The reduction should not apply to Canada. Care needs to be taken that such a provision is not inconsistent with any pre-existing publishing agreement otherwise the reduction might have to be absorbed totally from the writer's share of publishing income. The reduction should only apply to that part of the work which is in fact controlled.

Clause 19 The accounting clause should provide for direct accounting from the territory of source to the Artists. Record companies have been known to pay royalties via their various affiliates throughout the world thereby delaying payment to the Artists. Accounting clauses often provide for a foreign publisher to withhold taxes. This should only relate to taxes actually incurred and paid and any withholding tax credits should be passed on to the Artists.

Clause 21 The joint and several provision means that the Artists are responsible individually and collectively under the Agreement. If one member is found to be in breach of the Agreement the other members can be sued.

5. PUBLISHING HEADS OF AGREEMENT (AGREEMENT)

1. Date of Agreement:

2. Writer:

3. Publisher:

4. Services:
The writer agrees to provide the writer's exclusive services as a songwriter to the publisher during the term and throughout the territory.

5. Term:
The period of five (5) years commencing on the date of this Agreement. The term shall extend if necessary to include the release of four (4) qualifying albums. A qualifying album must contain works which in total are at least 80% written by the writer and which have previously been unrecorded.

6. Territory:
The World.

7. Compositions:
All compositions written during the term and any compositions which have been the subject of a prior publishing agreement and which revert to the writer during the term or which were written prior to the commencement of this Agreement and which are not subject to a prior publishing agreement.

8. Rights:
The publisher shall have the exclusive rights to commercially exploit the compositions throughout the territory during the term and the retention period. The compositions and all rights therein are hereby assigned to the publisher who agrees to reassign them to the writer

on expiry of the retention period. Use of the compositions in films and commercials is subject to the reasonable approval of the writer.

9. <u>Retention Period:</u>
Fifteen (15) years after the end of the term.

10. <u>Royalties:</u>
Mechanicals: 75/25 writer/publisher.
Synchronisation: 75/25 writer/publisher.
Performance: 75/25 writer/publisher.
Covers/other: 70/30 writer/publisher.
Sheet music royalties: 50% of net sums writer/publisher.
All royalties are calculated on net sums actually received by the publisher.

11. <u>Advance:</u>
The writer will be paid an advance of $20,000 on signing the Agreement and $20,000 on release of each qualifying album.

12. <u>Accounting:</u>
The company agrees to account and pay to the writer all income received in each six-month period ending 30 June and 31 December in every year during the term and retention period. The accounting and payment will occur within ninety (90) days of the end of that period. All reasonable and usual rights of audit will apply.

13. <u>Joint & Several:</u>
Where there is more than one writer they are jointly and severally (individually and collectively) liable under this Agreement.

14. <u>Applicable Law:</u>
The Agreement is subject to the laws and the sole jurisdiction of the State and Courts of Victoria.

15. Formal Agreement:

As soon as possible the parties will conduct good-faith and expeditious negotiations to enter into a formal agreement which will be based on this Agreement. In the interim this Agreement will be binding on the parties.

Comments:

Clause 3 If the company is not a major, a key-person clause might be appropriate. A clause allowing the writer to terminate the Agreement if the publisher defaults or is unable to pay its debts on time should also be included. On termination all copyrights should revert immediately.

Clause 5 The term of five years or four qualifying albums whichever is the longer should be negotiated. Three years would be reasonable with two albums. If the greater commitment is conceded then that should be reflected in the advance.

There may be a situation where a second album is not delivered, for example the record company might not take up an option and this could lead to the term being extended indefinitely. Because of this there should be some maximum period which would apply should the albums not be delivered. The earlier of five years or when the publisher is recouped might be reasonable. The writer should have the right to repay any unrecouped balance in these circumstances.

Clause 10 The publisher will sometimes receive a greater share of income for covers. This should only apply to covers obtained by the publisher. Since royalties are calculated on net sums there should be a cap on the percentages which can be paid to a licensee, particularly anyone associated with the publisher. Otherwise the royalties payable to the writer could be diluted. An alternative is for the royalties to be calculated 'at source', that is on the gross income generated in the country of source.

Clause 11 The advance is a 'signing-on' advance with future advances in relation to albums. The signing-on advance might still be unrecouped at the time the advance is payable in relation to the album. The publisher should not be entitled to use the album advance to recoup the unrecouped portion of the signing-on advance. This would defeat the purpose of the exercise which is to provide cash flow.

Clause 12 Accounting should be direct from the country of source. It should also be expeditious. Provision is often made for a foreign publisher to withhold taxes. This should only relate to taxes actually paid and withholding-tax credits should be passed on to the songwriter.

Clause 13 The joint and several clause only applies when there is more than one writer. Ideally this should never occur because each writer should sign an agreement separately. Otherwise an unsuccessful writer would receive a share of an advance which would then be recouped from the income of the successful writer.

6. PRODUCER AGREEMENT

This Agreement is made the day of 200 .

Between: of ('the Artist')

AND of ('the Producer')

AND of ('the Company')

Whereas:
The Company has engaged the Producer to produce recordings by the Artist ('the Producer's services') for the Company.

The Parties Agree as follows:

1. Definitions

The following words have these meanings:

1.1 'Artist's Agreement' means the Recording Agreement between the Artist and the Company in respect of the Artist's recording services (as it may from time to time be modified, extended, renewed or substituted).

1.2 'Album' is the album entitled [ ] containing the recorded performances of the Artist and including the following tracks:

____

____

1.3 'Master' means every recording of sound produced by the Producer whether or not coupled with a visual image reproduced on magnetic recording tape, disc recording or the digital tape equivalent of the original multi-track recording or any other material whether or not now known which is used in the recording, production or manufacture of Records.

1.4 'Record' has the meaning ascribed to it in the *Copyright Act 1968* (Cth). For the avoidance of doubt it shall include compact discs, DAT and any other sound carrier now known or not known including video.

1.5 'Recording Costs' has the same meaning that term has in the Artist's Agreement but for the purposes of this Agreement shall exclude touring advances and personal advances actually received by the Artist or the Artist's manager.

1.6 'Recordings' means the Recordings (and each of them) of the Artist's performance produced by the Producer whether alone or with others which make up the album.

1.7 'Territory' is the world.

In addition to the above definitions the terms defined in the Artist's Agreement shall apply to this Agreement where they are applicable.

2. Royalties

2.1 The Artist agrees that the Company shall as consideration for the Producer's services rendered for the production of the Album and for all rights granted to the Company pay to the Producer a royalty at the rate of 4%. It shall be calculated at and paid on the same basis and in the same manner in time and in respect of the same sales as the royalty payable to the Artist pursuant to the terms of the Artist's Agreement.

2.2 The Producer shall be entitled to receive a share of any flat fee to which the Artist is entitled based upon the proportion that the royalty rate set out in this Agreement bears to the Artist's royalty rate in the Artist's Agreement, that is if it is 10% of the Artist's royalties the Producer will receive 10% of the flat fee.

2.3 Where only a part of a Record comprises Recordings made under the terms of this Agreement, the Producer's royalty will be calculated by multiplying the royalty by a fraction, the numerator of which shall be the number of the Recordings embodied in such

Record and the denominator shall be the total number of sound Recordings embodied in it.

2.4 In the event that any single or EP release as defined in the Artist's Agreement embodies a master not produced by the Producer, the Producer shall nevertheless be paid the Producer's full royalties under this Agreement as if the Master had been produced by the Producer, that is there will be no pro-rata reduction of the Producer royalties.

2.5 The Producer's entitlement to royalties will not commence until the Artist has recouped Recording Costs pursuant to the Artist's Agreement.

3. Accounting

3.1 The Company shall furnish to the Producer accounting statements at the same time statements are provided to the Artist. Those statements will show the number of Records embodying Recordings made under the terms of this Agreement sold by the Company during the last preceding period, or sold by any licensee of the Company and accounted for by such licensee to the Company during the last preceding period. They will show the royalties due to the Producer in respect to the records sold in that period.

3.2 The Company will pay the Producer the royalties due under this Agreement less any withholding tax which it is obligated to, and does in fact, pay at the same time the accounting statements are provided. The Producer will be provided with all necessary documentation to allow the Producer to claim a tax credit in relation to any such withholding tax.

3.3 In the case of Records sold outside Australia, the Company's obligation to pay royalties to the Producer shall be limited to the amounts actually received by or credited to the Company in Australia by way of or on account of royalties.

3.4 The royalties and advances (if any) specified in this clause 3 constitute the sole remuneration payable to the Producer for the Producer's services.

3.5 The Producer shall have the same audit rights as have been granted to the Artist pursuant to the Artist's Agreement.

4. Ownership of Recordings

All Recordings made pursuant to this Agreement and any copyrights subsisting therein are the sole property of the Company. It shall be entitled to the sole and exclusive rights in relation to any such Recordings to use them free from any claim whatsoever (save for royalties payable to the Producer) in any country and in any manner at its sole discretion.

5. Warranty and Indemnity

5.1 The Producer warrants that the Producer is under no obligation of any nature to any person which could prevent the Producer fulfilling all of the terms and conditions of this Agreement or which could prevent the Company from fully and freely exercising any of the rights granted to it under this Agreement.

5.2 The Producer indemnifies and will keep indemnified the Company against any loss, damage, claims, costs (including reasonable legal costs) or demands sustained by, or made against the Company or any person, arising out of or relating to a breach by the Producer of any of the terms of this Agreement.

6. Promotion of Recordings

6.1 The Producer grants to the Company the irrevocable, non-exclusive right and licence to use the Producer's name, approved photograph and other representations of, and biographical material relating to, the Producer in any manner whatsoever for the purpose of advertising and promoting the sale of Records made pursuant to this Agreement.

2.2 The Company shall incorporate a credit on the label and packaging of all Records embodying Recordings made hereunder as follows:

'Produced by   '.

2.3 If the Company inadvertently fails to incorporate the credit the Company shall use all reasonable endeavours to rectify the error. Such inadvertent failure will not be a breach of this Agreement.

7. Notices

1.1 Any notice under this Agreement will be sufficiently served if:

(1) Delivered personally to the party to be served.

(2) Left at or two (2) days after having been sent by prepaid post to:

(a) The address of the party to be served as set out in this Agreement; or

(b) The last known place of abode or business of the party to be served; or

(c) The registered office of any party to be served which is a company; or

(3) Sent by facsimile transmission or email to the last known facsimile number or email address of the party to be served in which case it will be deemed to have been duly served at the time the facsimile transmission or email is sent.

1.2 In order for any notice to the Company to be binding upon the Company it must be addressed to the Business Affairs Manager of the Company.

8. Assignment Prohibited

The Producer will not assign the Producer's rights under this Agreement without the prior written consent of the Company, which consent will not be unreasonably withheld.

9. Applicable Law

This Agreement will be construed and given effect to in accordance with the laws of the State ofVictoria and the parties agree to submit to the exclusive jurisdiction of the Courts of that State.

Signed by the Producer ....

in the presence of: ....

Signed by the Artist ....

in the presence of: ....

Signed by a duly authorised officer of the Company in the presence of:

....

Comments:

A Producer of international standing would insist on being paid an advance per track. He or she might also ask for royalties to be paid at a rate specified by the Producer and from record one, that is not after recoupment of recording costs. It would be rare for this to be accepted. It is more common, but still subject to negotiation, for a producer to receive royalties from the sale of 'record one' but only after recording costs have been recouped. The Producer's fee may or may not be an advance against royalties being paid to the Producer. The Producer would probably insist on direct payment from the record company. It is important that an example as to how Artist's royalties are to be reconciled with the Producer's royalties is provided by the record company.

Sometimes a Producer might insist on the right to have a credit removed if the Producer is not satisfied with a final mix which the Producer does not control.

GLOSSARY

Adaptation: A rearrangement, arrangement or transcription of an original work. Copyright can exist in an adaptation as a new work if it is substantially different from the original work.

Administration Agreement: An agreement whereby a songwriter or a label licenses a publisher to administer copyrights. The copyright remains with the songwriter or label. The licence is usually short term and because the obligation is restricted to collecting and distributing income the fees are quite small, that is 10-15% of monies collected. There is no obligation on an administrator to place songs in films, obtain covers, liaise with songwriters or to carry out the traditional functions of a publisher.

Advance: A payment to an artist, songwriter or label of a lump sum in anticipation of future income. Recording advances may be paid on signing a contract, exercising an option, commencement of recording or production of a video, delivery of an album or in relation to a tour. Publishing advances may be paid on signing a contract, on recoupment of a previous advance or on exercising an option. Advances are recoupable against the anticipated future income. They are not returnable or repayable in the event that the future income does not eventuate.

An Agent: In the music industry an agent is a booking agent, that is he or she is responsible for booking tours and performances. An agent is usually paid 10% of the gross income. A theatrical agent does the same thing only in a broader context. Theatrical agents can charge from between 5% to 15% of the gross. The agent is the intermediary between the artist and the promoter/producer.

Ancillary Income: Income derived from activities other than the principal activity undertaken. The principal activity of a film producer is to exploit the film in a theatrical or other release. Ancillary income would be income from selling records or merchandise. The term is used more commonly in the film industry than it is in the music industry.

Arrangement: A transfer of a work from one medium to another. For example, a work written for piano may be arranged for an orchestra.

Artist & Repertoire (A & R) Manager: In a record company the A & R person is responsible for sourcing, nurturing and assisting artists in the development of their careers and their artistic output.

Artist Royalty: A royalty paid by a record company to an artist in return for that artist providing his or her exclusive services as a recording artist to the company. It is a percentage of the Royalty Base Price (see definition) of each unit sold less certain reductions and deductions.

Assignment: A written document which transfers an interest in copyright or other rights from the owner ('the assignor') to someone else ('the assignee'). In publishing agreements the rights assigned almost always revert to the songwriter who is the initial copyright owner after a certain period of time (the Reversion Period). In recording agreements there is no need for an assignment because the copyright in the master recordings is vested in the record company from the outset.

Australasian Mechanical Copyright Owners Society (AMCOS): A Society which administers mechanical rights in musical works in Australia and New Zealand. Principally it licenses record companies and individuals to reproduce musical works (songs) on records. The income collected is fixed by agreement between the representatives of the publishers and recording companies subject to the overall supervision of the Copyright Tribunal. Income collected is distributed to its members who assign their mechanical reproduction rights to the Society.

Australian Music Publishers Association (AMPAL): This Association represents Australian music publishers. It is mainly responsible for lobbying government.

Australasian Performing Right Association (APRA): APRA represents composers and music publishers who assign their public performance, broadcast and diffusion rights to it. APRA licenses these rights on behalf of its members and collects income which is distributed to members. Licences are issued to radio and television stations, venues and anyone who requires a licence to publicly perform, communicate and broadcast music. Licensees are required to provide information as to the use of the work. Income is distributed to members on the basis of the frequency of usage. APRA conducts its licence scheme throughout Australia and New Zealand and has reciprocal arrangements with similar societies throughout the world.

Australian Record Industry Association (ARIA): The major record companies and most of the independents are represented by ARIA. It is an industry advocate and supervises the annual music industry awards. It also has some supervision over the certification of sales figures and chart positions.

Audiovisual Rights: The rights to couple and exploit audio and visual performances.

Barrister: A lawyer who predominantly practises in court. Barristers are briefed by solicitors who provide the link between the barrister and the client. Sometimes the barrister and the solicitor are one and the same person although separate roles are often maintained in practice.

Biography (Bio): A list of a performer's professional qualifications and experience.

Bridge: A section of a musical work which connects a chorus and a verse. It can involve a change from one key to another or a different chord progression from the verse or chorus. It can be interchanged with the term 'middle eight'.

Business Affairs Manager: The person in a record company who is responsible for business affairs. Once the A & R person has sourced the artist it is then the responsibility of the Business Affairs Manager to prepare, negotiate and exchange signed contracts. If there is any disputation in relation to the commercial arrangement between an artist and a record or publishing company this will be resolved by the Business Affairs Manager.

Business Name: A name under which an artist or a company conducts business. Business names are registered State by State. Registration represents compliance with the State business-name registration formalities and does not confer any ownership of the name.

Catalogue: A publisher is in the business of acquiring a catalogue of publishing assets, that is copyrights of music and lyrics. Record companies acquire catalogues of masters. Film companies build a library of films. They are all acquiring a collection of copyrights.

Chord: A group of three or more notes which form an harmonic unit.

Collection Society: APRA, AMCOS and PPCA are collection societies. They acquire rights from owners and license those rights for use. APRA issues licences for the public performance and broadcast of musical works. AMCOS licenses rights to reproduce musical works on tape, disc or other software configuration. PPCA licenses the right to broadcast and play recorded masters.

Container Charge: [See Packaging Deduction].

Compact Disc (CD): A digitally encoded disc which can reproduce sound and visual images which are read and transmitted by means of a laser.

Company: A company is a separate entity for legal purposes. In Australia it is designated by 'Pty' or 'Ltd' or both. In America it is designated by 'Inc.'. Being a separate entity a company can provide protection to its shareholders against debts and liabilities being incurred. A company is managed by its directors and owned by its shareholders. Shareholders appoint directors. Directors appoint the Executive Officers. A company is incorporated Australia wide, not registered State by State as with business names.

Compilation: This occurs when tracks off several albums are configured and released as one album such as a Greatest Hits or Best Of. A compilation can involve tracks from different artists which are licensed for use 'The Hits of The Eighties' would be an example.

Composition: A musical work.

Contract: An agreement entered into between two or more people or parties by which one agrees to provide a service and the other agrees to make a payment or forgo something of value. In the recording industry contracts involve parties, a term, exclusive services being provided in a defined territory, payment of an advance and/or royalties and exclusive rights being created, assigned or licensed.

Contract of Service: An arrangement whereby one party employs another. It is important in the copyright context because this can result in the employer owning the copyrights resulting from creative endeavours undertaken by the employee in the course of the employment.

Contract for Services: This is an arrangement with a contractor (self-employed person or company) rather than a traditional employer/employee relationship. The principal contractor does not acquire ownership of the copyright in any works created as a result of the commercial arrangement unless there is an agreement to the contrary.

Controlled Composition: A musical work written, owned or controlled wholly or in part by the artist concerned. It can have important implications in America and sometimes in Canada in that many record contracts provide for mechanical royalties to be paid at a reduced rate in relation to controlled compositions. The reduction is usually three quarters of the statutory rate which otherwise would apply.

Convention: An international agreement between member countries which is in writing and governed by international law.

Copyright: A property right which gives the copyright owner or licensee the exclusive right to prohibit or to do certain acts. The rights are distinct from the rights in the medium itself. Copyright in Australia is governed by the *Copyright Act 1968* (Cth) and conventions and international agreements to which Australia is a party. Copyright subsists from the moment the subject matter is reduced to a material form. Copyrights can be assigned or licensed in writing and are divisible.

***Copyright Act 1968* (Cth):** Commonwealth legislation which governs copyright in Australia.

Copyright Tribunal: A Tribunal established under the auspices of the *Copyright Act 1968* (Cth) to determine matters relating to copyright.

Cover: A recording of a song previously recorded and released by another artist.

Credits: Credits identify and acknowledge the artists, songwriters and producer. Record credits include label and liner notes. In theatre and film the most sought-after credits are those which appear 'above the title'.

Cross-collateralisation: This applies when an advance payable in relation to one particular activity and recoupable from income generated from that activity is also recoupable from income from another source, that is, it is cross-recouped. A common example would be where an advance payable to a recording artist in relation to one album is recoupable from income from another album. An extreme and unacceptable example would be a record contract providing that a recording advance can be recouped against mechanical royalties, that is, publishing income.

Cue Sheet: This is provided by a composer of a soundtrack to a film or TV producer. It sets out the nature, extent and exact timing of the composition as synchronised into the soundtrack.

Cut Out/Deletion: Records which have been deleted from the current catalogue of a record company. They are usually sold at a very low price and are royalty free.

Deal: Industry-speak for an agreement.

Demo: Songs recorded in a very basic way on a demonstration tape or CD for presentation to a record or publishing company.

Diffusion Service: A transmission which is wider in its application than a traditional television or radio broadcast.

Direct Signing: Occurs when an artist signs a recording contract directly with a record company. It is very common and involves the artist agreeing to provide the artist's exclusive recording services to the company over a period of time. The company agrees to advance monies necessary to fund a certain number of recordings which are recoupable from artist royalties. The company also agrees to manufacture, promote and distribute those records. Generally the company owns the copyright in the masters recorded and the artist is paid a royalty based on units sold.

Discography: A list of an artist's recordings.

Distribution Deal: An arrangement where an artist funds his or her own recording and licenses the record company to distribute the records. The artist can earn more but the financial risk is higher. The artist owns the copyright in the masters.

Door Deal: This is when a performer agrees to take a percentage of entry fees to a venue. It should be contrasted with a guarantee. Under a guarantee the venue agrees to pay a certain fee plus a percentage of the door after enough customers to recover the fee have paid. It is important that the artist has a representative on the door.

Domain name: An address for internet purposes.

Dramatic Context Performance: A performance of a song in a dramatic performance. See also grand and small performance rights.

Dramatic Work: A work which is intended to be performed rather than narrated. It is usually distinguished by dialogue, action, gesture, costumes and effects.

Engineer: The person who looks after the technical aspects of the recording process. Often an engineer is attached to a particular studio.

Favoured Nations Clause: Applies when two or more artists of equal status are performing or recording together. If one negotiates a favourable clause they all benefit, that is, it will be read into the contracts of all the principal participants.

Gatt: The General Agreement on Tariffs and Trade to which Australia is a signatory. This has an intellectual property component.

Gold Record: A gold record in Australia signifies sales in excess of 35,000 units. In America it is 500,000 units.

Grand Performing Rights: These rights relate to the use of a musical work or song in a dramatic or theatrical context. Grand rights apply when there is a storyline connecting the various musical works which are composed especially for that production. An example would be Anthony Warlow singing Music of the Night during a performance of Phantom of the Opera. APRA does not administer grand rights. They are negotiated directly with the publisher or songwriter. See also 'small performance rights' and 'dramatic context performance'.

Hype: Industry slang for hyperbole. It can be shortlived and does not necessarily have anything to do with the talent of the performer.

Independent Promotion: A practice which was popular in the early eighties in America. It involved the use of independent promoters to get radio airplay for a record. Many of these practices were corrupt and resulted in a clean-out in the American industry at that time. Nevertheless many American record companies still rely on independent promoters for the success of their records.

Indie: Jargon for independent record company. Denotes a company which is not one of the majors.

Joint and Several: A legal term which applies when an obligation is imposed individually and collectively. If a loan is made to five members of a group and only one has money, that person can be sued for the full amount of the loan, not just one-fifth.

Key-person Clause: This clause is appropriate when there is a particular person in a company who is fundamental to the relationship. It allows an artist to terminate a contract if that person leaves the company or stops being involved in the day to day activities of the group. Major record or publishing companies will rarely (if ever) agree to clauses of this kind.

Label: A separate entity which is interposed between a record company and an artist or a publishing company and a songwriter. It is often controlled by the manager or the artist involved.

Libretto: The text as distinct from the music of an opera or musical. It is Italian for "Little book".

Licence: This occurs when a copyright owner (licensor) but licenses someone else (licensee) to exploit certain aspects of the copyright. It is limited in time, territory and scope. For example synchronisation rights in a song might be licensed to a film producer.

Literary Work: A work which is intended to convey information or instruction or which is to provide literary enjoyment. There is no requirement that the work be of any particular literary merit. A list of words, figures or symbols or even a computer program can constitute a literary work.

Lyrics: The words which form part of a song. Technically lyrics are a literary rather than a musical work.

Major: One of the six major record companies - SONY, BMG, WARNER MUSIC, EMI, UNIVERSAL MUSIC and FESTIVAL MUSHROOM RECORDS. They change over time because of mergers and acquisitions. Throughout 2003 there was much talk about EMI acquiring Warner Music and Sony "merging withÓ BMG. Internationally there are really only five. Festival Mushroom is an Australian phenomenon.

Manager: An individual or company who enters into an agreement with an artist to manage the affairs of that artist over a certain period of time for which the manager is paid a percentage of the artist's income. In America business managers are often differentiated from personal managers. In Australia they are usually one and the same. A manager in the contemporary music industry should be distinguished from a booking agent. In theatre, theatrical agents are more common.

Master Recording: The master tape of the finished recorded product. It includes the necessary material to make the parts which are required to manufacture a record. There is a separate and distinct copyright in the master.

Mechanical Right: The right to reproduce a musical work or song on disc, tape or software. The right is granted by the owner of the musical work, i.e. the composer or publisher.

Mechanical Royalties: The royalties payable to composers and/or their publishers for reproducing music on records. This is publishing income in that it is paid by record companies to publishers. It is usually collected by

AMCOS which controls the mechanical rights of many publishers and songwriters. Mechanical royalties are payable on the basis of the number of units sold. With small pressings of less than 1000 they will often be paid on the number of records pressed.

Merchandising: Relates to the sale of merchandise, T-shirts, programs, posters and the like. In practice merchandising rights are often licensed to a specialist merchandiser, particularly when a major tour is contemplated.

Middle Eight: This term is interchangeable with 'bridge'. It was originally an eight-bar structure used to differentiate between the verse and chorus.

Mix: The process of mixing or balancing the music recorded on two or more tracks of a multi-track recording onto the master tape.

Moshing: This occurs when audience members become inspired by a performance to such an extent that they feel the need to become part of it. They climb onto the stage and dive back into the audience. Sometimes a formal 'mosh pit' is provided for this purpose.

Musical Work: A work which comprises sounds and/or rhythms. There is no definition of musical work in the *Copyright Act 1968* (Cth). Nor is there any requirement that a piece of music be melodic or harmonic for the purposes of copyright protection.

Option: A clause in a contract allowing a publisher or a recording company to extend the term of a contract to include a further term and/or product. Options in recording contracts usually relate to records to be delivered. In a publishing context they apply to years although they can sometimes relate to albums. The effect is to extend the term during which exclusive services as a recording artist or songwriter are to be provided.

Packaging Deduction: A deduction from the royalty base price. It is supposed to cover the cost of packaging the record although it has no real basis in fact.

Parallel Import: A record legally manufactured outside Australia with the consent of the owner of the copyright in the master which is imported into and marketed in Australia by a company other than the Australian exclusive licensee of the copyright owner.

Patent: An exclusive right conferred by statute to exploit and to licence others to exploit, an invention in a territory for a certain period of time. The invention becomes public property when the patent term expires.

Passing Off: An action which arises when it can be established that one person is holding out or representing that the goods and services of another person are his or her own. A passing-off action protects goodwill associated with a business. It requires proof that there is a reputation to be protected, a misrepresentation and actual or likely damage.

Pay for Play: Refers to the fees payable by broadcasters to record companies for the right to play records. Licences are granted and income is collected by PPCA. That income is distributed to the record companies who may or may not pass it on to the artists depending on their contract with the record company. Even if a portion is payable to the artist it is often used for recoupment purposes.

Per Diem: This is Latin for 'per day'. It is an industry term for a daily payment to cover accommodation and living expenses when on tour.

Performance Income: Income collected by APRA for the public performance of musical works (publishing income) and PPCA for the public performance of records (recording income). A public performance in the general sense can include performing a song or playing a record at a night club, on radio or T.V. in a shop or business or "on holdÓ on a telephone.

Phonographic Performance Company of Australia (PPCA): The PPCA grants licences to play records in public.

Pipeline Income: A term used by publishers to calculate what advance (if any) they should pay to songwriters. It is an estimate of mechanical royalties, APRA money and other publishing income which is due but unpaid or paid but not yet accounted to the songwriter.

Pirate Recording: A recording which is manufactured without the consent of the owner of the copyright in the master and with no intention of paying mechanical royalties to the songwriter. This is a criminal activity.

Platinum Record: In Australia this signifies sales of 70,000 units. In America it denotes sales of 1,000,000 units.

Point (Royalty): A point is one percent. It is usually defined in the context of a royalty base price against which there are certain deductions and reductions.

Pressing & Distribution (P & D): Applies when artists have recorded their own master recording and license it to a record company to press and distribute records. The artists pay the record company a fee for carrying out this function. This involves the artists taking all the financial risk so obviously the returns are considerably greater.

Print: The use of musical works in a printed form, e.g. sheet music and song books.

Promoter: The person who puts on the event. Often the promoter will source artists or acts from a booking agent and sometimes from the manager direct. The promoter is responsible for paying all expenses associated with the concert or tour and retains any profits. He or she is also responsible for any losses that are incurred. The promoter is the supreme risk taker in the music industry.

Public Domain: A work which is no longer protected by copyright, and which can be used without compensation to the original owner.

Publisher: A publisher in the music industry acquires and commercially exploits music copyrights.

Publishing Income: Income derived from the commercial exploitation of music copyrights. It includes mechanical royalties (AMCOS), performance income (APRA) and sundry income from print and licensing for use in commercials, films and TV.

Publisher's Share: The share of income to which a publisher is entitled under the publishing contract.

Recording Income: Income derived from the commercial exploitation of the copyright in a master recording. It includes income from the sale of records, public performance of records and sundry income from licensing for use in commercials, films and TV.

Record Producer: The record producer liaises between the engineer and the artists in the studio. He or she is primarily responsible for ensuring that a commercial record is produced on budget and on time.

Recoup: To recover an advance.

Reversion Period: The period after which rights revert. The term is particularly appropriate to publishing agreements where it applies to publishing copyrights reverting. The period is usually ten to fifteen years. It should be distinguished from the term of the contract which is the term during which exclusive services as a songwriter are provided and which is usually three years. Whilst publishing copyrights almost always revert, recording copyrights almost never do.

Rhythm Section: The bass player, the drummer and rhythm guitarist in the conventional pop band configuration.

Rider: A clause attached to a contract. It sets out terms which relate to travel, accommodation, lighting, security, catering and other matters which are specific to that artist.

Riff: A melody which repeats and gives a song its identity.

Royalty Base Price: The price which is the base for calculating royalties. Traditionally it was the retail selling price less sales tax and packaging. The wholesale price then became common and today it is more likely to be the published price to dealer less the packaging deduction.

Sample: Sampling occurs when a sound which may be a guitar riff, drum sound or even part of a vocal is reproduced from a record. This can be done legitimately by seeking consent and paying a fee. More often than not it is done without consent. This is a breach of the copyrights in both the sound recording and the musical work.

Sideman Clause: A clause whereby an artist who is signed exclusively as a recording artist reserves the right to perform as a session player on recordings by other artists.

Small Performance Rights: A performance which is neither an exercise of a grand right nor in a dramatic context. An example would be Anthony Warlow singing Music of the Night in 'The Main Event'.

Songwriter: This is a common word in the contemporary music industry. It describes a person who writes songs. It can be contrasted with a composer who composes music and a lyricist who writes lyrics.

Soundtrack: A record which is released in conjunction with a musical or a film. It may include both original music and licensed tracks.

Statutory Rate: The mechanical royalty rate which applies in the United States of America which is fixed by statute. In Australia the rate is set by agreement between the recording and publishing representatives subject to the overall supervision of the Copyright Tribunal.

Synchronisation: The use of music in film, video, television and audiovisual presentations.

Trademark: A sign which could include a name or logo used or intended to be used to distinguish goods and services in the course of trade. Trademarks can be registered or unregistered. The trademark may be protected either by remedies under the Trade Marks Act 1995 or by a passing-off action.

Unit: A unit is an interest in a unit trust. Unitholders have a fixed entitlement to the assets and income of a trust based on their unitholding. This should be contrasted with a beneficiary in a discretionary trust who has no units or fixed entitlement to income or assets but, rather, is dependent upon the exercise of a discretion by a trustee. Trusts describe a relationship between one party (a trustee) who holds and administers assets on behalf of another (a beneficiary). They are regulated by a trust deed.

Writ: A document issued by a superior court or with judicial authority ordering a person to do, or not to do, something. A writ usually includes a statement of claim which sets out the basis of the claim. Issuing and serving a writ are necessary prerequisites to bringing a matter before the superior courts.

Writer: A word often used to describe a songwriter. See songwriter.

Writer's Share: In Australia the writer's share means the share that the songwriter receives under a publishing agreement. In America it is used in a more technical sense in the context of performance income. There it describes the minimum share that a writer can receive, namely 50%. Writers in America then negotiate with the publisher in relation to what portion of the publisher's share the writer will receive. The end result is not much different to the position in Australia. The splits are usually somewhere between 75/25 in favour of the writer in a publishing agreement and 90/10 in favour of the writer in an administration agreement.

END NOTES

CHAPTER 1 – THE ICEMAN

1. Tommy Tycho, *The Tommy Tycho Story – Music, Maestro Please*, Brolga Publishing Pty Ltd, 1995, p. 170.

CHAPTER 2 – GOOD VIBRATIONS

1. Glenn Wheatley, *Paper Paradise – Confessions of a Rock 'n' Roll Survivor*, Bantam, 1999, p. 60.
2. Toby Creswell, *Too Much Ain't Enough – Jimmy Barnes (The Authorised Biography)*, Random House Australia, 1993, p. 32.
3. Ibid p. 48.
4. Renée Geyer, *Confessions Of A Difficult Woman – The Renée Geyer Story*, HarperCollins Publishers, 2000, p. 52.
5. Ibid.
6. Michael George Smith, 'Ozrock: The State Of Play', (1994) 135 *Overland*, p. 21, p. 24.
7. Clinton Walker, 'Young and Restless', *The Age* (Melbourne), 10 December 1994, Saturday Extra p. 5.
8. *Regina v I. H. Saxon* (Unreported, Supreme Court of NSW, Dunford J, 1 August 1996).
9. David Lesser, 'The Hit Man', (1991) Spring *HQ* (Sydney), p. 72, p. 77.
10. James Freud, *I am the Voice left from Drinking – The Models – From the Burbs to Barbados and Beyond*, HarperCollins Publishers, 2002, p. 225.

CHAPTER 3 – MEN OUT OF WORK

1. Submission by the Australian Council of Trade Unions to the Prices Surveillance Authority, 19 November 1990.
2. Fredric Dannen, *Hit Men – Power Brokers and Fast Money Inside the Music Business,* Vintage, 1991, p. 226.
3. Stan Soocher, 'Madonna, Bruce And Grubman Indursky', *The National Law Journal*, 18 November 1991, pp. 1 & 30.

4. Michael Brereton, *International Tax Planning – An Analysis and Case Study*, October 1980.
5. Michael Brereton, 'Taxation Aspects of Importance to the Music Industry', 25 February 1984, pp 27-42.
6. Molly Meldrum, 'Men's Real Launch', *TV Week,* (NSW), 22 June 1985, p. 37.
7. Ralph Novak, 'Two Hearts – Men at Work', *People Weekly* (USA), 1 July 1985.
8. Ibid.
9. Glenn A. Baker, *Penthouse* (Australia), 1985 or thereabouts, p. 129.
10. Ibid.

CHAPTER 4 – IF YOU LEAVE ME CAN I COME TOO

1. Peter Wilmoth, 'Men at Work – A Hole in the Road', *The Age* (Melbourne), 13 July 1985, Saturday Extra p. 1.
2. Wheatley, above Chapter 2 note 1.
3. Geyer, above Chapter 2 note 4, p. 59.
4. Ibid.
5. Peter Wilmoth, 'The Mark of the Dragon', *The Age* (Melbourne), 20 May 1985, p. 11.
6. Bernard Zuel, 'The Sun Sets on Midnight Oil', *The Age* (Melbourne), 4 December 2002, p. 13.
7. Wilmoth, above Chapter 4 note 1.
8. Peter Wilmoth, 'A House Divided', *The Sunday Age* (Melbourne), 11 August 1996, Agenda p. 1.
9. Ibid.
10. Ibid.
11. Tess Lawrence, 'LRB on top of the Wave', *The Bulletin,* (NSW), 24 October 1978, p. 78.
12. *We Two Pty Ltd v Shorrock* (2002) FCA 875.
13. Wilmoth, above Chapter 4 note 7, p. 1.
14. Peter Holmes, 'Neil Finn', (1992) 10 *APRA Magazine* (Australia), pp. 6-7.
15. Tycho, above Chapter 1 note 1, p. 118.
16. Ibid.

17. Michael Watts, 'Confession of an Elitist', *Melody Maker*, (UK), February 1978.
18. Geyer, above Chapter 2 note 4, p. 69.
19. *Elvis Presley Enterprises Inc v Sid Shaw ElvislyYours* [1999] EWCA CIV 964.

CHAPTER 5 – TALK TO MY MANAGER

1. Elly McDonald, 'No Trouble in Paradise', *Ram Magazine*, 11 September 1985.
2. Sally Loane, 'The Rich', *The Age* (Melbourne), 26 June 1989, p. 11.
3. Christopher Webb, 'Losses are Double or Nothing at Two', *Herald Sun* (Melbourne), 20 November 1991, p. 73.
4. Yasmine Kartal, 'The Ivy my Biggest Mistake – Wheatley', *The Sunday Sun* (Melbourne), 29 July 1990, p. 7.
5. Gerard Wright, 'Godinski', *The Sunday Age* (Melbourne), 28 November 1993, Agenda p. 12.
6. Ibid p. 1.
7. David Lesser, 'The Hit Man', (1991) Spring *HQ* (Sydney), pp. 72 & 75
8. Ibid p. 78.
9. Ibid.
10. Ibid p. 79.
11. Ibid p. 77.
12. *Nigel Martin-Smith v Robert Peter Williams* (1999) UK C of A.
13. *Brenner & Another v First Artists' Management Pty Ltd & Another* [1993] 2 VR 221, p. 250.
14. Ibid.
15. Ibid p. 236.
16. Ibid.
17. Larry Schwartz, 'The Demos Inside Daryl', *The Sunday Age* (Melbourne), 1 September 1996, Agenda p. 4.
18. Transcript of Proceedings, *Adrian Roland Leonard Barker v Sean Kelly and Others* (Supreme Court of Victoria, Byrne J, 26 November 1992).
19. Ibid p. 4.
20. James Freud, above Chapter 2 note 9, p. 265.

21. Ibid.
22. *Churchers Pty Ltd v Positive Dream Pty Ltd*. Victorian Supreme Court No 6162 of 1999
23. *Biscayne Partners Pty Ltd v Valance Corp Pty Ltd & Ors* [2003] NSW SC 874

CHAPTER 6 – KYLIE IS A T-SHIRT

1. *Minogue v Grundy Television Pty Ltd* (Unreported, Supreme Court of Victoria, Beach J, 16 November 1989).
2. *Corporations Act 2001* (Cth), section 147.
   Corporations Regulations 2001 (Cth), schedule 6.
3. *Honey v Australian Airlines Ltd and Another* (1989) 14 IPR 264.
4. Ibid.
5. *Honey v Australian Airlines Ltd and Another* (1990) 18 IPR 185.
6. *Pacific Dunlop Ltd v Hogan* (1989) 23 FCR 553.
7. *Talmax Pty Ltd and Another v Telstra Corporation Pty Ltd* (1996) ATPR 41-484.
8. *Talmax Pty Ltd v Telstra Corporation Pty Ltd* [1997] 2 Qd R 444.
9. *Silvio Foschini v Victorian Football League* (Unreported, Supreme Court of Victoria, Crockett J, 15 April 1983).

CHAPTER 7 – THEY CAN'T DO THAT

1. *CBS Productions Pty Ltd v O'Neill* [1985] 1 NSWLR 601.
2. *Fahey and Others v Stephens Publishing Pty Ltd and Another* 1988 No. VG 459 (Unreported, Federal Court of Australia, Sweeney J, 15 November 1991).
3. *Cruise and Kidman v Southdown Press Pty Ltd* [1993] 26 IPR 125.

CHAPTER 8 – YOU CAN HAVE MY GIRLFRIEND TOO (JUST LEAVE THE CAT)

1. *Schroeder Music Publishing Co. Ltd v Macaulay* [1974] 1 WLR 1308.
2. *Clifford Davis Management Ltd v WEA Records Ltd* [1975] 1 WLR 61.
3. *Industrial Relations Act 1996* (NSW), section 106.
4. *Trade Practices Act 1974* (Cth), section 51AA.

CHAPTER 9 – BRICKS AND MORTAR

1. *Boosey v Whight* [1900] 1 Ch 122.
2. Dean Ellinson, 'Intellectual Property Protection for Performers', (1989) 9 *Victorian Law Institute Journal*, pp. 839 & 841.
3. At first instance:
   Alexandre Rachmaninoff and others v Gaumont Buena Vista International, Momentum Films Pty Ltd, David Hirschfelder, Universal International Music BV Universal Music SA, Universal Music Publishing, TG 1, Paris 1st Chamber Section 1, 24 May 2000.
   On appeal:
   Alexandre Rachmaninoff and others v Gaumont Buena Vista International, Momentum Films Pty Limited, David Hirschfelder, Universal International Music BV Universal Music SA, Universal Music Publishing, Court of Appeals, Paris 4th Chamber Section A, 12 June 2002.
4. Stuart Gibson, 'Protecting Film and Television Formats' (2003) 77(5) *Law Institute Journal* (Victoria), p. 46.
5. *TCN Channel Nine Pty Ltd v Network Ten Ltd* [2001] ATPR 91–699.
6. *Schott Musik International GMBH Co. & Ors v Colossal Records of Australia Ltd & Ors* [1996] 1033 FCA 1.
7. Victoria Pellicano, 'Dance and Copyright' (1997) 2 *Media And Arts Law Review,* Nadine Meisner, 'Stealing A Dance' *The Australian Financial Review,* 13 December, 2002.
8. Simon Minahan, 'Copyright – the Devil and the Detail', *The Age* (Melbourne), 1 April 2003, Next p. 6.
9. Rachael Osman, 'Pirates Rule the Cyber Waves', *The Australian Financial Review*, 2 May 2003, p. 3.
10. Ibid.
11. Ibid.
12. *Metro-Goldwyn-Mayer Stydios Inc. et al v Grokster Ltd et al; Jerry Lieber et al v Consumer Empowerment BV aka Fasttrack* (United States District Court – Central District of California), CV01-08541 – SVW; CV01-09923 – SVW.
13. Ibid.
14. Ibid.
15. Michael Wolf, 'Entertainers Lose Battle with Virtual Bandits', *The*

Australian Financial Review, 7 May 2003, p. 63.

16. Ibid.
17. Ibid.
18. Brett Foley, 'Medicine Makers Face Tougher Penalties', *The Australian Financial Review*, 14 May 2003, p. 3.
19. Garry Barker, 'Record Industry Backs Napster's Return', *The Sunday Age* (Melbourne), 25 May 2003, News p. 6.
20. Ibid.
21. Ibid.
22. Ibid.
23. Eric Savitz, 'iTunes is Sweet Music for Apple Investors', *The Australian Financial Review*, 28 May 2003, p. 55.
24. John Davidson, 'Record Chief's Deal to Sell with Kazaa' *The Australian Financial Review,* 17 September 2003, p.53.

CHAPTER 10 – OUT OF THE CLOSET

1. Copyright Law Review Committee, The Importation Provisions of the *Copyright Act 1968* (Cth), (1988).
2. Prices Surveillance Authority, *Inquiry into Book Prices*, Report No. 25, (1989).
3. Australian Council of Trade Unions, 'Background Submission to the Prices Surveillance Authority', (1990).
4. Australian Council of Trade Unions, 'Final Submission to the Prices Surveillance Authority Enquiry into the Price of Sound Recordings', (1990).
5. Tony Burchill, 'Record Firms in Spin on Imports', *The Australian Financial Review*, 12 December 1990, p. 10.
6. Ibid.
7. Prices Surveillance Authority, *The Prices of Sound Recordings*, Report No. 35, (1990).
8. ACTU, 'PSA Recommends Benefits for Australian Musicians and Composers', 18 December 1990.
9. Glenn A. Baker, 'Aussie Govt Report Angers Industry', *Billboard* (USA), 12 January 1991, p. 1.

10. Geyer, above Chapter 2 note 4.
11. Brett Thomas, 'Music Stars Storm Canberra', *Sydney Morning Herald* (Sydney), 4 August 1991, p. 1.
12. Ibid.
13. Ibid.
14. Tim Dodd, 'Rich Rock Stars Fighting to Retain the Consumer Rip-Off', *The Australian Financial Review*, 7 August 1991, p. 2.
15. Tom Burton, 'The Artless Culture Policy', *The Australian Financial Review*, 18 October 1994, p. 15.
16. Email from Phil Tripp, 21 May 1998.
17. *Copyright Amendment Act (No. 2) 1998* (Cth)
18. *Copyright Amendment Act (No. 1) 1998* (Cth), Schedule 2.
19. ACCC, 'Threats to CD Supplies Cost Record Companies $1M'., 6 March 2002'.
20. Ibid
21. *Universal Music Australia Pty Ltd v Australian Competition & Consumer Commission* [2003] FCAFC 193 [22 August 2003].

CHAPTER 11 – WIPEOUT

1. Neil Murray, *Sing For Me, Countryman*, Sceptre Books, 1993.
2. Andrew McMillan, *Strict Rules*, Hodder & Staughton, 1993.
3. *Bulun Bulun & Anor v R & T Textiles Pty Ltd & Anor* 41 IPR 513.
4. *Yumbulul v Reserve Bank of Australia & Ors* 21 IPR 481.
5. Annabel Crabb, 'Aboriginal Art, Culture to get Better Protection', *The Age* (Melbourne), 19 May 2003, News p. 6.

CHAPTER 12 – THE FILUM

1. *Hayden Productions Pty Ltd v TCN Channel 9 Pty Ltd* (Unreported, Supreme Court of NSW, Carruthers J, 7 August 1987).
2. Andiee Paviour, 'Tears of a Clown', (1993) 57 *WhoWeekly* (Australia), p. 43.
3. Michaela Boland, 'Troubled Waters', *The Australian Financial Review*, 9 January 2003, p. 39.

CHAPTER 13 – EIGHT SHOWS A WEEK

1. John Bell, *The Time of My Life*, Allen & Unwin, 2002, p. 166.
2. Clark Forbes, 'If this is Australia, then Farewell', *The Sun* (Melbourne), 18 January 1988.
3. Ibid.
4. Ibid.
5. Ibid.
6. Leonard Radic, 'A Passing Parade of Aussie History', *The Age* (Melbourne), 18 January 1988, p. 14.
7. Ibid.
8. Ibid.
9. Ibid.
10. Ibid.
11. Alan Attwood, 'Irreverent Anthems', (1988) 4 *Time* (Australia), p. 10.
12. Ben Hills, 'How the Carlton Push Became History', *The Herald* (Melbourne), 18 March 1988, p. 11.
13. Christopher Webb, 'Jacobsen Punters Led on a Song and Dance', *The Age* (Melbourne), 15 May 2003, Business p. 3.
14. Norman Lebrecht, *When the Music Stops*, Pocket Books, 1997.

CHAPTER 15 – NOTHING CHANGES

1. Patrick Donovan, 'Bands on the Brink', *The Age* (Melbourne), 5 April 2003, Insight p. 5.

BIBLIOGRAPHY

ARTICLES

Attwood, Alan, 'Irreverent Anthems', (1988) 4 *Time* (Australia), p. 10.

Baker, Glenn A., *Penthouse* (Australia), 1985 or thereabouts, p. 129.

Baker, Glenn A., 'Aussie Govt Report Angers Industry', *Billboard* (USA), 12 January 1991, p. 1.

Barker, Garry, 'Record Industry Backs Napster's Return' *The Sunday Age* (Melbourne), 25 May 2003, News p. 6.

Boland, Michaela, 'Troubled Waters', *The Australian Financial Review*, 9 January 2003, p. 39.

Burchill, Tony, 'Record Firms in Spin on Imports', *The Australian Financial Review*, 12 December 1990, p. 10.

Burton, Tom, 'The Artless Culture Policy', *The Australian Financial Review*, 18 October 1994, p. 15.

Crabb, Annabel, 'Aboriginal Art, Culture to get Better Protection', *The Age* (Melbourne), 19 May 2003, News p. 6.

Dodd, Tim, 'Rich Rock Stars Fighting to Retain the Consumer Rip-Off', *The Australian Financial Review*, 7 August 1991, p. 2.

Donovan, Patrick, 'Bands on the Brink', *The Age* (Melbourne), 5 April 2003, Insight p. 5.

Ellinson, Dean, 'Intellectual Property Protection for Performers', (1989) 9 *Victorian Law Institute Journal*, p. 839.

Foley, Brett, 'Medicine Makers Face Tougher Penalties', *The Australian Financial Review*, 14 May 2003, p. 3.

Forbes, Clark, 'If this is Australia, then Farewell', *The Sun* (Melbourne), 18 January 1988.

Gibson, Stuart, 'Protecting Film and Television Formats' (2003) 77(5) *Law Institute Journal* (Victoria), p. 46.

Hills, Ben, 'How the Carlton Push Became History', *The Herald* (Melbourne), 18 March 1988, p. 11.

Holmes, Peter, 'Neil Finn', (1992) 10 *APRA Magazine* (Australia), p. 6.

Kartal, Yasmine, 'The Ivy my Biggest Mistake – Wheatley', *The Sunday Sun* (Melbourne), 29 July 1990, p. 7.

Lawrence, Tess, 'LRB on top of the Wave', *The Bulletin,* NSW, 24 October 1978, p. 78.

Lesser, David, 'The Hit Man', (1991) Spring *HQ* (Sydney), p. 72.

Loane, Sally, 'The Rich', *The Age* (Melbourne), 26 June 1989, p. 11.

McDonald, Elly, 'No Trouble in Paradise', *Ram Magazine*, 11 September 1985.

Meldrum, Molly, 'Men's Real Launch', *TV Week,* NSW, 22 June 1985, p. 37.

Meisner, Nadine, 'Stealing a Dance' *The Australian Financial Review*, 13 December 2002.

Minahan, Simon, 'Copyright – the Devil and the Detail', *The Age (Next)* (Melbourne), 1 April 2003, p. 6.

Novak, Ralph, 'Two Hearts – Men at Work', *People Weekly* (USA), 1 July 1985.

Osman, Rachael, 'Pirates Rule the Cyber Waves', *The Australian Financial Review*, 2 May 2003, p. 3.

Paviour, Andiee, 'Tears of a Clown', (1993) 57 *Who Weekly* (Australia), p. 43.

Pellicano, Victoria, 'Dance and Copyright' (1997) 2 *Media and Arts Review*.

Radic, Leonard, 'A Passing Parade of Aussie History', *The Age* (Melbourne), 18 January 1988, p. 14.

Savitz, Eric, 'iTunes is Sweet Music for Apple Investors', *The Australian Financial Review*, 28 May 2003, p. 55.

Schwartz, Larry, 'The Demos Inside Daryl', *The Sunday Age* (Melbourne), 1 September 1996, Agenda p. 4.

Smith, Michael George, 'Ozrock: The State Of Play', (1994) *Overland* 135, p. 21.

Soocher, Stan, 'Madonna, Bruce And Grubman Indursky', *The National Law Journal*, 18 November 1991, p. 1.

Thomas, Brett, 'Music Stars Storm Canberra', *Sydney Morning Herald* (Sydney), 4 August 1991, p. 1.

Walker, Clinton, 'Young and Restless', *The Age* (Melbourne), 10 December 1994, Saturday Extra p. 5.

Watts, Michael, 'Confession of an Elitist', *Melody Maker*, UK, February 1978.

Webb, Christopher, 'Losses are Double or Nothing at Two', *Herald Sun* (Melbourne), 20 November 1991, p. 73.

Webb, Christopher, 'Jacobsen Punters Led on a Song and Dance', *The Age* (Melbourne), 15 May 2003, Business p. 3.

Wilmoth, Peter, 'The Mark of the Dragon', *The Age* (Melbourne), 20 May 1985, p. 11.

Wilmoth, Peter, 'Men at Work – A Hole in the Road', *The Age* (Melbourne), 13 July 1985, Saturday Extra p. 1.

Wilmoth, Peter, 'A House Divided', *The Sunday Age* (Melbourne), 11 August 1996, Agenda p. 1.

Wolf, Michael, 'Entertainers Lose Battle with Virtual Bandits', *The Australian Financial Review*, 7 May 2003, p. 63.

Wright, Gerard, 'Godinski', *The Sunday Age* (Melbourne), 28 November 1993, Agenda p. 1.

Zuel, Bernard, 'The Sun Sets on Midnight Oil', *The Age* (Melbourne), 4 December 2002, p. 13.

BOOKS

Bell, John, *The Time of My Life*, Allen & Unwin, 2002.

Brown, Peter and Gaines, Steven, *The Love You Make – An Insider's Story of the Beatles*, McGraw Hill, 1983.

Creswell, Toby, *Too Much Ain't Enough – Jimmy Barnes – The Authorised Biography*, Random House Australia, 1993.

Coupe, Stuart, *The Promoters – Inside Stories from the Australian Rock Industry*, Hodder Headline Australia Pty Ltd, 2003.

Dannen, Fredric, *Hit Men – Power Brokers and Fast Money Inside the Music Business*, Vintage, 1991.

Freud, James, *I am the Voice Left from Drinking – The Models – From the Burbs to Barbados and Beyond*, HarperCollins Publishers, 2002.

Gee, Mike, *The Final Days of Michael Hutchence*, Omnibus Press, 1998.

Geyer, Renée, *Confessions of a Difficult Woman – The Renée Geyer Story*, HarperCollins Publishers, 2000.

Hayward, Philip (ed.), *From Pop to Punk to Post Modernism*, Allen & Unwin, 1992.

King, Tom, *The Operator – David Geffen Builds, Buys and Sells the New Hollywood*, Broadway Books, 2000.

Lebrecht, Norman, *When the Music Stops*, Pocket Books, 1997.

McHenry, Paul, Spencer, Chris, and Zbig, Nowara (eds), *Who's Who of Australian Rock*, The Five Mile Press, 4th ed., 1996.

McMillan, Andrew, *Strict Rules*, Hodder & Staughton, 1993.

Murray, Neil, *Sing for Me, Countryman*, Sceptre Books, 1993.

Simpson, Shane, *Music Business – Making Music Work*, Omnibus Press, 2002.

Soocher, Stan, *They Fought the Law – Rock Music Goes to Court*, Schirmer Books, 1999.

Tayler, Michele, *Music Speak – A Music Business Lexicon*, Victorian Rock Foundation, 1992.

Tycho, Tommy, *The Tommy Tycho Story Music, Maestro Please*, Brolga Publishing Pty Ltd, 1995.

Butler, Bruce, *Young Players Guide*, The Push, 3rd ed., 1992.

Walker, Clinton, *Stranded*, McMillan, 1996.

Wheatley, Glenn, *Paper Paradise – Confessions of a Rock 'n' Roll Survivor*, Bantam, 1999.

CASES

Adrian Roland Leonard Barker v Sean Kelly and Others (Supreme Court of Victoria, Byrne J, 26 November 1992).

Alexandre Rachmaninoff and others v Gaumont Buena Vista International, Momentum Films Pty Ltd, David Hirschfelder, Universal International Music BV Universal Music SA, Universal Music Publishing, TG 1, Paris 1st Chamber Section 1, 24 May 2000.

Alexandre Rachmaninoff and others v Gaumont Buena Vista International,

Momentum Films Pty Limited, David Hirschfelder, Universal International Music BV Universal Music SA, Universal Music Publishing, Court of Appeals, Paris 4th Chamber Section A, 12 June 2002.

Boosey v Whight [1900] 1 Ch 122.

Biscayne Partners Pty Ltd v Valance Corp Pty Ltd & Ors, [2003] NSWSC 874

Brenner & Another v First Artists' Management Pty Ltd & Another [1993] 2 VR 221, p. 250.

Bulun Bulun & Anor v R & T Textiles Pty Ltd & Anor 41 IPR 513.

CBS Productions Pty Ltd v O'Neill [1985] 1 NSWLR 601.

Clifford Davis Management Ltd v WEA Records Ltd [1975] 1 WLR 61.

Cruise and Kidman v Southdown Press Pty Ltd [1993] 26 IPR 125.

Elvis Presley Enterprises Inc. v Sid Shaw Elvisly Yours [1999] EWCA CIV 964.

Fahey and Others v Stephens Publishing Pty Ltd and Another 1988 No. VG 459 (Unreported, Federal Court of Australia, Sweeney J, 15 November 1991).

Hayden Productions Pty Ltd v TCN Channel 9 Pty Ltd (Unreported, Supreme Court of NSW, Carruthers J, 7 August 1987).

Honey v Australian Airlines Ltd and Another (1989) 14 IPR 264.

Honey v Australian Airlines Ltd and Another (1990) 18 IPR 185.

Metro-Goldwyn-Mayer Studios Inc. et al v Grokster Ltd et al; *Jerry Lieber et al v Consumer Empowerment BV aka Fasttrack* (United States District Court – Central District of California), CV01-08541 – SVW; CV01-09923 – SVW.

Minogue v Grundy Television Pty Ltd (Unreported, Supreme Court of Victoria, Beach J, 16 November 1989).

Nigel Martin-Smith v Robert Peter Williams (1999) UK C of A.

Pacific Dunlop Ltd v Hogan (1989) 23 FCR 553.

Regina v I H Saxon (Unreported, Supreme Court of NSW, Dunford J, 1 August 1996).

Schott Musik International GMBH Co. & Ors v Colossal Records of Australia Ltd & Ors [1996] 1033 FCA 1.

Schroeder Music Publishing Co. Ltd v Macaulay [1974] 1 WLR 1308.

Silvio Foschini v Victorian Football League (Unreported, Supreme Court of Victoria, Crockett J, 15 April 1983).

Talmax Pty Ltd and Another v Telstra Corporation Pty Ltd (1996) ATPR 41–484.

Talmax Pty Ltd v Telstra Corporation Pty Ltd [1997] 2 Qd R 444.

TCN Channel Nine Pty Ltd v Network Ten Ltd [2001] ATPR 91–699.

We Two Pty Ltd v Shorrock (2002) FCA 875.

Yumbulul v Reserve Bank of Australia & Ors 21 IPR 481.

LEGISLATION

Copyright Act 1968 (Cth).

Copyright Amendment Act 1984 (Cth).

Copyright Amendment Act 1989 (Cth).

Copyright Amendment Act 1991 (Cth).

Copyright Amendment Act (No. 1) 1998 (Cth).

Copyright Amendment Act (No. 2) 1998 (Cth).

Copyright Amendment (Moral Rights) Act 2000 (Cth).

Corporations Act 2001 (Cth).

Corporations Regulations 2001 (Cth).

Entertainment Industry Act 1989 (NSW).

Income Tax Assessment Act 1997 (Cth).

Industrial Relations Act 1996 (NSW).

Trade Practices Act 1974 (Cth).

REPORTS, PAPERS AND SUBMISSIONS

ACCC, 'Threats to CD Supplies Cost Record Companies $1M, 6 March 2002'.

ACTU, 'PSA Recommends Benefits for Australian Musicians and Composers', 18 December 1990.

Australian Council of Trade Unions, 'Background Submission to the Prices Surveillance Authority', (1990).

Australian Council of Trade Unions, Final Submission to the Prices Surveillance Authority, Enquiry into the Price of Sound Recordings, (1990).

Michael Brereton, *International Tax Planning – An Analysis and Case Study*, October 1980.

Michael Brereton, 'Taxation Aspects of Importance to the Music Industry', 25 February 1984, p. 27.

Copyright Law Review Committee, The Importation Provisions of the *Copyright Act 1968* (Cth), (1988).

Prices Surveillance Authority, *Inquiry into Book Prices*, Report No. 25 (1989).

Prices Surveillance Authority, *The Prices of Sound Recordings*, Report No. 35 (1990).

Victoria Pellicano, Dance and Copyright, *Media And Arts Law Review*, Volume 2, September 1997

Nadine Meisner, Stealing A Dance, *The Australian Financial Review* 13 December 2002.

IMMEDIA! MUSIC BUSINESS BOOKS & OVERSEAS MUSIC INDUSTRY DIRECTORIES

These books and overseas directories are available by mail order from IMMEDIA! Prices effective until December 30, 2004.

THE AUSTRALASIAN MUSIC INDUSTRY DIRECTORY ©2004

The print edition of the AustralAsian Music Industry Directory is a complete, concise & up-to-date music industry sourcebook that contains all the contacts you will need within 70+ sections. It's the ultimate contact book for doing business in AustralAsia. **PRICE $40** (Internet subscription prices are covered on the following pages)

ALL AREA ACCESS: Management Guide for Unsigned Musicians ©1997

How to market your act & music without a manager, but how to attract the right one. Starting up, booking gigs, press and the media, doing deals, touring, finance & managing your agent or manager. Essential book for musos.

PRICE $60

ALL YOU NEED TO KNOW ABOUT THE MUSIC BUSINESS ©2000

Written by a top American dealmaker lawyer, it's a three level hardcover that delivers the music business from bottom to top. An insider's guide to every legal & financial aspect of the business of music filled with advice, anecdotes & answers at an easy pace or fast tracked.

PRICE $70

THE ART OF MUSIC PRODUCTION ©2002

Revealing what it takes to become a successful record producer it runs from how to start, what kind of music to produce, how to deal with artists, record companies and publishers as well as the career strategies needed for long term success. Answering all the practical questions the aspiring producer needs to know, the book also contains witty anecdotes as well as looking towards expanding into other new media.

PRICE $45

BEYOND THE CHARTS ©2000

A detailed history of MP3 & the digital music revolution which has changed the way music is consumed, distributed & marketed. Tracks the evolution of this technology and its stakeholders, debates the pros, cons & its impact on consumers, artists, music industry heavyweights & society.

PRICE $45

CONFESSIONS OF A RECORD PRODUCER – How To Survive The Scams and Shams Of The Music Industry ©2002

Protect your rights & preserve your assets with this brilliant book, dissecting major and indie record deals, publishing and production agreements, plus it shows the shadier side of the biz, using 15 years of examples by this anonymous producer. One of the best we have!

PRICE $45

CRAFT AND BUSINESS OF SONGWRITING ©2002

Practical guide to create and market artistic and commercially successful songs, teaching the craft of song construction and revealing secrets of the music biz. Anecdotes, exercises and examples from dozens of top songwriters. 300+ pages.

PRICE $45

EVERYTHING YOU'D BETTER KNOW ABOUT THE RECORD INDUSTRY ©1996

Written by a major producer & songwriter with best advice on selecting managers, accountants & lawyers plus publishing and indie label considerations. Ins and outs of royalties, budgets, contracts and agreements. Complete contracts analysed point by point.

PRICE $90

EXPLODING: The Highs, Hits, Hype, Heroes and Hustlers of the Warner Music Group ©2003

From the ultimate Warner insider, Stan Cornyn, it reads like other scandalous books such as "Hit Men", "Stiffed" and "Mansion on the Hill". 480 pages that traces the history of the Warner Music Group from decades of riotous fun and booming business to when it went 'splat' in the 90s. An epic look at the evolution and resulting confusion that's a result of the record business becoming one branch of multi-national media conglomerates.

PRICE $35

HOW TO BE YOUR OWN BOOKING AGENT – The Musician's and Performing Artist's Guide to Successful Touring ©2004

Step-by-step method. Comprehensive guide for any performer wanting to be a successful touring artist. Seasoned veteran Goldstein shares secrets on running your own mini-business. Topics include negotiating contracts; developing effective press kits; using the media to your advantage; maximising label relationships; booking successful tours & expanding audiences, plus sharpening negotiation skills. A DIY Masterpiece!

PRICE $60

HOW TO HAVE YOUR HIT SONG PUBLISHED ©1988

A step by step sequence that songwriters can use to prepare & educate themselves in the ways of music publishing. Essential guide for anyone associated with the music business or songwriting needs for constant reference. Includes sample contracts, how to read music trades and crucial contact tips.

PRICE $40

HOW TO MAKE AND SELL YOUR OWN RECORDING ©1999

Offers all the technical information, practical tips & business guidelines for self production of CD, cassette, even vinyl. Covers every angle from recording to marketing including worksheets & budget outlines for each step. For first time recorders or indie label chiefs and Indians. The world's best book on rolling your own records and one of our top sellers!

PRICE $75

HOW TO WRITE A HIT SONG ©2001

"How to Write a Hit Song" covers every topic aspiring songwriters must know to be successful from creating memorable lyrics, composing melody & crafting song structure to collaborating, finding a publisher & recording. Our least expensive songwriter book.

PRICE $27

HOWLING AT THE MOON – The Odyssey of a Monstrous Music Mogul in an Age of Excess ©2004

Outspoken, outrageous & phenomenally successful former Sony CEO traces his staggering journey as he rocketed up the 70s and 80s corporate monolith. Yetnikoff's hilarious account of how he became Michael Jackson's godfather confessor, prompted David Geffen to give his mistress oral sex lessons, chased the Rolling Stones around the world nearly coming to blows with Jagger, plus tales from feeding his craving for power, sex, liquor and cocaine. Shocking account of a man who led the most remarkable run of success -- and self-destruction -- ever seen in the industry.

PRICE $50

KOHN ON MUSIC LICENSING (a.k.a. The Art Of Music Licensing) ©2002

Third Edition–Also known as The Art of Music Licensing, this global guide to music publishing's revenue side covers all aspects of licensing music to disc, new media, computer software, games, film and TV, online and other areas of music exploitation. At over 1000 pages with a disc, it covers how to clear a license, negotiate fees, copyright renewal and contains exhaustive, concrete examples for publishers who wish to exploit their copyrights as well as those seeking permission to use music.

PRICE $375

LIVE SOUND MIXING ©1997

Written by Australian sound expert Duncan Fry, the first book to show how to pull great sound out of a PA system. Jam packed with useful info, diagrams and hints, explains basic principles of how a PA system works to trouble shooting.

PRICE $50

MAKING IT IN THE MUSIC BUSINESS ©2004

A business & legal guide for songwriters and performers makes copyright easy, band partnerships, names, dealing with agents and managers plus the important role of a music lawyer & how to find the right one. Discusses contracts & points with a glossary of legal terms.

PRICE $35

MUSIC BUSINESS ©2002

Our most popular and best selling book on all aspects of doing business in the music industry. Written by music & copyright lawyer Shane Simpson it has an extensive chapter on new technologies and music as well as everything you need to know about establishing a music business presence and dealmaking point-by-point. Sections on record and publishing deals, band structures and agreements, managers, collection societies, copyrights and much more explains music legalities & business realities for Australia.

PRICE $60

A MUSIC BUSINESS PRIMER ©2003

Rapaport–author of top selling book 'How To Make & Sell Your Own Recording'–explores relationships between music businesses vs creativity and talent of musicians or performers. All music industry areas are covered; controversial free file sharing issue exploring artists' creative rights; licensing & sampling; marketing & promoting; publishing deals, including collaborator/songwriter agreement, plus more. Perfect for musicians and future music pros who want a comprehensive industry overview.

PRICE $60

MUSIC INDUSTRY MANAGEMENT ©2002

Music Industry Management was designed as an Australian resource for musicians, songwriters and others who want to manage their own careers, or take a more informed role in the work that's done on their behalf. A practical, comprehensive introduction to the realities of managing bands, music events and copyright. Features more than 20 sample contracts and working documents, as well as some useful case studies. Used by many schools in music business courses.

PRICE $45

THE MUSIC MANAGERS MANUAL ©2002

Created by the Australian Music Managers Forum in late 2002, this loose-leaf, ring bound 175 page book was created to deal with many of the things that will confront a new manager or self-managed artist. Edited by top music journalist Christie Eliezer, it contains invaluable advice sourced from a broad range of music industry professionals. It's the ultimate Australian-based guide for those either self managing or for the emerging artist manager.

PRICE $75

MUSIC MONEY AND SUCCESS ©2000

A must for every songwriter, performer and musician, as well as required reading for every music lawyer, manager agent, producer or publisher. Featuring 3 New Chapters: the Internet; Sampling; Co-ventures and Joint Ventures Plus: * New Mechanical Royalty Rates for the Years 2002-2007 New Synchronization Rates for Putting Songs in Movies, Television Series And Advertising Commercials * New Technology Areas: Downloads, Streaming, DVDs, Web site Licensing, etc. * Internet's Effect on Recording and Publishing Contracts.

PRICE $60

MUSIC PUBLISHING – The Real Road To Music Business Success ©2000

Covers all aspects of publishing including how to set up your own publishing entity. Newly updated, you can learn how to forecast sales, calculate advances, evaluate copyright purchases, negotiate favorable contracts and licenses. Market product effectively, manage personnel and company affairs efficiently and maximise commercial potential.

PRICE $100

MUSICIANS BUSINESS AND LEGAL GUIDE ©2001

2nd edition. A thick book by the Beverly Hills Entertainment Lawyers Assn., providing information on key legal and business issues. Thoroughly & exhaustively covers all aspects of the commercial & legal areas of a musician. Foreign contracts are analysed by points. Range of info is staggering.

PRICE $90

THE REAL DEAL: How To Get Signed To A Record Label ©2002

A revised and completely updated edition of industry classic that offers specific advice to musicians on getting that all-important record deal. Included are all the business necessities, creative aspects, and marketing strategies needed for musicians to survive and thrive. Learn, step-by-step, how to prepare a presentation package and reach the right person at the record labels, and discover dozens of no-fail procedures and time-tested techniques for making it in this competitive business.

PRICE $45

RUTHLESS SELF-PROMOTION IN THE MUSIC INDUSTRY ©1999

How to become a promotion fanatic with all you need to know about how to get new business. Gather marketing information about your segment of the music industry and use networking or other strategies to achieve success. A fascinating book on driving yourself into the industry.

PRICE $55

SECRETS OF NEGOTIATING A RECORD CONTRACT – The Musician's Guide to Understanding & Avoiding Sneaky Lawyer Tricks ©2001

By the author of our hugely popular "Confessions of a Record Producer; How to Avoid the Scams and Shams of the Music Industry", this 300 page book is a streetwise guide to deciphering music recording agreements crafted by today's top major label lawyers. Clause by clause Moses deconstructs actual contracts and translates them into plain English with the originals and decoded versions shown side by side.

PRICE $55

SONGWRITING AND THE CREATIVE PROCESS ©1995

Provides the direction and inspiration needed to develop songwriting skills with sections on all the basic elements of songwriting & transforming ideas from concept to song. Easy to understand sections on all the basic elements of songwriting: melody, harmony, song structure, rhythm, lyrics and 'hooks'. Tips from songwriting professionals plus lessons in creativity.

PRICE $55

START AND RUN YOUR OWN RECORD LABEL ©2003

An industry insider, Daylle Deanna Swartz, offers sound advice and successful strategies to novices and professionals alike... information, ideas and observations from over 100 industry pros including founders and presidents of prominent indie labels. Concise and inspiring, topics discussed range from working with contracts, marketing & promoting, touring & aspects of Internet marketing.

PRICE $50

SUCCESSFUL LYRIC WRITING ©1988

The complete guide to writing professional lyrics from theory, principles and song forms to how to create titles, song ideas, avoid pitfalls and choose the best music form for words. Inside you'll find a series of "student tested" exercises, practice critiques and quizzes that reinforce songwriting theory each step of the way and prepare you for the books main feature - ten specially designed lyric writing assignments.

PRICE $50

THE PROMOTERS ©2003

It will probably be called the "Hit Men" of the Australian music industry-a revealing probe into the sometimes criminal aspects as well as the hilarious escapades of concert promoters Down Under. It strips back the veneer of respectability of entrepreneurs & impresarios and scrapes the scum off the soft, putrid underbelly of the talent exploitation industry. The smoke and mirrors of promotion, the scraping of razor blades aimed at throats and noses and the big guns of the industry are laid bare.

PRICE $35

THIS BUSINESS OF ARTIST MANAGEMENT ©1997

The new, updated, definitive manual for professional artists & those involved in developing an artist's career. Formerly known as "Successful Artist Management" it's got the best guidance on performance, recording & publishing, working in film & TV plus career planning strategies. The best book for managers, those considering a career in management or cluey artists who want to manage themselves.

PRICE $55

THIS BUSINESS OF MUSIC ©2003

This authoritative guide to the legal, practical and procedural aspects of the industry now includes up to date information on music technology, contracts, record clubs, DAT, licensing, copyrights, work-for-hire rules and show music among many other crucial topics. Published by Billboard and in its 8th edition, it's a classic.

PRICE $80

THIS BUSINESS OF MUSIC MARKETING AND PROMOTION ©2003

A complete, practical guide to carrying out a music marketing and promotion plan. In the competitive world of music, creating the sounds is only half the battle. Actively selling those sound to the listening public is just as vitally important. This Business of Music Marketing and Promotion provides a comprehensive array of techniques, tools, and strategies - both standard and alternative - needed to get music to the marketing, promote it effectively, and ensure the highest possible sales.

PRICE $55

THE ULTIMATE SURVIVAL GUIDE TO THE NEW MUSIC INDUSTRY – Handbook for Hell ©2004

Easy-to-read book with topics ranging from how to successfully release independent albums & attract top managers; creating revenue through licensing, self-distribution rights, soundtrack opportunities, merchandising, & more. Includes crucial CD-ROM with recording & publishing contracts & valuable music business forms, plus interviews with A&R managers and other industry pros.

PRICE $50

WHAT THEY'LL NEVER TELL YOU ABOUT THE MUSIC BUSINESS ©2002

This insider guide discloses the hidden dynamics and often unfortunate consequences of what really happens when a deal is prepared, contracts are signed, and promises are made-and alerts musicians, attorneys, songwriters, and anyone else interested in the music business to the potent dangers lurking beneath.

PRICE $60

2004 OVERSEAS MUSIC INDUSTRY DIRECTORIES

U.S. RECORDING INDUSTRY SOURCEBOOK

©2004

In new lay-flat binding format, 2004's 500+ pages it's the definitive, all-inclusive contact book for North America. They've added radio stations and venues to the extensive listings of labels, distributors and majors; managers, agents, promoters, publishers, lawyers, studios, associations, PR, music media, websites record pools, CD & tape manufacturers and much more. Comes with Sourcebook CD of all information that works with Mac and Windows. The best overall guide to the US & Canada. **PRICE $200**

U.S. POLLSTAR BOOKING AGENCY ROSTERS

©2004

Over 188 pages which features virtually all US Booking agencies with full personnel contact details including emails and website addresses. All companies list their artist roster which is also cross referenced to be able to source specific artists quickly. It's the best way to find agents to book your artist within a specific genre or territory as well as sourcing overseas acts to tour Australia. **PRICE $150**

U.S. POLLSTAR RECORD COMPANY ROSTER

©2004

132 pages comprehensively listing major & indie labels, plus national distribution, label personnel & artist rosters with a personnel index & artist index that makes it an up to the minute recording label & A&R resource. For easy reference there is a fax & phone index for each listing.The Roster also has a Publishers & Distribution Group section. Published twice yearly, it's the best, most current & accurate contact guide for the US recording industry. **PRICE $150**

U.S. POLLSTAR TALENT BUYER DIRECTORY

©2004

Over 356 pages with every major concert promoter, and all the bookers of nightclubs, colleges, fairs, festivals and theme parks that buy touring artists. It includes overseas contacts as an added bonus as well as a complete personnel index. The Talent Buyers is used by agents everywhere, companies are broken up state by state to make locating easier. It's published bi-annually for as up to date information as possible. **PRICE $150**

UK MUSIC WEEK DIRECTORY

©2004

Published by the UK music weekly trade magazine, "Music Week" this 300+ page directory covers all aspects of the English/Ireland/Scotland/Wales music industry biz including retailers, record companies, publishers, agents, distributors and legals to name a few. Artists are cross referenced by managers and labels. A very broad range of business services, complete music media (print and electronic) and studios. **PRICE $175**

U.S.—THE MUSICIAN'S ATLAS

©2004

Now in its fifth edition, the 2004 Musician's Atlas provides access to over 15,000 music businesses and key industry contacts in more than 25 categories. Current names, phone and fax numbers, e-mail and website addresses, detailed submission policies and the styles of music preferred is just some of the information you'll find as well as city-by-city lists of vital contacts for media, gigs, retailers and even places to eat! **PRICE $80**

SECURE ONLINE MUSIC BOOKSTORE

WWW.IMMEDIA.COM.AU/BOOKS

Though we have been selling music business books and overseas music industry directories online and from our Sydney office since 1995, our new secure website for 2004 introduces a new look and design for your convenience and shopping security.

Regulary updated, the IMMEDIA! online secure books website contains over 60 books, directories and services that can assist, amuse or inform everyone from aspiring musicians to managing directors.

There are hundreds of titles from around the world on the business of music and thousands on how to play instruments or fiddle with technology. We limit ourselves to the best and most useful books for those music industry professionals who want to do business, find out how to create their own product or businesses and also read a few scandalous titles for professional amusement.

OUR BOOK CATEGORIES INCLUDE:

- Music Industry Directories
- Publicity, Promotion & Marketing
- Legal
- General Music Business
- Songwriting & Publishing
- Record Production & Release

...and much more.

Plus we offer online subscriptions to the AustralAsian Music Industry Directory and the Platinum and Gold In Music and Media Daily News Subscription Services.

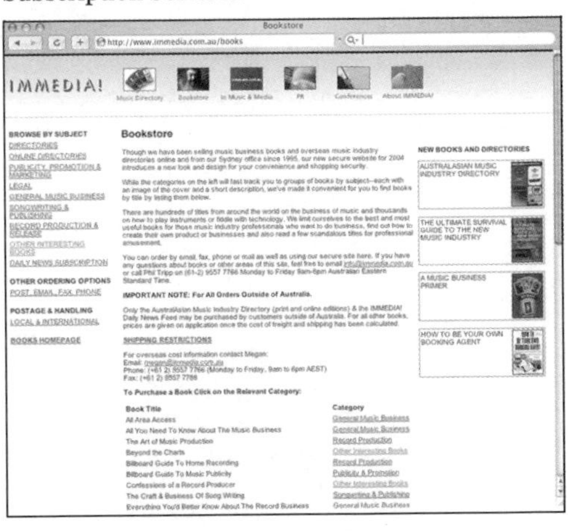

AUSTRALASIAN MUSIC INDUSTRY DIRECTORY

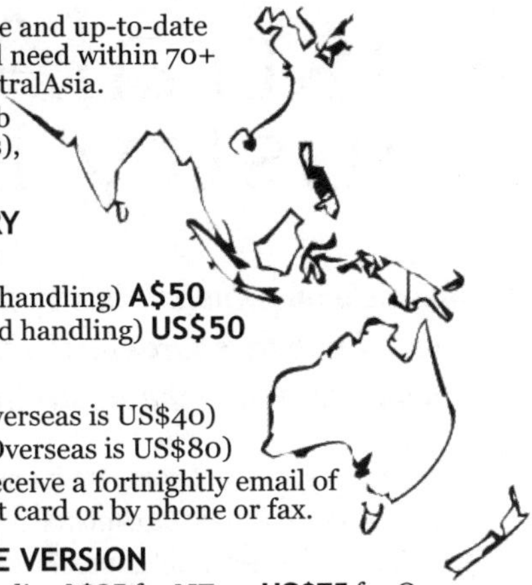

The AustralAsian Music Industry Directory is a complete, concise and up-to-date music industry sourcebook that contains all the contacts you will need within 70+ sections. It's the ultimate contact book for doing business in AustralAsia.

Available as a print edition & online subscription service to a web edition (updated fortnightly with email alerts sent to subscribers), both are published every January and July.

• GET THE CURRENT PRINT EDITION OF THE DIRECTORY

Shipped within Australia (postage & handling included) **A$40**
Shipped to any New Zealand address (including postage and handling) **A$50**
Shipped to Asia/Pacific & rest of World (including postage and handling) **US$50**

• ONLINE SUBCRIPTION

6 months access—A$40 (Aust orders only) (NZ is A$50 & Overseas is US$40)
12 months access—A$80 (Aust orders only) (NZ is A$85 & Overseas is US$80)
You'll have 24 hour access to our continually updated site and receive a fortnightly email of changes and additions. You can register & pay online with credit card or by phone or fax.

• GET A CURRENT PRINT COPY AND ACCESS TO ONLINE VERSION

6 months online + the latest print directory is **A$75** within Australia, **A$85** for NZ, or **US$75** for Overseas
12 months online + both directories is **A$125** within Australia, **A$150** for NZ, or **US$125** for Overseas

• TO ACCESS THE ONLINE DIRECTORY (http://www.immedia.com.au/amid)

Free access only available for January 1997 edition (now over 7 years old) is for sampling or research purposes but listings are old and inaccurate.
Access to continually updated listings from our latest edition is by paid subscription only.

ORDER A BOOK OR DIRECTORY WITH IMMEDIA!

Contact IMMEDIA! — 20 Hordern Street, Newtown, NSW, 2042, AUSTRALIA
Phone within Australia: (02) 9557 7766 International: (61-2) 9557 7766
Fax within Australia: (02) 9557 7788 International: (61-2) 9557 7788
Secure online website: http://www.immedia.com.au/books

HOW TO PAY:

CREDIT CARD

We accept Visa, Mastercard & Bankcard (Australian Bankcards only), your order will be processed within 3 days. No AMEX or Diners.

CHEQUE

Please make out your cheque to IMMEDIA! PTY LTD. It is our firm policy that cheque orders (personal or company) must be cleared by our bank before shipment. This will incur a 10 day clearance delay before shipping. NO EXCEPTIONS! Please note that there is a cheque dishonour fee of $15.

POSTAL MONEY ORDER OR BANK DRAFT

Please make out your money order or draft to IMMEDIA! PTY LTD. Your order will be processed within 3 working days.

IMPORTANT DELIVERY DETAILS:

We generally ship by air courier so we need a daytime street address where someone will be during the day to sign for the shipment.

Otherwise, please specify a secure postal address. See below shipping details.

AUSTRALIA — Please add A$8.80 to your first book, on your second a total of $10, on your third a total of $12.50, on your fourth a total of $15 and $2.50 per book thereafter. This covers handling and delivery. Please allow 3 working days for delivery. If payment is by cheque then allow for a 10 day delay while cheque is being cleared.

OVERSEAS — Shipping prices on application. Unless specified we will ship by Air Mail. Phone, fax, or email admin@immedia.com.au for further details.

AustralAsian Music Industry Directory

The AustralAsian Music Industry Directory is a complete, concise and up-to-date music industry sourcebook that contains all the contacts you will need for doing business within the AustralAsian music industry.

If you want the most current contacts for over 70 categories of music businesses (Agents, Managers, Record Labels, Publishers, Promoters Venues, Music Media, Studios, Uni Bookers, Artists and Songwriters plus many more) you can't afford to be without the AustralAsian Music Industry Directory.

Available as a print edition & online subscription service to a web edition (updated fortnightly with email alerts sent to subscribers), both are published every January and July.

Purchase the Directory

Purchase a print Directory for $30 at our offices ($40 posted to you), 6 month online subscription for $40 (12 months for $80) or get combinations of both. Visit or contact IMMEDIA!

IMMEDIA! 20 Hordern St, Newtown, NSW, 2042
Phone - (02) 9557 7766 Fax - (02) 9557 7788
Email - admin@immedia.com.au
Further Info - http://www.immedia.com.au/amid
Purchase - http://www.immedia.com.au/books

online music bookstore

WWW.IMMEDIA.COM.AU/BOOKS

Recently redesigned and regulary updated, the IMMEDIA! online secure books website contains over 60 books, directories and services that can assist, amuse or inform everyone from aspiring musicians to managing directors.

Our book categories include:

- Music Industry Directories
- Publicity, Promotion & Marketing
- Legal
- General Music Business
- Songwriting & Publishing
- Record Production & Release

...and much more.

For a detailed print catalogue of what's available you can also contact IMMEDIA! directly.

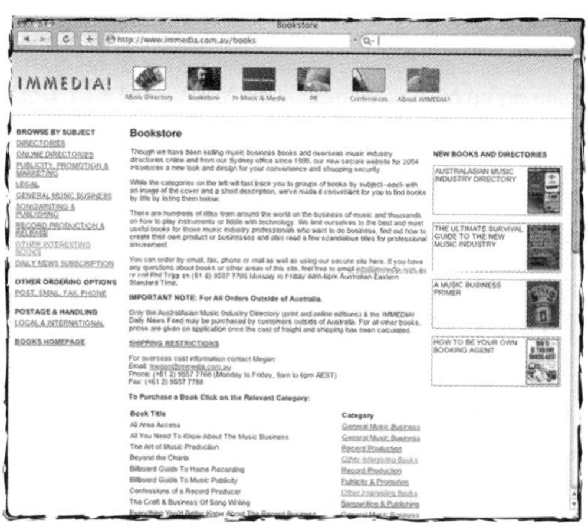

IMMEDIA! 20 Hordern St, Newtown, NSW, 2042
Ph. (02) 9557 7766 **Fx.** (02) 9557 7788
E. admin@immedia.com.au

NOTES

NOTES